THOMAS SHADWELL
HIS LIFE AND COMEDIES

THOMAS SHADWELL

HIS LIFE AND COMEDIES

By

ALBERT S. BORGMAN

BENJAMIN
New York

BLOM, INC.
1969

First Published 1928
Reissued 1969 by
Benjamin Blom, Inc., Bronx, New York 10452

Library of Congress Catalog Card Number 68-56540

Printed in the United States of America

PREFACE

ONE of the most unlucky figures in the literary history of the seventeenth century is Thomas Shadwell. Poet-laureate to William and Mary, friend of many of the wittiest men of his age, dramatist who could count more successes than failures, he, nevertheless, is remembered as one who "never deviates into sense." Dryden's satirical lines—among the most trenchant ever penned—have given Shadwell an unenviable reputation. But no person who has read with an open mind even the least happy of Shadwell's comic ventures can properly dismiss him as dull.

This monograph, which is an attempt to bring together the facts of Shadwell's life and to review each of his thirteen plays, was in the hands of the publishers before Mr. Montague Summers' valuable edition of Shadwell with its long prefatory essay was published. In two such studies pursued independently, it is inevitable that the writers will happen upon many of the same facts. It is likewise inevitable that each writer will discover material which is unknown to the other. Among the various items which I have presented and which are not found in Mr. Summers' essay may be mentioned the references to Shadwell's children in the registers of St. Bride's, the uncomplimentary portrait of the Whig poet in *Scandalum Magnatum*, and the use of Hooke's *Micrographia* as the source for a few of the passages in *The Virtuoso.*

In my quotations from Shadwell's plays I have used the collected edition of 1720; but, whenever the wording differed from that in the first quartos, I have substituted the earlier reading. A list of the places where my quotations from Shadwell differ from the 1720 text is found in a footnote on page 12.

This monograph is a doctoral dissertation, with additions and omissions. In its original form, it was written under the direction of Professor George Pierce Baker, then of Harvard University. I wish to thank the custodians of the British Museum, of the New York and Boston Public Libraries, and of the libraries of Harvard, Yale, and New York Universities for many courtesies. I owe debts of gratitude to the Rev. A. Taylor, for permission to examine the registers of St. Bride's; to the Rev. F. W. G. Sidebotham, rector of Weeting, and the Rev. H. Tyrrell Green, rector of Santon, for kindly answering my queries, and to Professors George P. Baker, Hyder E. Rollins, Allardyce Nicoll, and B. Sprague Allen, for many helpful suggestions. Finally, for their editorial supervision of publication, I extend thanks to Professor Arthur H. Nason, Director, and Miss Hannah E. Steen, of the New York University Press.

A. S. B.

January 15, 1928.

CONTENTS

THOMAS SHADWELL

HIS LIFE AND COMEDIES

PART I

SHADWELL'S LIFE

CHAPTER I

EARLY LIFE

> To make quick way I'll leap o'er heavy blocks,
> Shun rotten Uzza, as I would the pox;
> And hasten Og and Doeg to rehearse,
> Two fools that crutch their feeble sense on verse;
> Who, by my Muse, to all succeeding times
> Shall live in spite of their own dogg'rel rhymes.

IN writing these lines, Dryden was prophet as well as poet, for Shadwell and Settle, nearly two hundred and fifty years later, are known primarily not as dramatists but as victims of his satire. Posterity's treatment of the "heroically mad" Doeg is undoubtedly justified. Any person of to-day who wades through the tragedies of Settle realizes that they are merely phenomena of literary history rather than works of permanent value as literature. One may at first be inclined to feel the same about the plays of Shadwell, especially if one approaches them with the expectation of finding the polished wit of Etherege or Congreve. But, although they lack the continued brilliancy which one associates with these masters of Restoration Comedy, at their best they contain an abundant vitality; and the reader cannot help feeling, if his interest lies in social history, that Shadwell is one of the keys necessary to unlock the England of Charles II. For that reason, if for no other, a study of the life and comedies of this dramatist is worth attempting.

The monograph which follows is in two parts. The first contains the facts of Shadwell's life: his education, his success as a writer of comedies and operas for the Duke's Theatre, his literary combats, his political quarrels and his enforced retirement from playwriting, his return to the theatre, and his none-too-happy efforts as poet-laureate. The second considers, in turn, each of his thirteen comedies—their relationship to earlier and contemporary drama, and their echoes of the life of the time.

According to the *Account of the Author and his Writings,* prefaced to the edition of his plays published in 1720 and doubtless written from material furnished by his son, Thomas Shadwell came "of an ancient Family in *Staffordshire*, the Eldest Branch of which [had] enjoyed an Estate there of at least five hundred Pounds *per Annum* for above three hundred Years, without any Honours or Publick Business." In 1537, arms described as "Per pale Or and Az[ure] on a chev[ron] betw[een] three annulets, four escallop shells, all counterchanged" had been granted to a Thomas Shadwell of Linedon, Staffordshire.[1] One hundred years later, on December 9, 1637, another Thomas Shadwell, the "third son of Edward Shadwell of Lindon, Staffordshire, esq., deceased," was admitted to the Middle Temple.[2]

It may have been the last-mentioned Thomas Shadwell, who, on May 16, 1639, was "bound with John Pay" at the admission of a member of another branch of his family to the Middle Temple. The person in question, described as "Mr. John, son and heir of George Shadwell of London, gent; deceased,"[3] had in 1637/8 been granted the degree of B.A. by the University of Cambridge.[4] Born at Thetford,[5] he had, after completing his preliminary education, matriculated at Pembroke College as pensioner during Easter term, 1634.[6] While he was a member of the Middle Temple, his name appeared three times in the lists of persons "fined as usual" for absence from readings on May 15 and October 30, 1640, and on May 14, 1641.[7] In the *Account*, we are told that John Shadwell did not much trouble himself with the practice of law, "having more than a competent Fortune left him by an Uncle"; that he "had eleven Children to maintain in the time of the Civil Wars, wherein he was a great Sufferer for the King, which forc'd him to sell and spend good part of his Estate"; and that he "was in Commission for the Peace in three

[1] Arthur J. Jewers, "Grants and Certificates of Arms" (*The Genealogist*, New Series, XXV, 252). Mentioned by D. M. Walmsley (London *Times Literary Supplement*, April 16, 1925).

[2] *Middle Temple Records, Minutes of Parliament* (London, 1904-5), II, 864.

[3] *Ibid.*, II, 880.

[4] *Book of Matriculations and Degrees . . . in the University of Cambridge from 1544 to 1659* (compiled by John Venn and J. A. Venn, Cambridge, 1913), p. 599.

[5] In a letter dated August 21, 1675, John Shadwell refers to Thetford, "which gave me my first being" (*Cal. State Papers*, Dom. Series, 1675-1676, p. 267).

[6] Not at Caius College, as is stated in the *Account*.

[7] *Middle Temple Records, Minutes of Parliament*, II, 892, 899, 906.

Counties in *England, Middlesex, Norfolk,* and *Suffolk,* and behav'd himself with great Ability and Integrity."[8]

The place and date of the birth of his son, Thomas, can probably never be exactly determined. The *Account* states that he "was born at *Santon-Hall* in *Norfolk,* a Seat of his Father's" and that he died in 1692, "in the 52d Year of his Age." On the other hand, the *Liber Matriculationis* of Gonville and Caius College records that Shadwell was born at Broomhill, near Brandon, Norfolk, and that he was admitted at the age of fourteen as "pensioner to the bachelors' table" on December 17, 1656.[9] Thus, two dates have been suggested for his birth, 1640 and 1642, and two places, Santon Hall and Broomhill.[10]

Parish records do not furnish us with corroborative evidence for the truth of either of these assertions. Although the registers of the combined parishes of St. Mary's and All Saints', Weeting, in which Broomhill House stood, have been preserved since the time of Elizabeth, they contain no reference—so I have been informed by the present rector—to a Thomas Shadwell. They do, however, record the births to "John Shadwell Esq. and Sarah his Wife" of a daughter Susan on November 28, 1654, and a son Edward on August 14, 1656.[11] If, on the other hand, the *"Santon-Hall* in *Norfolk"* of the *Account* was the "manor or farm-house" in Santon, designated by Blomefield in the eighteenth century as "now

[8] The name of John Shadwell occasionally appears in records for the years 1644-1662, but one is not justified in saying that the father of the dramatist is meant in every instance. In 1644, a John Shadwell was King's Escheator at Wolverhampton (*Collections for a History of Staffordshire,* 1886, &c., VII, pt. ii, 110). On March 9, 1652/3, a John Shadwell was assigned a whole chamber in the new brick buildings of the Middle Temple. On May 20, 1653, he was called to the degree of the Utter Bar, and on June 6, 1655, the whole chamber was to be assigned, on his surrender, to Francis Dove (*Middle Temple Records,* III, 1046, 1048, 1080). In May, 1656, a John Shadwell was commissioner for monthly assessments in Norfolk (R. H. Mason, *History of Norfolk,* 1884, p. 323). Would one who was "a great Sufferer for the King" have been employed in this manner? The father of the dramatist was more likely the John Shadwell, who, on July 31, 1662, was appointed member of a commission in the county of Norfolk to receive subscriptions in compliance with the Act for a "free and voluntary present to his Majesty" (Mason, p. 332).

[9] *Admissions to Gonville and Caius College, 1558-1678* (ed. J. and S. C. Venn, London, 1887), pp. 239-240.

[10] Also spelled "Bromehill" and "Bromhill."

[11] Information kindly furnished by the Rev. F. W. G. Sidebotham, Rector of Weeting, who also writes that a note in the hand of a former rector, the Rev. R. A. Oram, states, "The poet was brought here when about 14 years of age. He was born at Stanton Hall, Norfolk." Mr. Oram, however, did not give the source of his information.

a depopulated village,"[12] we are no better off; for the date of the earliest entry in the register of the church there is 1770.[13] Lacking the assistance of the parish records to confirm either of the statements, we are forced to decide which is the more convincing source of information, the *Account* written twenty-eight years after Shadwell's death or the *Liber Matriculationis* with its contemporary entries. Probably the latter; and, for that reason, I am willing to accept 1642 as the date of Shadwell's birth.[13a]

To be consistent, one ought to accept Broomhill House as the place; but I am inclined to be inconsistent and to favor Santon Hall. The registers of Weeting, as we have seen, contain entries of the births of Susan and Edward Shadwell in 1654 and 1656. If the family had been living in that parish from 1642, it seems strange that the names of a few of the nine other children do not appear. A plausible assumption is that the Shadwells were residing elsewhere, and Santon Hall seems to be the only possibility for the place. But all this theorizing is futile. No matter in which of the houses Shadwell was born, the district in which he spent his boyhood would be the same since the parishes of Weeting and Santon join on the Norfolk side of the Little Ouse River. Of

[12] Francis Blomefield, *Essay Towards a Topographical History of the County of Norfolk* (London, 1805), II, 155. The Rev. H. Tyrrell Green, Rector of Santon, Norfolk, informs me that the "present farm house next the church at Santon is probably that mentioned by Blomefield, but about 200 yards West of the Church are the foundations of a house surrounded by a dry moat 'which' (to quote Mr. W. G. Clarke, 'Breckland Wilds,' p. 195) 'are all that remain of Santon House, where it is said that Thomas Shadwell, the poet laureate, was born.'" "On the Ordnance Survey Map (6 inch) the present farm house is marked as Santon House Farm and the Moat is marked as Santon House (Site of)."

[13] A. M. Burke, *Key to the Ancient Parish Registers of England and Wales* (London, 1908), p. 134.

[13a] Mr. Montague Summers (*Works of Thomas Shadwell,* 1927, I, xxiv-xxv) presents evidence that 1641 may be the year of Shadwell's birth. He quotes a letter from the Bursar of Gonville and Caius, Mr. J. F. Cameron, who at his request examined the original entry in the *Liber Matriculationis:* "The entry occurs in the half year 'a Computo Annunciationis 1656'; the next half year being 'a Computo Michaelis 1656.' The reference to age in the entry is . . . annos natus 14 admittitur in commeatum Baccalaureorum Decemb. decimo septimo . . . it would seem however that in the entry as first made a space was left for the date, for the words 'decimo septimo' are crowded, and the whole date 'Decemb. decimo septimo,' though in the same handwriting as the rest of the entry seems to be in rather different ink. Also 17 December does not fall in the half year in question. The two preceding entries are dated 12 April, 1656. I cannot explain these facts, but it seems to me that the date is more probably 17 December, 1655, than 17 December, 1656. If so he would be born in 1641. If 'æt. suæ 52' could mean in his 52nd year that would be

one thing, however, we are certain: his home at the time he matriculated at the university was Broomhill House.[14]

Thomas Shadwell, who described himself in the dedicatory epistle to *The Libertine* as having the "Birth and Education, without the Fortune, of a Gentleman," was taught at home for five years by a Mr. Roberts and then sent to the King Edward VI Free Grammar School at Bury St. Edmunds, at that time under the headmastership of Thomas Stephens.[15] Although a "noted Cavalier," Stephens held this position during the period of the Civil War and Commonwealth with the exception of two years, from October 15, 1645, to September 11, 1647. Roger North, who was a student at the school a few years after Shadwell's residence there, describes the headmaster as "pedant enough, and noted for high flights in poetry and criticism, and what we now call jingling, not

right for the date of his death in November, 1692." The "æt. suæ 52" was part of the inscription which was intended for the laureate's monument in Westminster Abbey; the words on the monument as finally erected were, however, "Ætat. Suæ 55," doubtless a mistake on the part of the sculptor. I might add that the bursar of Gonville and Caius in 1655 and 1656 was not particular about listing the new students in the order of their matriculation. For instance, on March 28, 1655, Henry Rixe was admitted sizar; this entry is followed by that of John Ruddle, who was admitted sizar on October 19, 1654; the next entry is dated June 15, 1655 (*Admissions to Gonville and Caius College*, ed. Venn, p. 238).

[14] This building, which arose out of the ruins of Bromehill Priory, stood about a mile south-east of the town of Weeting. See Blomefield, *op. cit.*, II, 163-167.

[15] The records for the early years of Bury School are incomplete. The list of students for 1656 has, however, been preserved. In it appears the name of "Johannes Shadwell filius Johannis Shadwell de Bromhill in Com. Norf. armigeri." Mr. S. H. A. Hervey, the editor of the *Biographical List of Boys Educated at King Edward VI Free Grammar School, Bury St. Edmunds. From 1550 to 1900* (Suffolk Green Books, No. XIII) thinks a mistake may have been made here and "John" written instead of "Thomas." This inference seems to me unwarranted. In the list, the boys are arranged in forms, John Shadwell being in the fourth. Richard Short, whose name appears among those in the fourth form, was admitted to Christ's College, Cambridge, on February 24, 1658/9, aged 16, and William Worts (or Woortes), also a member of the fourth form, was admitted to the scholars' table at Gonville and Caius on February 3, 1658/9, aged 16. Of those in the highest form, Erasmus Warren was admitted to Christ's on February 10, 1656/7, Henry Boldero on March 31, 1657, and John Heigham on March 31, 1657, whereas John Pistor and Giles Kedington (or Kerrington) were admitted to Gonville and Caius on February 2, 1656/7, and on September 10, 1657. It seems certain that Thomas Shadwell, who was admitted pensioner to the bachelors' table at Gonville and Caius on December 17, 1656, an earlier date than any of those just mentioned, is not the "Johannes Shadwell" of the list. Probably Thomas Shadwell was a pupil at Bury School in 1655.

a little derived from the last age."[16] "The worst of him was," continues North, "what his corpulence declared, the being a wet epicure, the common vice of bookish professions." In his family he "used the forms of loyalty and orthodoxy"; but, in order "to hold his school," he was forced "to use outwardly an occasional conformity, by observing the church duties, and days of super-hypocritical fastings and seekings, wherewith the people, in those days, were tormented." But near the dawn of the Restoration he would attend a "Church of England conventicle" with some of his boarders. After the return of Charles II, he showed his loyalty in many ways, one of which was to dress his pupils in cloaks of scarlet, the king's color, and parade them through Bury to church.

In his zeal to keep alive loyalty to the king and to the Church, Stephens did not neglect to instruct his pupils thoroughly in the "rules of grammar and the learning of the Latin and Greek tongue." His method was to require "all his scholars to fill a quarter of a sheet of paper with their Latin themes, and write the English on the opposite page." Then, in the presence of one or two of the lower forms as an audience, a boy was required to stand at a desk in the middle of the school and read his theme in English or Latin, as the master designated.

The headmaster's greatest fault seems to have been his proneness to play favorites among his pupils. He thought very highly of John North, a lad of studious habits, but had small patience with his brother Dudley, a boy of "much spirit, which would not be suppressed by conning his book, but must be rather employed in perpetual action." Stephens "most brutally abused" Dudley, "correcting him at all turns, with or without a fault, till he was driven within an ace of despair, and . . . making away with himself. . . . This ill usage made an impression upon his spirits, that did not wear out in all his life, but, to his dying day, he resented it. And he often spoke of it in a kind of passion, and declared that he wanted only the satisfaction of talking to this man, and showing where he used him ill, and had denied him common justice."

[16] The characterization of Stephens and his school is found in Roger North's *Lives of . . . Francis North, Baron Guilford, . . . the Hon. Sir Dudley North, . . . and the Hon. and Rev. Dr. John North* (London, 1826), I, 11; II, 291-292; III, 277-282. Dudley and John are in the list of 1656; Francis was admitted to St. John's, Cambridge, on June 8, 1653. Roger entered Jesus College, Cambridge, on October 30, 1667.

It is, of course, useless to speculate as to whether or not Shadwell was favored by his headmaster. He could not have stood among the lowest in Stephens' estimation. Some thirty years later, in the epistle dedicatory to his translation of the Tenth Satire of Juvenal, he wrote that he did not have the reputation either at school or at college of being deficient in Greek or Latin. But, in addition to obtaining the book knowledge necessary for entrance to the university, Shadwell doubtless picked up information of another sort during his year's sojourn at Bury. He could not have helped learning something about the famous fair, which he was later to introduce in one of his best comedies.

The atmosphere was quite different at Gonville and Caius College, Cambridge, where Shadwell matriculated on December 17, 1656, as "pensioner to the bachelor's table."[17] Royalist sympathy, which Stephens represented, was lacking here. In fact, the royalist master, Thomas Batchcroft, had been ejected in April, 1649; and his place had been taken by William Dell, a chaplain in the Parliamentary Army. The Parliamentary Committee for Regulating the Universities had also appointed fellows to replace those who had been forced out. Academic responsibilities seem to have rested lightly upon the shoulders of Dell; for he neglected to attend meetings and was seldom in residence.[18]

Shadwell, who had entered the precincts of this college through the Gate of Humility, did not remain within the walls long enough to be able to depart as candidate for a degree through the Gate of Honour. In little more than a year and a half after his matriculation, he became a member of the Middle Temple. Among the admissions on July 7, 1658, is the name of "Mr. Thomas, son and heir-apparent of John Shadwell of the Middle Temple, esq., specially; bound with his father and Mr. Francis Jermy of the Utter Bar."[19] Possibly the father, like Sir Edward Belfond, was able to obtain the services of a "modest, learned Lawyer, of little Practice" to instruct his son in "some old Common-Law Books, the Statutes, and the best Pleas of the Crown, and the Constitution

[17] John Venn in his *Biographical History of Gonville and Caius College, 1349-1897*, III, 271-273, says that the charges for pensioners to the bachelors' table were on a somewhat higher scale than for those admitted to the two lower tables.

[18] *Ibid.*, III, 94-95, 102-103.

[19] *Middle Temple Records, Minutes of Parliament*, III, 1125.

of the old true *English* Government."[20] In addition to studying the law, Shadwell, at this time, had an opportunity to observe the life of the adjoining district of Whitefriars, then a refuge for rogues, thieves, and prostitutes—a locality of which he was later to make dramatic capital in *The Squire of Alsatia.*

While he was residing in the Temple, Shadwell doubtless continued his interest in music. The *Account* speaks of "his Great Skill" in that art. In his dedicatory epistle to his translation of the Tenth Satire of Juvenal, he replies to Dryden's satirical fling at him for playing upon the lute by saying "that that and all other Gentleman-like Exercises, which [he] was capable of Learning, [his] Father was at the charge of." Also, in his preface to *Psyche,* he tells of how he had written the words of that opera "not so much [for] . . . the Wit or Fancy of 'em, as the making of 'em proper for Musick; in which [he] cannot but have some little Knowledge, having been bred for many Years of [his] Youth to some Performance in it." His skill was remembered after his death by Tom Brown, who, in one of his *Letters from the Dead to the Living,* describes the "thrumming upon an old broken Theorbo" of "*Tom Shadwell,* who still keeps up his Musical Talent in these gloomy Territories."[21]

Shadwell was perhaps indebted for his early interest in music to John Jenkins, to whom he referred in 1680 as the "*Worthiest Master of my Youthful Days.*"[22] Musician in ordinary to both Charles I and Charles II, Jenkins was one of the best composers and performers of his time. For a great part of his life he had lived in the homes of different Norfolk gentlemen, among them being Sir Hamon L'Estrange. Roger North, whom he had taught, describes him as "a person of much easier temper than any of his

[20] Shadwell, IV, 44. Unless otherwise specified, all references to the plays of Shadwell are from the four-volume edition published in 1720. In the following instances I have substituted the readings in the first quartos: p. 20, l. 20, "that" for "the"; p. 20, l. 30, "to" for "at"; p. 42, l. 7, "it" added; p. 149, l. 12, "they'd" for "they"; p. 158, l. 29, "perpetually" added; p. 188, l. 21, punctuation; p. 197, l. 20, "bestow" for "bestrew"; p. 209, l. 35, "Vices" for "Vice"; p. 225, l. 30, "Rank" for "Ranks"; p. 248, l. 18, p. 249, ll. 4, 13, "Beau" for "Beaux."

[21] *Works of Mr. Thomas Brown* (London, 1720), II, 165. D. M. Walmsley (*Review of English Studies,* I, 350-352) calls attention to two songs, the music of which is ascribed to Shadwell. They are both in the British Museum MS. Addl. 19,759.

[22] In the poem, "To my Much Respected Master, and Worthy Friend, Signior Pietro Reggio, On the Publishing his Book of Songs."

faculty." "He was neither conceited nor morose, but much a gentleman, and had a very good sort of wit, which served him in his address and conversation, wherein he did not please less than in his compositions."[23] Since he was "welcome to the house[s] of all lovers," it is unlikely that the doors of Broomhill would be closed to him. Shadwell was probably given lessons by Jenkins at the time when he was being taught at home by Mr. Roberts.

For a few years following his admission to the Middle Temple, definite references to Shadwell are lacking. The *Account* states that, after he had "spent some Time" there, he "went abroad to improve himself by travelling." To his experiences on the Continent he makes no allusion, unless we may consider that the itinerary of the Younger Belfond somewhat resembled his own. After seeing two campaigns in France and studying there "History, Civil Laws, and Laws of Commerce," Belfond "made the Tour of *Italy*, and saw *Germany*, and the *Low-Countries*."[24] But if Shadwell neglects to make definite mention of his travels on the Continent, he does refer to the fact that he spent four months in Ireland when he was twenty-three years old.[25] He was doubtless there with his father, who held the offices of Recorder of Galway and Attorney General for Connaught.[26]

[23] *Autobiography of the Hon. Roger North* (ed. Augustus Jessopp), (London, 1887), pp. 79-81.

[24] Shadwell, IV, 44.

[25] Epistle Dedicatory to his translation of the Tenth Satire of Juvenal.

[26] John Shadwell was Recorder of Galway from 1665 (*Cal. State Papers*, Dom. Series, 1671, p. 498) to September 29, 1670, when William Sprigge was elected to the position (*Hist. MSS. Comm. Tenth Report, Pt. V*, p. 503). Although he attempted to be reinstated, he had not been successful by September 23, 1673 (*Cal. State Papers*, Dom. Series, 1673, p. 553). In 1666, John Shadwell, "Attorney of Connaught," was paid 20 *l.* "out of [the] revenues in Ireland" (*Cal. State Papers*, Ireland, 1666-1669, p. 75). On March 12, 1682/3, in a "list containing all the payments to be made for civil affairs to begin from 1682, Christmas," is "John Shadwell, Att[orney] Gen[eral] of Connaught" (*Cal. Treas. Books*, 1681-1685, Vol. VII, Pt. II, p. 1005). He was Attorney-General at Tangier, under William O'Brien, second Earl of Inchiquin from 1675 to 1677 (*Cal. State Papers*, Dom. Ser., 1675-1676, pp. 267, 268; *Cal. State Papers*, Dom. Ser., 1677-1678, p. 295). On August 6, 1677, because of complaints mutually brought against each other by the earl on the one hand, and Shadwell and the magistrates of Tangier on the other, all parties to the dispute were ordered to appear before the King in the Robes Chamber to justify the complaints and to defend themselves. On December 5, 1678, he told the Committee for Examinations of the Popish Plot what he remembered of the trial of the Archbishop of Tuam (*Hist. MSS. Comm. Eleventh Report, Pt. II*, pp. 21-22). In 1680, John Shadwell appeared as "put in or kept in" in a book listing Justices of the Peace (*Hist. MSS. Comm. Eleventh Report, Pt. II*, p. 186). In 1684, he died and was buried at Oxburgh, Norfolk (Blomefield, VI, 197).

Sometime between 1663 and 1667, Shadwell was married to a member of the Duke's Company of players, Mistress Ann Gibbs, daughter of Thomas Gibbs, proctor and public notary of Norwich. The prompter Downes, in his *Roscius Anglicanus,* published in 1708, lists "Mrs. Ann Gibbs" as appearing in the rôles of Olivia in *Twelfth Night* and Lucia in *Cutter of Coleman Street,* and "Mrs. Gibbs" as acting Julia in *The Duchess of Malfi* and Lucia in *Epsom-Wells.* The first of the plays mentioned was seen by Pepys on September 11, 1661, the second on December 16, 1661, and the third on September 30, 1662. The fourth was not performed until December, 1672. In the edition of Sir Robert Stapylton's *The Slighted Maid,* published in 1663, the name of "Mrs. Gibbs" appears opposite the important part of Decio. This play was seen by Pepys on February 23, 1662/3, and it is likely that the cast in the quarto is of that performance. The marriage must have taken place then after that date.[27]

There still remains the problem of explaining the "Mrs. Gibbs" who appeared in *Epsom-Wells* in 1672. Is she the same person as the "Mrs. Gibbs" who acted in at least eleven plays during the years 1676-1678?[28] Possibly, if we may assume that she was a member of the Duke's Company and that, after appearing in an important part, she was not heard of again for four years. The cast of *Epsom-Wells,* as given by Downes, must be that of the original performance and not of a later revival; for the names of Angel and Mrs. Johnson are not found in the lists of actors in plays produced after 1673. I am inclined to believe that Downes,

[27] D. M. Walmsley, in "New Light on Thomas Shadwell" (London *Times Literary Supplement,* April 16, 1925), thinks this Ann Gibbs was "in all probability the same person who married one Thomas Gaudy, of Claxton, Norfolk, at St. Clement Danes, July 12, 1662." She is described as "of Norwich, . . . spinster, about 17" and was married with "consent of father, Thomas Gibbs, of Norwich, gent., alleged by Thomas Gibbs, of Furnival's Inn, gent. [who signs Thomas Gibbs, jun.]." J. Foster, *London Marriage Licences* (London, 1887), col. 535.

[28] Mrs. Gibbs, according to casts printed in the first quartos, acted the following parts: Henrietta (Otway's *Don Carlos,* 1676), Beatrice (Ravenscroft's *The Wrangling Lovers,* 1677), Mrs. Essence (Rawlins' *Tom Essence,* 1677), Arbella (D'Urfey's *Madam Fickle,* 1677), Clara (Otway's *Cheats of Scapin,* 1677), Iras (Sedley's *Antony and Cleopatra,* 1677), Clarina (*The Counterfeit Bridegroom,* 1677), Maundy (Behn's *Sir Patient Fancy,* 1678), Chloe (Shadwell's *The History of Timon of Athens, the Man-Hater,* 1678), Victoria (Otway's *Friendship in Fashion,* 1678), Flora (Leanerd's *The Counterfeits,* 1679). The last-mentioned play, however, was acted on May 28, 1678 (Nicoll, *History of Restoration Drama,* p. 311).

who has been shown more than once to be inaccurate in detail, may have again made a mistake here and carelessly written the maiden name of the actress, "Mrs. Gibbs," instead of the married name, "Mrs. Shadwell," opposite the part of Lucia in *Epsom-Wells*.

The name of "Mrs. Shadwel" first appears in a quarto of D'Avenant's *The Rivals*, published in 1668.[29] This comedy, however, was presented as early as September 10, 1664. In his comments on that performance, Pepys refers to the singing of Mrs. Gosnell; and, on December 2, 1664, he commends the "good actings of Betterton and his wife and Harris." Since the names of neither Mrs. Gosnell nor Mrs. Betterton appear in the quarto of 1668, it seems likely that the cast there given is of the revival in November, 1667.[30] The time of the marriage must therefore have been between February 23, 1662/3, and November, 1667.[31]

Several years later, Nat Thompson, the "Popish Intelligencer," precipitated a discussion[32] as to whether or not Shadwell had been a Catholic and "*married by a* Popish Priest." The editors of two of the Whig news sheets, Richard Janeway and Langley Curtis—both men who would not be likely to falsify the facts concerning an upholder of their cause—had something to say of the matter. Curtis wrote of a conversation reported to him by a certain "Mr. S——," who, on Christmas, 1681, had talked about Shadwell's "high Whiggism" to an unnamed gentleman. This gentleman, an old acquaintance of the dramatist, "*said he wondred to hear the said Poet was so violent against the Papists, since he had frequently*

[29] The name of "Mrs. Shadwell" appears twice in Downes, as Lady Cockwood in *She Would If She Could* and Emilia in *The Sullen Lovers*. According to casts printed in the contemporary editions, Mrs. Shadwell acted the following parts: Heraclia (D'Avenant's *The Rivals*, 1668), Cleora (Orrery's *Mustapha*, 1669), Celinda (Edward Howard's *The Six Days Adventure*, 1671), Clarina (Edward Howard's *The Women's Conquest*, 1671), Joanna (Crowne's *Juliana*, 1671), Irene (Crowne's *The History of Charles the Eighth of France*, 1672), Caelia (Payne's *The Fatal Jealousie*, 1673), Rose (Payne's *The Morning Ramble*, 1673), Gertrard (*sic*) (*Hamlet*, 1676), Dutchess of Eboli (Otway's *Don Carlos*, 1676), Julia (Webster's *Duchess of Malfi*, 1678), Melissa (Shadwell's *The History of Timon of Athens, the Man-Hater*, 1678), Lucinda (Maidwell's *The Loving Enemies*, 1680), and Gonerill (Tate's *The History of King Lear*, 1681).

[30] The Lord Chamberlain's Records list a performance on November 19, 1667 (Nicoll, p. 309).

[31] Montague Summers, in the London *Times Literary Supplement* of May 7, 1925, states that Sarah, a daughter of Shadwell and Ann Gibbs was baptized on March 9, 1665, but he cites no authority.

[32] See pp. 55-58.

to him owned himself to be a Papist and that he was Marryed by a Popish Priest, and that during the time of his professing himself such, he brought the Gentleman acquainted with Sir George Wakeman, *with whom the said Poet had an intimate acquaintance*" and that he "*never knew he professed himself to be other than a* Roman *Catholick till the Plot broke out.*" On the authority of Janeway, we learn that "Mr. S——" later confronted Shadwell with these statements and that Shadwell had replied that "it was not the *first Lye* his Author had told, and that 'twas true, that he had (about Twenty years since) been attempted by Priests, and (being intangled by their Sophistry) had, for some small time, been inclining to the Church of *Rome,* but never had by any Act, joyned himself with that Church." The problem to be solved then is which is the more credible witness: Shadwell speaking through Janeway or "Mr. S——" reporting through Curtis what he had heard from another person. In my opinion, the question is still an open one. There is no evidence in any of his works that Thomas Shadwell was ever a Catholic.[33]

[33] The dramatist's father, John Shadwell, was not unfavorably disposed towards Catholics. In 1687, Edward Shadwell [see p. 90n.] petitioned for a place in the customs or excise, "he and his ancestors having been ever loyal and great sufferers, and in the late plot his father was very active in Norfolk and Suffolk as a Justice of the Peace and in assisting the Roman Catholics." *Cal. Treas. Books,* 1685-1689, VIII, pt. iii, 1630.

CHAPTER II

DRAMATIC WORK, 1668-1680

The Itch of writing Plays, the more's the pity,
At once has seiz'd the Town, the Court, and City.
Amongst the Rest, the Poet of this Day
By meer Infection has produc'd a Play.

THUS writes Shadwell in the epilogue to *The Sullen Lovers* and makes his excuse for entering the profession of dramatic poet. After begging his readers to look upon this first attempt as a work composed in haste by a young writer, he adds, "Nor can you expect a very correct Play, under a Year's Pains at the least, from the Wittiest Man of the Nation; It is so difficult a thing to write well in this Kind."[1] Despite the fact that it was a first play hastily written, *The Sullen Lovers* seems to have been a considerable popular success. This the author judges was due to the "great Favour and Countenance it receiv'd from His Majesty and their Royal Highnesses. But [he] could not perswade [him]self that they were so favourable to the Play for the Merit of it, but out of a Princely Generosity, to encourage a young Beginner, that did what he could to please them, and that otherwise might have been baulk'd for ever: 'Tis to this [he owed] the Success of the Play, and [is] as far from Presumption of [his] own Merits in it, as one ought to be, who receives an Alms."

We are fortunate in being able to watch its early performances through the eyes of Samuel Pepys. On May 2, 1668, anticipating the interest which would be taken in the new play, he arrived at the theatre "at a little past twelve, to get a good place in the pit." Then "setting a poor man to keep [his] place," he was able to spend an hour at his bookseller's. Upon his return, he found the theatre quite full: "But I had my place, and by and by the King comes and the Duke of York; and then the play begins, called *The Sullen Lovers; or, The Impertinents*, having many good humours in it, but the play tedious, and no design at all in it.

[1] Preface to *The Sullen Lovers.*

But a little boy, for a farce, do dance Polichinelli, the best that ever anything was done in the world, by all men's report: most pleased with that, beyond anything in the world, and much beyond all the play."

On May 4, he was again at the Duke of York's house; but *The Impertinents* filled him with less pleasure than before, "it being but a very contemptible play, though there are many little witty expressions in it; and the pit did generally say that of it." He seemed determined to give this comedy a fair trial, however, and, on May 5, visited the playhouse once more and saw *The Impertinents*, "now three times, and the three only days it hath been acted. And to see the folly how the house do this day cry up the play more than yesterday! and I for that reason like it, I find, the better too." Then he adds what may explain in part his change of attitude and the interest of the public in the performance: "by Sir Positive At-All, I understand is meant Sir Robert Howard." On the next day, at Westminster Hall, he heard among other things that "my Lord St. John is meant by Mr. Woodcocke, in *The Impertinents*."[2]

By May 8, the success of the play was assured. "But Lord! to see how this play of Sir Positive At-All, in abuse of Sir Robert Howard, do take, all the Duke's and everybody's talk being of that, and telling more stories of him, of the like nature, that it is now the town and country talk, and, they say, is most exactly true." On June 24, Pepys had reached the conclusion that *The Impertinents* was "a pretty good play"; and, on April 14 of the following year, he was willing to call it "a play which pleases me well still."[3]

Downes, recalling the comedy in his old-age, asserts that *The Sullen Lovers* was "Admirably Acted" and that it "had wonderful Success, being Acted 12 Days together." The players were apparently well fitted for the characters they impersonated. The part of Sir Positive, the boastful knight whose antics delighted the audi-

[2] For Sir Robert Howard, see p. 131 ff. Oliver St. John, who became Chief Justice of the Common Pleas in 1648 and afterwards Lord Chief Justice of the Upper Bench, was one of Cromwell's lords. Pepys, on October 12, 1662, described him as "a very plain grave man." He died on December 31, 1673, at the age of seventy-five.

[3] On August 29, 1668, Pepys records, "Carried Harris to his playhouse, where, though four o'clock, so few people there at *The Impertinents*, as I went out; and do believe they did not act."

ence, was taken by Harris. Angel and Nokes appeared as the other "impertinents," acting the rôles respectively of the "familiar loving Coxcomb" Woodcock and the "conceited Poet" Ninny.[4] Smith and Mrs. Shadwell were the "sullen lovers," Stanford and Emilia.[5]

When *The Sullen Lovers* was published later in the year, it was dedicated to William Cavendish, Duke of Newcastle. In the epistle dated September 1, 1668, Shadwell wrote of the "great Obligations I have had the Honour to receive from Your Grace." These obligations continued; and the author took the opportunity to acknowledge them in the dedications of four other plays. In the epistle to *The Humourists* addressed to "the Most Illustrious Princess, Margaret, Dutchess of Newcastle,"[6] he wrote, "I have been more obliged by my Lord *Duke* than by any Man." Two years later, in the dedication to *Epsom-Wells*, after naming Newcastle "the only *Mecaenas* of our age," Shadwell asserted:

> You are He, who still preserves and maintains the Magnificence and Grandeur of our ancient Nobility; and being one that's truly great in Mind as well as Fortune, you take delight in rewarding and encouraging of Art and Wit: And while others detract from Poetry, or at least neglect it, your Grace not only encourages it by your great Example, but protects it too. *Welbeck* is indeed the only place, where the best Poets can find a good Reception.

[4] See poem "On Poet Ninny" by John Wilmot, Earl of Rochester (*Collected Works*, ed. John Hayward, 1926, p. 63).

[5] Downes, *Roscius Anglicanus* (facsimile reprint of rare original of 1708, London, 1886), p. 29.

[6] The dedication of *The Humourists* is the subject of three letters by Shadwell which were printed in *Letters and Poems in Honour of the Incomparable Princess, Margaret Dutchess of Newcastle* (1676), pp. 127-130. In the first, dated "London, April 20, 1671" and addressed to the Duke, Shadwell writes: "Had I not been out of Town a great part of the last Summer, and almost all this Winter, I had written to your *Grace* long since. . . . But (my Lord) the Printing of the *Humourists* has given me a new occasion of troubling you, and desiring your Favour to be an Advocate, for me, to my Lady Dutchess, to procure me her Pardon, and a favourable reception of that little Comoedy. . . . Your *Grace* saw this *Comoedy* (before the Sting was taken out) and was pleased to approve it, which is to me more than the Plaudit of a Theatre: As it is, it stands more in need of Pardon, and Protection, which I hope your *Grace*, and my Lady Dutchess will have the Mercy to afford it." In the second letter, dated April 20 and addressed to the Duchess, the author begs her pardon for the imperfections of his play, and expresses the conventional humility of the dedicator. In the third, dated May 25, 1671, he writes: "Being an Hundred and fifty miles from *London*, at a place called *Chaddeston*, near *Manchester:* I had an account, but the last Post, of the receit of your *Graces* Noble present" given in appreciation of his dedication.

But what Dryden called the "northern dedications" did not cease with *Epsom-Wells;* for, in 1676, Shadwell, on two occasions, acknowledged favors from his patron. In the epistle dedicatory to *The Libertine*, after piling praise upon praise until the foundation seems ready to crumble, Shadwell wrote:

> All these Heroick Qualities I admired, and worshipped at a Distance, before I had the Honour to wait upon your Grace at your House. For so vast was your Bounty to me, as to find me out in my Obscurity, and oblige me several Years before you saw me at *Welbeck;* where (when I arrived) I found a Respect so extreamly above the Meanness of my Condition, that I still received it with Blushes; having had nothing to recommend me, (but the Birth and Education, without the Fortune, of a Gentleman) besides some Writings of mine, which your Grace was pleased to like. Then was soon added to my former Worship and Admiration infinite Love, and infinite Gratitude, and a Pride of being favour'd by one, in whom I observ'd a Majesty equal with greatest Princes, yet Affability exceeding ordinary Gentlemen; a Greatness, that none e'er approached without Awe, or parted from without Satisfaction.
>
> Then (by the great Honour I had to be so daily admitted into your Grace's publick and private Conversation,) I observed that admirable Experience and Judgment surmounting all the Old, and that Vigorousness of Wit, and Smartness of Expression, exceeding all the Young I ever knew; and not only in sharp and apt Replies, the most excellent Way of pursuing a Discourse; but (which is much more difficult) by giving easie and unforced Occasions, the most admirable Way of beginning one; and all this adapted to Men of all Circumstances and Conditions: Your Grace being able to discourse with every Man in his own way; which, as it shews you to be a most accurate Observer of all Mens Tempers, so it shews your Excellency in all their Arts. But when I had the Favour daily to be admitted to your Grace's more retir'd Conversation, when I alone enjoyed the Honour, I must declare, I never spent my Hours with that Pleasure, or Improvement; nor shall I ever enough acknowledge that, and the rest of the Honours done me by your Grace, as much above my Condition as my Merit.

This adulation was continued in the epistle to *The Virtuoso.* Here Shadwell declared, "Whatever I Write, I will submit to Your Grace, who are the greatest Master of Wit, the most exact Observer of Mankind, and the most accurate Judge of Humour, that ever I knew." Favors from the family did not cease with the death of William Cavendish on Christmas Day, 1676. We learn from the epistle to *The Woman-Captain*, published in 1680 and addressed to Henry, Lord Ogle, that Shadwell had been recommended to this nobleman's "Kindness and Protection" by his "Excellent Father," Henry, Duke of Newcastle, the son of the dramatist's former patron.

Encouragement from one who served as a link between the present and the past meant much to Shadwell. Not only had Newcastle shown kindnesses to the older dramatists, Jonson, Ford, Brome, and Shirley, but he was also generous to Dryden, Flecknoe, and Settle.[7] Somewhat of a dabbler in playwriting, he had seen his comedies, *The Country Captain,* in which Shirley had a large share, and *The Variety,* produced by the King's Men at Blackfriars. After the Restoration, he contributed something to Dryden's *Sir Martin Mar-all,* wrote *The Humorous Lovers,* and, with aid from Shadwell, prepared *The Triumphant Widow* for the stage. It may be that Newcastle exerted his greatest influence upon the younger writer not as a patron or dramatist but as former acquaintance of Jonson. In addition to supplying numerous epitaphs for members of the Cavendish family, Jonson had written two epigrams upon the duke and two masques presented upon the occasions of his entertaining Charles I. According to his wife, Newcastle said "he never heard any man read well but B. J." Doubtless some of the duke's admiration for Ben was passed on to his Restoration protégé during those moments of "more retir'd Conversation" to which Shadwell was admitted.

The author of *The Sullen Lovers* showed his enthusiasm for Jonson countless times in prologue, epilogue, and dedication. On September 19, 1668, Pepys, who sat next to him at a performance of *The Silent Woman,* records that he was "big with admiration" of that play. Shadwell is mentioned elsewhere in the Diary. On September 20, 1668, he and Harris disappoint Pepys, who had invited them to dinner; and, on April 16 of the following year, he informs the diarist that the new comedy *Guzman* is the work of the Earl of Orrery. Less than two months before the last-mentioned conversation, his second play had been produced.

[7] For the subject of Newcastle as a playwright and a patron of dramatists, see H. T. E. Perry, *The First Duchess of Newcastle and Her Husband as Figures in Literary History,* pp. 86-95, 100-118, 142-166.

The success of *The Sullen Lovers* did not embolden the author to tempt fate immediately with another comedy of humours. His next dramatic effort was of a very different nature—an adaptation of a blank verse tragi-comedy "wrote in single Scenes," *The Rewards of Virtue*, by a certain Mr. John Fountain of Devonshire. Finding many things in that work which pleased him and thinking that it might "be made a pleasant Entertainment for the Audience,"[8] Shadwell rearranged certain of the scenes, presented in action incidents which were narrated in the original, and added some lyrical passages. The result was *The Royal Shepherdess*, produced for the first time at the Duke's Theatre on February 25, 1668/9. Plays in the pastoral vein with musical interludes were not entirely distasteful to Restoration audiences; and Shadwell may have been influenced to revise *The Rewards of Virtue* by noticing the success of Beaumont and Fletcher's *The Faithful Shepherdess*, revived by the King's Company in October, 1668, but played by them as early as June 13, 1663, at which time it had been "much thronged after, and often shown."[9]

Pepys, who was present at the first performance of *The Royal Shepherdess*, does not comment favorably on that play: "To the Duke of York's house, and there before one, but the house infinite full, where, by and by, the King and Court come, it being a new play, or an old one new vamped, by Shadwell, called *The Royal Shepherdesse;* but the silliest for words and design, and everything, that ever I saw in my whole life, there being nothing in the world pleasing in it, but a good martial dance of pikemen, where Harris and another do handle their pikes in a dance to admiration; but never less satisfied with a play in my life." On the next day, February 26, the diarist went to the King's House to see their rival offering, again Beaumont and Fletcher's *Faithful Shepherdess*. "But, Lord! what an empty house, there not being, as I could tell the people, so many as to make up above £10 in the whole house! The being of a new play at the other house, I suppose, being the cause, though it be so silly a play that I wonder how there should be enough people to go thither two days together, and not leave more to fill this house." Despite Pepys' disapproval, Shadwell's play managed to live six days.[10]

[8] Preface to *The Royal Shepherdess.*

[9] Pepys also records performances on October 12 and October 14, 1668, and on February 26, 1668/9.

[10] Downes, p. 31.

In the following year, Shadwell returned to the comedy of humours, a type of play which he frequently asserts is more difficult to write than one depending primarily upon plot. But the reception of *The Humourists* was a great disappointment to him: it came "upon the Stage with all the Disadvantages imaginable." After he had finished writing it, he was forced to blot out the main design because it had given offence; when he had satisfied all the exceptions which were made against it, a numerous party resolved "to damn it, right or wrong, before they had heard or seen a Word on't"; to add to his confusion, the actors were imperfect in their parts. The play, thinks Shadwell, would have fallen beyond redemption, had it not been revived after the second day "by her Kindness (which I can never enough acknowledge) who, for four Days together, beautified it with the most excellent *Dancings*, that ever had been seen upon the Stage. This drew my Enemies, as well as Friends; till it was something better Acted, Understood, and Liked, than at first: By this means the poor Play's Life was prolonged."[11]

After the comparative failure of *The Humourists*, Shadwell did not present another play for at least a year unless his unpublished *The Hypocrite* belongs to 1671. We know of the latter work merely through references by Dryden and Settle. The author of *MacFlecknoe*, after picturing the "worlds of *Misers*" that ought to flow from Shadwell's pen, writes:

> *Humorists* and Hypocrites it should produce,
> Whole *Raymond* Families and Tribes of *Bruce*.

Settle, in the course of his paper combat with Shadwell, to be discussed later, wrote in the preface to *Ibrahim* (published in 1677) some harsh, but by no means entirely unjustifiable, criticism of the works of his fellow-dramatist. There he classes *The Hypocrite* with *The Humourists* and *The Miser* as plays written in Shadwell's "humbler and modester days" before he had become "flusht with the Trophies of his *Epsom-Wells*." He also brands Shadwell's remark concerning his own drudging for three years upon *The Conquest of China* as being "as notoriously false, as that his *Hypocrite* was Acted six days."

[11] Preface to *The Humourists*. It is not unlikely that the dancer who came to the rescue was Mrs. Johnson. See p. 26.

Unlike his earlier offerings, Shadwell's next extant play was produced anonymously at the King's Theatre in Covent Garden before the fire which destroyed that house on January 25, 1671/2.[12] The sting of the failure of *The Humourists* may still have been upon him when he turned to the task of adapting Molière's *L'Avare* to the English stage. When he saw that the play in which he had attempted to exemplify his theories of comedy was received at first unfavorably and then saved, not through any merit of its own, but by the interpolation of "excellent Dancings," he threw aside for the time being all thoughts of interesting the public in further studies of humours and took what seemed the easiest road to success. He had every reason to believe that another reworking of a "French Farce" would win acclamation. He had merely to recall that Lacy had derived an amusing play, *The Dumb Lady, or The Farrier made Physician,* from two of Molière's comedies,[13] that Medbourne had rendered *Tartuffe* "into English with much Addition and Advantage,"[14] and that Caryl had pleased the court and the city more than once with his adaptation of *L'école des femmes* called *Sir Salomon, or, The Cautious Coxcomb.*[15]

In his prologue, Shadwell shows his disgust with the audience for approving this type of play:

> *Our Poet never doubts the good Success*
> *Of Farce, that's in half* French, *half* English *Dress:*
> *And this was made with little Pains and Wit,*
> *As any cobbling Poet e'er wrote yet,*
> *And therefore he's resolv'd not to submit.*
> *The Fortune of his Fellows he has seen,*
> *Who in dull Farce have so successful been,*
> *That could he write true Wit, he is in doubt*
> *Whether you would endure to sit it out.*

In a vein of blundering ill-nature, he writes in the preface: "*I think I may say without Vanity, that* Molière'*s Part of it has not suffer'd in my Hands; nor did I ever know a* French *Comedy made*

[12] Preface to *The Miser.* Percy Fitzgerald, in *A New History of the English Stage* (London, 1882), I, 137, prints a ballad "On the Unhappy Conflagration of the Theatre Royal, January 25, 1672."

[13] Probably acted in 1669, although not published until 1672.

[14] Published in 1670.

[15] This play and *The Sullen Lovers* were presented at Dover on the occasion of the visit of the Duchess of Orlèans in May, 1670. See p. 121.

use of by the worst of our Poets, that was not better'd by 'em. 'Tis not Barrenness of Wit or Invention, that makes us borrow from the French, *but Laziness.*" Then he makes what later becomes a frequently repeated boast—that he constructs his plays with great rapidity. *The Miser,* he says, was "*wrote in less than a Month.*"[16]

Despite his lack of sympathy with this play, Shadwell was not slow to dedicate it to Charles Sackville, Lord Buckhurst, later to become the Earl of Dorset and Middlesex. At this time, Sackville was known as the author of a lyric or two, the person to whom Dryden had dedicated his *Essay of Dramatic Poesy,* and the man who, in his youth, had gained the reputation of being very much of a rake. He was now apparently ready to settle down to his career of generosity to men of letters. His frequent favors are mentioned by Shadwell in the epistle to *The Miser.* There is no doubt that Sackville liked the company of the dramatist. Some six years later, Nell Gwyn, in a letter to "Mr. Hide," wrote: "My lord of Dorscit apiers wonse in thre munths, for he drinkes aile with Shadwell & Mr Haris at the Dukes house all day long."[17] After the Revolution, it was Dorset who, as Lord Chamberlain, secured Shadwell's appointment to the office of poet-laureate.

Although the first comedy Shadwell dedicated to Sackville was not a work to which he, as author, could point with pride, he was willing to declare that he was "more fond of [his next play], than of anything [he had] ever wrote."[18] *Epsom-Wells,* presented by the Duke's Company at their theatre in Dorset Garden in December, 1672,[19] was well liked by the town, and, says Downes, "in general being Admirably *Acted,* produc'd great Profit to the Company."[20] The cast contained the best players in the troupe. The

[16] Many of the dramatists of this time liked to brag of their rapidity in composition. Ravenscroft in his prologue written for the performance of *The Citizen Turn'd Gentleman* (London, 1672) at the Middle Temple alleges that "*A fortnights sickness did this Play produce.*" Revet avers that his *The Town-Shifts* (London, 1671) was "*thought on, begun, and finished, in a fortnight.*" Nevil Payne says that *The Morning Ramble* (London, 1673) was "*nine days work.*"

[17] "Letters from the Collection of William Tite, Esq.," pp. 25-26 in *Camden Miscellany,* Vol. V.

[18] Epistle Dedicatory to *Epsom-Wells.*

[19] The Lord Chamberlain's records list performances on December 2 and December 4, 1672, and December 5, 1673, at the theatre and on December 27, 1672, and February 20, 1680/1, at Court. Printed in Nicoll, *History of Restoration Drama,* pp. 309, 310, 312.

[20] P. 33.

parts of the three "Men of Wit and Pleasure," Raines, Bevil, and Woodly, were taken by Harris, Betterton, and Smith, while the low comedy rôles of the citizens, the comfit-maker Bisket and the haberdasher Fribble, were acted by Nokes and Angel. Underhill was "a delightful Brute" "in the course, rustick Humour of Justice *Clodpate*."[21] Mrs. Betterton appeared as the "silly affected" Mrs. Jilt; Mrs. Gibbs[22] and Mrs. Johnson were the "Young Ladies of Wit, Beauty, and Fortune," Lucia and Carolina. Mrs. Johnson,[23] whose name is found for the first time in theatrical records as Betty in *Sir Salomon* (produced in 1669) did not remain in the Duke's Company very long after the production of *Epsom-Wells*, for Downes writes that "*in this Comedy, Dancing a Jigg so Charming well, Love's power in a little time after Coerc'd her to Dance more Charming, elsewhere.*"

An interesting reference to Shadwell was made by John Aubrey in a letter to Anthony à Wood on October 26, 1671: "I am writing a comedy for Thomas Shadwell, which I have now almost finished since I came here, et quorum pars magna fui. And I shall fit him with another, *The Countrey Revell*, both humours untoucht, but of this, mum! for 'tis very satyricall against some of my mischievous enemies which I in my tumbling up and down have collected."[24] These words admit of more than one interpretation. Aubrey may merely be referring in a jocose way to the fact that he is writing a play in the manner of Shadwell's comedies of humour. Or he may intend his words to be taken more literally, and wish Wood to understand that he is writing a comedy for Shadwell with the hope that the latter might use his influence to get it produced. In the decade of the 1670's, Shadwell was doubtless influential with the management of the Duke's theatre. His wife was one of the chief actresses. He was apparently a close friend of Henry Harris. He was urged by Betterton to write

[21] In the prologue to *Win Her and Take Her*, Cave Underhill mentions his "*part in* Epsom-Wells *the Justice*."

[22] Or was it Mrs. Shadwell? See pp. 14-15.

[23] She also acted Statyra in Edward Howard's *The Women's Conquest* (pub. 1671), Honour Muchland in Payne's *The Morning Ramble* (pub. 1673), Ismena in Arrowsmith's *The Reformation* (pub. 1673), and Morena in Settle's *The Empress of Morocco* (pub. 1673).

[24] Quoted in a note by Andrew Clark in his edition of Aubrey's *Brief Lives* (Oxford, 1898), I, 52. Of the first of the plays mentioned, Clark has found no trace; of the second, there is a rude draft in MS. Aubr. 21.

Psyche, and he hurriedly put together *The Libertine* in three weeks because the theatre needed a play. According to Settle, *The Triumphant Widow* was "given him to bring into the Duke's House." For these reasons, I am inclined to favor the second interpretation of Aubrey's words—that Shadwell as a person of influence was able to bring plays to the attention of the management of the theatre.

His close association with the management may account also for the fact that he was asked to transform *The Tempest* of D'Avenant and Dryden from comedy to opera. This work, which Shadwell never saw fit to acknowledge, has been shown by Mr. W. J. Lawrence to be contained in the quarto of *The Tempest* published in 1674.[25] The opera was evidently produced for the first time around the latter part of April, 1674. Shadwell's changes consisted in rearranging the material in some of the scenes and in adding passages of a lyrical and spectacular nature. Since "all things" in *The Tempest* were "perform'd . . . so Admirably well," says Downes, "not any succeeding Opera got more Money."[26] In fact, its popularity was so great that the rival company was moved to produce a burlesque by Thomas Duffett called *The Mock-Tempest: or The Enchanted Castle*.[27]

To 1674 probably belongs another play in which Shadwell had a hand, *The Triumphant Widow, or the Medley of Humours*, published in 1677 as the work of the Duke of Newcastle. Following a suggestion made by Sir Charles Firth, Mr. H. T. E. Perry[28] has compared the characters of Sir John Noddy in *The Triumphant Widow* and Sir Humphrey Noddy in *Bury-Fair*, and, after noting that "nowhere in the Duke's other writings is there [a] strong tendency towards knockabout farce," feels rightly that Shadwell, in the later play, "was only reclaiming his own property." Mr. Perry also thinks that the portion of the comedy in which Crambo, "an heroick poet," and Codshead, "a coxcomb," are presented, show

[25] "Did Thomas Shadwell write an Opera on The Tempest" in W. J. Lawrence, *The Elizabethan Playhouse and Other Studies*, 1st series, pp. 193 ff. See also discussion by G. Thorn-Drury and D. M. Walmsley in *Review of English Studies*, I (1925), 327-330; II (1926), 463-466; III (1927), 204-208, 451-453.

[26] P. 35.

[27] Acted on November 19, 1674. Nicoll, p. 307.

[28] I have here summarized Mr. Perry's conclusions. The discussion is found in his *The First Duchess of Newcastle and Her Husband as Figures in Literary History*, pp. 157-165.

"further unmistakable traces of Shadwell." The basis upon which the latter assumption is founded appears in Settle's preface to *Ibrahim.* Here it is stated: "Having a Play, call'd the *Triumphant Widdow,* given him to bring into the Duke's Play-house, he [i.e., Shadwell] spitefully foists in a Scene of his own into the Play, and makes a silly Heroick Poet in it, speak the very words he had heard me say, and made reflexions on some of the very lines he had so sencelessly prated on before in the *Notes.*" Although it is impossible to identify the "very words" or the "very lines," which do not appear in the version of the play as printed, the heroic poet is a character Shadwell enjoyed ridiculing and it is not inconceivable, even if it cannot be absolutely proved, that the Crambo-Codshead portion of *The Triumphant Widow,* in Mr. Perry's words, "is only one more attack made by the future laureate upon his unfortunate enemy," Settle.[29] Except for Justice Spoilwit, later to do service as Mr. Oldwit in *Bury-Fair,* it is impossible further to disentangle the work of Shadwell from that of Newcastle.

The success of the operatic version of *The Tempest* led the management of the Duke's Company to produce a work of a similar nature the following year. At Betterton's request, Shadwell had, in the latter part of 1673, adapted the *Psiché* of Quinault, Molière, and Corneille. Some sixteen months later, he made a few slight changes in his text,[30] and the resulting work, the opera *Psyche,* was acted for the first time on February 27, 1674/5.[31] Having "a Continuance of Performance about 8 Days together it prov'd very Beneficial to the Company," records Downes.[32]

Shadwell's attitude towards what he terms his "*first Essay in Rhime*" is not unlike that taken towards his earlier adaptation of Molière, *The Miser.* He makes clear that this play is not one to which he can point with pride, but rather a piece of hack-work dashed off "*in those few Hours . . . snatch'd from Friends and Wine.*" "*In a thing written in five Weeks, as this was, there must needs be many Errours, which I desire true Criticks to pass by; and which perhaps I see my self, but having much Business, and indulging myself with some Pleasure too, I have not had leisure to*

[29] See the account of Shadwell's quarrel with Settle in the next chapter.

[30] Preface to *Psyche.*

[31] The Lord Chamberlain's Records on that day list "Psyche first Acting." It was also performed on March 2, 1674/5 (Nicoll, p. 310).

[32] Pp. 35-36.

mend them, nor would it indeed be worth the Pains, since there are so many splendid Objects in the Play, and such variety of Diversion, as will not give the Audience leave to mind the Writing; and I doubt not but the Candid Reader will forgive the Faults, when he considers that the great Design was to entertain the Town with variety of Musick, curious Dancing, splendid Scenes and Machines; and that I do not, nor ever did intend to value my self upon the writing of this Play." Associated with the "poet" in this enterprise were Matthew Lock, "*that long known able, and approved Master of Musick,*" "*Composer to His Majesty, and Organist to the Queen,*" the writer of the vocal music; Seignior Giovanni Baptista Draghi, "*Master of the* Italian *Musick to the King,*" the composer of "*all the Instrumental Musick (which is not mingled with the Vocal)*"*;* Monsieur St. Andrée, the "*most famous Master of* France," the director of the dances; Mr. Stephenson, "*the ingenious Artist*" who painted the scenes; and Mr. Betterton, who bestowed "*great Industry and Care*" upon "*those things that concern the Ornament or Decoration of the Play.*"

Although *Psyche* was "Splendidly set out, especially in Scenes; the Charge of which amounted to above 800 *l.*," the town soon tired of the type of entertainment it represented; and, in the epilogue to his next play, *The Libertine,* Shadwell has Jacomo attempt to conciliate the spectators with some Articles of Peace, among which is the assurance, "*You'll no more be troubled with Machines.*" Elsewhere, he begs the audience to give him fair play so that he may "*write himself into Favour once again,*"[33] and explains his immoderate haste in the composition of this "tragedy" by saying that "*the Play-house* [*had*] *great Occasion for a Play.*"[34] *The Libertine,* notable not for any intrinsic merit but because it represents the initial appearance of Don Juan in English literature, was acted in June, 1675.[35] Although the author describes it as the "*most irregular Play upon the Stage,*" he had no reason to complain of its success; for he writes: "*It pleased those, whom, of all the World, I would please most. Nor was the Town unkind to it; for which Reason I must applaud my good Fortune, to have pleased with so little Pains.*" He could well make the last statement since *The Libertine* represented the work of only three weeks.

[33] Prologue.
[34] Preface.
[35] The Lord Chamberlain's Records list a performance on June 15, 1675 (Nicoll, p. 310).

Downes couples this play with *The Virtuoso*, when reporting that "they were both very well *Acted*, and got the Company great Reputation." Betterton's acting of Don John "Crown'd the Play."[36] No list of actors in the first performance of *The Libertine* has been preserved, but it is quite probable that the low comedian, Cave Underhill, who had "created" Justice Clodpate in *Epsom-Wells*, was selected for the part of Jacomo. Anthony Aston, the author of the supplement to Cibber's *Lives of the Late Famous Actors and Actresses*, speaks of Underhill as having no rival in "his dry, heavy, downright way in low comedy," but that when he "aim'd at any archness," as he did when playing Jacomo, he "fell into downright insignificance."[37]

Shadwell's contribution to the repertory of the Duke's Company in 1676 was *The Virtuoso*, a comedy of humours ridiculing the scientific movement. It is possible that the idea of a play on this subject may have occurred to the dramatist as early as 1670 or 1671. Dryden's line "Let *Virtuosos* in five years be writ" admits of other interpretations than that Shadwell "laboured at composition, and produced *The Virtuoso*, it is said, after a prolonged agony of five years."[38] The various activities of Shadwell between 1671 and 1676 and his generally hasty methods of composition do not convince one that he would be capable of a "prolonged agony" over a single work. Dryden, to whom Shadwell refers as his "particular Friend" in the preface to *The Humourists*, may have been shown a preliminary sketch of *The Virtuoso* in 1671. But the author was unwilling at that time to risk the production of another comedy of humours and so did not complete the play. Some years later, he showed what he had written to the Duke of Newcastle at Welbeck;[39] and, upon receiving that nobleman's approbation, he was encouraged to complete the work begun five years or so earlier. The amount of time elapsing between preliminary sketch and production would account for Dryden's line.

The Virtuoso, which was "very well *Acted* and got the Company great Reputation,"[40] was performed in May, 1676,[41] and

[36] P. 37.
[37] *Colley Cibber. Written by Himself*, II, 315.
[38] Edmund Gosse, *History of Eighteenth Century Literature* (London, 1889), p. 49.
[39] Epistle Dedicatory to *The Virtuoso*.
[40] Downes, p. 37.
[41] The Lord Chamberlain's Records list

succeeded "beyond [the author's] Expectation." Its only enemies were "some Women, and some Men of Feminine Understandings; who like slight Plays only, that represent a little Tattle-sort of Conversation, like their own."[42] It was received favorably by the royal family and, according to Langbaine, was applauded by the University of Oxford.[43] Anthony Leigh, who had become a member of the Duke's Company near the time of Angel's death in 1673 and who was later to act the leading comic rôles in many plays by Shadwell, was "Eminent" in the part of Sir Formal Trifle,[44] described in the dramatis personae as a "florid Coxcomb." Nokes, who had formerly been the poet Ninny in *The Sullen Lovers* and the citizen Bisket in *Epsom-Wells*, appeared as Sir Samuel Hearty,[45] a "brisk, amorous, adventurous, unfortunate Coxcomb." Available theatrical records give no information concerning the other members of the cast.

In his prologue, Shadwell assures the audience that

if with new Fops he can but please,
He'll twice a Year produce as new as these.

But he did not live up to this promise. In his epistle, he writes that he has "no Pension but from the Theatre, which is either unwilling, or unable, to reward a Man sufficiently for so much Pains as correct Comedies require" and that he cannot allot his whole time to the writing of plays, but is "forced to mind some other business of Advantage." Evidently this "other business" required the greater part of his attention for the next year and a half. Not until December, 1677, or January, 1677/8,[46] does a new play by Shadwell appear, and then it is not a comedy, but a revision of a Shakespearean tragedy in the light of Restoration practice.

a performance on May 25, 1676 (Nicoll, p. 310).

[42] Epistle Dedicatory.

[43] P. 451.

[44] Downes, p. 41.

[45] Sir Credulous in *Sir Patient Fancy* (Act IV, Scene I) says, "Very well, put me into this Basket, and cord me down, send for a couple of Porters, hoist me away with a Direction to an old Uncle of mine, one *Sir Anthony Bubleton* at *Bubleton-Hall* in *Essex;* and then whip slap-dash, as *Nokes* says in the Play, I'm gone, and who's the wiser?" *Works of Aphra Behn* (ed. Summers), IV, 70. "Whip slap-dash" is one of the favorite expressions of Sir Samuel Hearty, who is brought to Miranda in a chest (Shadwell, I, 415).

[46] *Timon of Athens* was registered on February 23, 1677/8.

Timon of Athens, or the Man Hater "was very well *Acted*, and the Musick in't well Perform'd; it wonderfully pleas'd the Court and City; being an Excellent Moral."[47] It seems to have set the fashion for a series of rewritings of Shakespearean tragedies and historical plays.[48] During the next few years, the Duke's Company brought out Dryden's *Troilus and Cressida*, Otway's version of *Romeo and Juliet* called *The History and Fall of Caius Marius*, Crowne's two plays based on *Henry VI*, and Tate's happily ending *King Lear*, while the Theatre Royal presented Ravenscroft's *Titus Andronicus*, Tate's *The Ingratitude of a Common-Wealth: Or, The Fall of Caius Martius Coriolanus*, and D'Urfey's reworking of *Cymbeline* with the title of *The Injured Princess, or The Fatal Wager*. Shadwell's *Timon of Athens*, which Mr. Odell has called "an excellent acting-medium,"[49] was presented with a more than adequate cast. Betterton was Timon; Smith, Alcibiades; Harris, Apemantus; Mrs. Betterton, Evandra; and Mrs. Shadwell, Melissa. The Senators of Athens were acted by Sandford, Underhill, Leigh, Norris, Percival, and Gillo. The part of the steward Demetrius was taken by the ill-fated Matthew Medbourne, himself a playwright and for many years a member of the Duke's Company, but soon to die in prison as a result of the Popish Plot. John Bowman, then at the beginning of his theatrical career, played Timon's servant Diphilus, and Thomas Jevon, also one of the younger members of the company and later to win reputation in comic parts, was the Poet. The other minor rôles of the Old Man, Chloe, Thais, and Phinias were taken by Richards, Mrs. Gibbs, Mrs. Seymour, and Mrs. LeGrand.

This play, an undoubted success, was followed by a comedy containing Jonsonian echoes called *A True Widow*. It was produced sometime between October 17, 1678, the day on which the body of Sir Edmund Berry Godfrey was found,[50] and February

[47] Downes, p. 37.

[48] Dryden's *All for Love* was probably produced before *Timon*. Although it is written "in imitation of Shakespear's stile," it is not an adaptation.

[49] George C. D. Odell, *Shakespeare from Betterton to Irving*, (New York, 1920), I, 48. See also Hazelton Spencer, *Shakespeare Improved* (Cambridge, 1927), pp. 281-287.

[50] The first four lines of the epilogue doubtless refer to the panic which followed the murder of Godfrey:

"*In troubled Times, like these—the Ancients chose*
T'exhibit Feasts, and Plays, and publick Shows;
By such Diversions to allay Men's Fears,
Compose their Minds, and mollifie their Cares."

16, 1678/9, the date of the dedication,—probably in November or December, 1678. Although it received the benefit of Sir Charles Sedley's "Correction and Alteration," it "met not with that Success from the Generality of the Audience, which [the author] hop'd for." The failure, Shadwell thinks, may have been due to "the Calamity of the Time, which made People not care for Diversions," "the Anger of a great many, who thought themselves concern'd in the Satyr," or "the want of Taste in others." He is satisfied that it deserved a better fate: "I have the Judgment of Men of the best Sense, besides the best of the Poets, on my side in this Point." In anger at those who condemn him, he writes: "And till I see more Variety of new Humour, than I have produced in my Comedies, and more naturally drawn, I shall not despair of bearing up near my Contemporaries of the first Rate, who write Comedy, and of always surmounting the little Poetasters of the fourth Rate."[51]

This play was dedicated to Sir Charles Sedley, who in 1679 was known as a dramatist, having written a comedy, *The Mulberry Garden*, and a dreary tragedy in couplets, *Antony and Cleopatra*. But those who were numbered among his acquaintances relished his spoken wit more than any of his literary attempts. In the dedication to *A True Widow*, Shadwell writes: "My greatest Satisfaction is, that I have the Honour of his Friendship, and my Comedies have had his Approbation, whom I have heard speak more Wit at a Supper, than all my Adversaries, with their Heads join'd together, can write in a Year." As we shall see later, during Shadwell's period of hardships, Sedley, like Dorset, was willing to do more than merely express approval.

Disappointed because of the failure of *A True Widow*, the author decided to suit his next comedy, *The Woman-Captain*, to the tastes of his audience.

> *He found, by's last, you would not like what's good,*
> *Though it was prais'd by all that understood.*
> *Remembring how you us'd that last he writ,*
> *He made this Low, so to your Level fit;*
> *Plenty of Noise, and Scarcity of Wit—*
> *The Devil's in you all, if this don't hit.*[52]

[51] Dedication to *A True Widow*.

[52] Epilogue.

Contemporary references to the first performances of this play are lacking; but, with Mrs. Elizabeth Barry in the lively part of Mrs. Gripe, it is hard to believe that they could have been failures. This actress, who for four years had appeared in both comic and serious rôles, was at this time on the eve of her great triumphs in the plays of Otway. Anthony Leigh, who in the prologue says "*I'll hang, if I don't make you laugh to Day*," was admirably cast as the penurious husband, Gripe.[53]

The Woman-Captain, which was acted before November, 1679,[54] was the last play written by Shadwell before he became enmeshed in the warfare of politics. Some "poetic" labors disassociated from his dramatic efforts, however, belong to the years we have been considering. In 1676, there was printed in a volume of *Letters and Poems in Honour of the Incomparable Princess, Margaret, Dutchess of Newcastle* an elegy by Shadwell on the Duchess's death.[55] As verse, it is heavy and monotonous, a forecast of what the writer was to do later in his official odes. In 1680, he furnished an epilogue, spoken by Mrs. Barry, for Laurence Maidwell's *The Loving Enemies*,[56] a play in which his wife appeared and which, in the character of Circumstantio, was imitative of Sir Formal Trifle in *The Virtuoso*.

But more interesting than either of these ventures into verse is the long poem in couplets, "To my Much Respected Master, and Worthy Friend, Signior Pietro Reggio, On the Publishing his Book of Songs," which was printed in the volume of *Songs set by Signior Pietro Reggio*.[57] Among the contents is a setting of "Arise, arise, yee subterranean winds," called "Song in the Tempest. The words by Mr Shadwell." Shadwell's poem to the composer flows along with monotonous smoothness. In his first lines, he realizes his shortcomings as a poet:

[53] See Genest, I, 283.

[54] Advertised in "A Catalogue of Books . . . Printed and Published at *London* in *Michaelmas* Term, 1679" (*Term Catalogues*, ed. Arber, I, 370).

[55] Entitled "An Elegy upon the death of the Incomparable Princess Margaret Dutchess of New-Castle" and printed on pp. 165-168 of the volume. The Duchess was buried in Westminster Abbey on January 7, 1673/4.

[56] This play may have been produced in 1679.

[57] In the British Museum copy is a note: "It was advertized in the London Gazette 1680 as 'A Choice collection of songs set by Signor Pietro Reggio to be engraved on copper in an extraordinary manner in very large folio, most of them out of Mr. A. Cowley's excellent Poems.' "

If I could write with a Poetick fire
Equal to thine in MUSICK, *I'd admire*
And Praise Thee fully: Now my Verse will be
Short of thy Merit, as I short of Thee.

After praising both the composing and performing of Reggio and commenting on the fact that "*the Pretenders of this Quacking Age*" are unable to suit the sound of their music to the sense of the poet, Shadwell continues:

In thy Invention, *and thy* Singing *too,*
Thy Fancy's *ever Various, ever New.*
Thou to each Temper canst the Heart Engage,
To Grief canst soften, and inflame to Rage.
With Horrour fright, with Love canst make us burn,
Make us Rejoyce one Moment, and next Mourn,
And canst the Mind to every Passion turn.
And to each Grace *and* Cadence, *thy great Art,*
Such soft Harmonious Sweetness *does impart,*
With gentle Violence thou dost storm a Heart.
How oft dost thou my Anxious Cares destroy,
And make me want, or wish no other Joy!
For when thy Ayres, *perform'd by Thee, I hear,*
No Wealth I envy, and no Power, I fear;
Nor Misery, nor Death I apprehend,
For Fame nor Liberty can I contend,
When I am charm'd by Thee, my Excellent Friend.

Near the end, Shadwell writes:

In your own Language Y' are a Poet *too.*
So good, I wish that Ours as well you knew.

Possibly the fact that Reggio knew English no better and therefore over-estimated the value of Shadwell's verses may account for the Sonetto contained in the same volume and addressed "Al' Signor *Tomaso Shadwel,* Poeta Dignissimo, per li suoi bellissimi Versi scritti in lode del' Autore." Since this poem contains what are, to my knowledge, the only verses of unqualified praise of Shadwell published during his lifetime, it is worth printing here:[57a]

[57a] The text of Reggio's poem printed here reproduces the wording in the British Museum volume. It differs in some respects from the text printed by Mr. Summers in his edition of Shadwell, I, clv.

CIgno Immortal, che col' tuo nobil' canto,
Radolciresti, al più crudo Aspe il core:
Ben tù di Preggio auanzi il Gran Cantore;
Che placò l'Ira del' Eterno pianto:

Egli có i dolci accenti, impetrò tanto,
Che ritrasse il suo Ben dal' cieco horrore.
Tù con là Cetra, à lè *CASTALIE* suore
L'alme rapisci: onde, è maggiore il vanto.

Sono lè rime tue Rivi correnti,
Che di Eloquenza in sen' chiudon tesori
Ricchi vié più dè gl'Indian Torrenti.

Sú i bei Colli di *PINDO* á coglier Fiori
M'inuita l'Harmonia dè tuoi concenti:
Mentre *APOLLO* t'intreccia il'crin di Allori.

From a statement in the manuscript of Aubrey's *Brief Lives*, we learn of Shadwell's friendship for a greater man than Reggio. Here the dramatist is pictured not as painfully tuning his lyre to a key of praise, but as engaged in the melancholy task of pall-bearer. Aubrey thus briefly describes the burial of Samuel Butler on September 27, 1680: "About 25 of his old acquaintance at his funerall. I myself being one [of the eldest, helped to carry the pall with Tom Shadwell, at the foot, Sir Robert Thomas and Mr. Saunders, esq., at the head; Dr. Cole and Dr. Davenant, middle]. His coffin covered with black bayes."[58]

Some few days before the funeral of Butler, Shadwell had participated in a more joyous event. On September 21, 1680, the parish register of St. Brides' records the christening of "Wm Son of Thomas Shadwell and Anne his wife."[59] During the period of the twelve years we have been considering, these registers contain also the entries on January 20, 1673/4, of the baptism of "George ye son of Thomas Shadwell and Ann his wife," and on February 21, 1677/8, of the burial of "George Shadwell." The Shadwells

[58] Aubrey, *Brief Lives* (ed. Andrew Clark), I, 136-137. The words in square brackets are struck out in the manuscript, "apparently only because Aubrey thought they went too much into detail," says Clark.

[59] On October 5, 1680, occurs this entry among the christenings: "William Son of Thomas Shadwell and Ann his wife." It is impossible to say whether this entry or that given in the text is correct. The entries from the register of St. Bride's are here printed for the first time. For other entries from this register see p. 71.

were evidently not living in this parish in 1671 at the time of the birth of their son John,[60] who was later to be knighted and become physician in ordinary to three of England's rulers.

Since his initial success with *The Sullen Lovers,* Shadwell had written partially or completely thirteen plays of varying degrees of merit. He had become acquainted with those gentlemen described by the author of the *Account* as "the most celebrated Persons of Wit and distinguished Quality in that Age." He had penned some occasional verse of no particular importance. He had also engaged in two paper combats. It is to these that we must now direct our attention.

[60] He matriculated at University College, Oxford, on May 15, 1685, aged 14. *Alumni Oxonienses* (ed. J. Foster), IV, Early Series, 1337.

CHAPTER III

LITERARY CONTROVERSIES, 1668-1680

SHADWELL began his controversial tilts in the preface to his first play, *The Sullen Lovers.* Here he stated forcefully his ideas on the condition of the contemporary stage and expressed his scorn for those writers who differed from him in their estimate of Ben Jonson. The author he had particularly in mind was Dryden, at that time the most active and popular of the dramatists writing for the London theatres. In *An Essay of Dramatic Poesy,* printed in 1668, Dryden had discussed, among other subjects, the comparative merits of the earlier dramatists and had referred to Jonson, not only as a "careful and learned observer of the dramatic laws," but also as "the most learned and judicious writer which any theatre ever had."[1] This high opinion of the author of *The Silent Woman,* however, did not cause Dryden to lose his sense of critical values or to overlook the fact that Shakespeare and Beaumont and Fletcher were greater wits than Jonson. "One cannot say he [i.e., Jonson] wanted wit, but rather that he was frugal of it. . . . Humour was his proper sphere; and in that he delighted most to represent mechanic people." And later, in the same essay, Dryden had written that Jonson did not possess a "luxuriant fancy"; "as he did not want imagination, so none ever said he had much to spare."

Shadwell, however, ignored the good things that were said about Jonson in this temperately-phrased essay; and, in the preface to *The Sullen Lovers,* he stressed the remarks which had unfavorable implications. Although he referred to the *persons* who were making these derogatory observations about his favorite dramatist, it appears that he was thinking primarily of Dryden. He calls those writers "Insolent" who had of late said that Jonson "wrote his best Plays without Wit; imagining, that all the Wit in Plays consisted in bringing two Persons upon the Stage to break Jests, and to bob one another, which they call Repartie; not considering that there is

[1] Unless otherwise indicated, all quotations from Dryden's prose works in this chapter are from W. P. Ker's edition of *Essays of John Dryden* (Oxford, 1900).

more Wit and Invention requir'd in the finding out good Humour, and Matter proper for it, than in all their smart Reparties. For in the writing of a Humour, a Man is confin'd not to swerve from the Character, and oblig'd to say nothing but what is proper to it." But Shadwell did not allow the matter to rest merely with these words in reply to the *Essay*. He added two other remarks which Dryden could well consider as having personal application. The first was a charge of plagiarism, an accusation which Shadwell was again to make in his epistle to *The Medal of John Bayes:* "I have the Example of some, that never yet wrote Play without stealing most of it; and (like Men that lye so long, till they believe themselves) at length by continual Thieving, reckon their stol'n Goods their own too." The second was an attack upon Florimel and Celadon, the principal characters in *Secret Love:* ". . . in the Plays, which have been wrote of late, there is no such thing as perfect Character, but the two chief Persons are most commonly a Swearing, Drinking, Whoring, Ruffian for a Lover, and an impudent ill-bred *Tomrig* for a Mistress, and these are the fine People of the Play; and there is that Latitude in this, that almost any thing is proper for them to say; but their chief Subject is Bawdy, and Profaneness, which they call *Brisk Writing.*"

The older writer did not reply immediately to the newcomer in the theatre. He had first to justify his position on the use of rhyme in the drama by answering Sir Robert Howard's preface to *The Great Favourite, or The Duke of Lerma.* In his "Defence of an Essay of Dramatic Poesy," Dryden wrote, "My chief endeavours are to delight the age in which I live. If the humour of this be for low comedy, small accidents, and raillery, I will force my genius to obey it, though with more reputation I could write in verse." The latter statement was taken up by Shadwell in the preface to his second play. Here he asserts that in *The Royal Shepherdess* have been strictly observed "the Rules of Morality and good Manners . . . (Virtue being exalted, and Vice depressed)" and ventures the opinion that "perhaps it might have been better received, had neither been done in it." He finds "it pleases most to see Vice encourag'd, by bringing the Characters of debauch'd People upon the Stage, and making them pass for fine Gentlemen, who openly profess Swearing, Drinking, Whoring, breaking Windows, beating Constables, *&c.*" "But it is said, by some"—and here is the slur at Dryden—"that this pleases the People, and a Poet's Business is only to endeavour that: But he, that debases himself to think of nothing but pleasing the Rabble, loses the Dignity of a Poet, and becomes as little as a Jugler, or a Rope-Dancer, who please more than he can do."

The reply to Shadwell's strictures is found in the preface to *An Evening's Love; or, The Mock Astrologer,* published in 1671. After calling Jonson the "only man, of all ages and nations," who has written humour well, and acknowledging that he "can be taxed with fewer failings than any English poet," Dryden begins his answer to the preface to *The Sullen Lovers:*

> I know I have been accused as an enemy of his writings; but without any other reason, than that I do not admire him blindly, and without looking into his imperfections. . . . I admire and applaud him where I ought: those who do more, do but value themselves in their admiration of him; and, by telling you they extol Ben Johnson's way, would insinuate to you that they can practise it. For my part, I declare that I want judgment to imitate him; and should think it a great impudence in myself to attempt it. To make men appear ridiculous on the stage, was, as I have said, his talent; and in this he needed not the acumen of wit but that of judgment. For the characters and representations of folly are only the effects of observation; and observation is an effect of judgment. Some ingenious men, for whom I have a particular esteem, have thought I have much injured Ben Johnson, when I have not allowed his wit to be extraordinary: but they confound the notion of what is witty, with what is pleasant. That Ben Johnson's plays were pleasant, he must want reason who denies: but that pleasantness was not properly wit, or the sharpness of conceit, but the natural imitation of folly; which I confess to be excellent in its kind, but not to be of that kind which they pretend.

He commends "the mixed way of Comedy; that which is neither all wit, nor all humour, but the result of both," and notes that the qualities "which Quintilian reckons up as the ornaments of wit . . . are extremely wanting in Ben Johnson." He finds repartee to be "the greatest grace of Comedy, where it is proper to the characters." To the charge that he makes "debauched persons . . . the chief persons of the drama" and that he makes them happy at the conclusion of the play, "against the law of Comedy, which is to reward virtue, and punish vice," he replies that no such law has "been constantly observed in Comedy, either by the ancient or modern poets." After he emphasizes the dictum that "the first end of Comedy is delight, and instruction only the second," he answers the accusation of plagiarism by conceding that whenever he has found a story in a romance, novel, or foreign play which he liked, he has "made no difficulty . . . to take the foundation of it, to build it up, and to make it proper for the English stage." In doing so, he is merely following the practise of Shakespeare, Jonson, and Beaumont and Fletcher. The forming of the material into acts and scenes,

> disposing of actions and passions into their proper places, and beautifying both with descriptions, similitudes, and propriety of language, is the principal employment of the poet; as being the largest field of fancy, which is the principal quality required in him. . . . Judgment, indeed, is necessary in him; but 'tis fancy that gives the life-touches, and the secret graces to it; especially in serious plays, which depend not much on observation. For, to write humour in comedy (which is the theft of poets from mankind), little of fancy is required; the poet observes only what is ridiculous and pleasant folly, and by judging exactly what is so, he pleases in the representation of it.

Then comes the conclusion, which is in the nature of a threat—a threat later to be fulfilled with disastrous effect to Shadwell's reputation: "I shall but laugh at them hereafter, who accuse me with so little reason; and withal contemn their dulness, who, if they could ruin that little reputation I have got, and which I value not, yet would want both wit and learning to establish their own; or to be remembered in after ages for anything, but only that which makes them ridiculous in this."

These ominous words may have caused Shadwell to employ a more restrained method of utterance in his reply to this essay than he had used heretofore. Certainly, there is nothing ill-natured in the preface to *The Humourists*. In this, the author politely takes "leave to dissent from those, who seem to insinuate, that the ultimate End of a Poet, is to delight, without Correction or Instruction." A poet should do all he can, "decently to please, that so he may instruct. To adorn his Images of Virtue so delightfully, to affect People with a secret Veneration of it in others, and an Emulation to Practise it in themselves: And to render their Figures of *Vice* and *Folly* so ugly and detestable, to make People hate, and despise them." Then, after discussing the various vices and fopperies that he would present in his comedies, he returns to Dryden and the preface to *An Evening's Love:*

> And here I must make a little Digression, and take Liberty to dissent from my particular Friend, for whom I have a very great Respect, and whose Writings I extremely admire; and though I will not say, his is the best way of Writing, yet, I am sure, his Manner of Writing it is much the best that ever was. . . . His Verse is smoother and deeper, his Thoughts more quick and surprising, his Raptures more mettled and higher; and he has more of that in his Writing, which *Plato* calls σώφρονα μανίαν, than any other Heroick Poet. And those, who shall go about to imitate him, will be found to flutter and make a Noise, but never rise. Yet (after all this) I cannot think it Impudence in him, or any Man, to endeavour to imitate Mr. *Johnson*, whom he confesses to have fewer Failings, than all the *English* Poets; which implies he was the most perfect, and best Poet: And why should not we endeavour to imitate him? because we cannot arrive to his Excellence? . . . Men of all Professions ought certainly to follow the best in theirs; and let not Endeavours be blamed, if they go as far as they can in the right Way, though they be unsuccessful, and attain not their ends. If Mr. *Johnson* be the most faultless Poet, I am so far from thinking it Impudence to endeavour to imitate him, that it would rather (in my Opinion) seem Impudence in me not to do it.

Furthermore, Shadwell "cannot be of their Opinion, who think [Jonson] wanted Wit." He also will not agree that "to the writing of his Humours . . . Wit was not required, but Judgment." "Nature . . . subjected Wit to the Government of Judgment, which is the noblest Faculty of the Mind. Fancy rough-draws, but Judgment smooths and finishes: nay, Judgment does indeed comprehend Wit; for no Man can have that, who has not Wit." He then considers another passage in Dryden's preface: "The Reason given by some, why *Johnson* needed not Wit in writing Humour, is, because Humour is the effect of Observation, and Observation the effect of Judgment; but Observation is as much Necessary in all other Plays, as in Comedies of Humour." After defining wit as "the Invention of remote and pleasant Thoughts, of what Kind sover," he declares that "there is as much Occasion for such Imaginations in the Writing of a curious Coxcomb's Part, as in Writing the greatest Hero's; and that, which may be Folly in the Speaker, may be so Remote and Pleasant, to require a great deal of Wit in the Writer." Jonson "put Wit into the Mouths of the meanest of his People, and . . . made it proper for 'em."

The argument was brought to a close by Dryden in his "Defence of the Epilogue; or an Essay on the Dramatic Poetry of the Last Age," printed with *The Conquest of Granada* in 1672. Loath to continue a discussion which must have been wearisome, he was willing to state: "For Ben Johnson, the most judicious of poets, he always writ properly, and as the character required; and I will not contest farther with my friends who call that wit: it being very certain, that even folly itself, well represented, is wit in a larger signification; and that there is fancy, as well as judgment, in it, though not so much or noble."

Thus the preface-skirmish between Shadwell and Dryden ended. Although touching incidentally upon plagiarism and the purpose of comedy, it was concerned primarily with the academic question as to whether or not Jonson had used wit in writing his plays of humour. Dryden had finally to admit that there was some truth in his antagonist's main contention; and Shadwell, who had at first expressed his opinions with some degree of heat and not a little ill-nature, had been won—either by threat or by example—to a more sober method of statement.

There is no indication that these writers were not on friendly terms at the conclusion of the controversy. In fact, Shadwell was soon to assist Dryden in an attack upon a fellow-dramatist, Elkanah Settle, who, in the dedication to *The Empress of Morocco*, addressed to Henry, Earl of Norwich, in 1673, had made some rather irritating remarks:

> *Thus a Dedication which was formerly a Present to a person of Quality, is now made a Libel on him, whilst the Poet either supposes his Patron to be so great a sot to defend that in Print, which he hist off the Stage: or else makes himself a greater, in asking a Favour from him which he nere expects to obtain. However, that which is an abuse to the* Patron, *is a Complement to the* Bookseller, *who whispers the* Poet, *and tells him, Sir, Your Play had misfortune, and all that—but if you'd but write a Dedication, or Preface—The Poet takes the hint, picks out a person of Honour, tells him he has a great deal of Wit, gives us an account who writ Sence in the last Age, supposing we cannot be Ignorant who writes it in This; Disputes the nature of* Verse, *Answers a Cavil or two, Quibles upon the* Court, *Huffs the* Critiques, *and the work's don. 'Tis not to be*

imagin'd how far a sheet of this goes to make a Bookseller *Rich, and a* Poet *Famous.*

But my Lord, whilst I trouble you with this kind of discourse, I beg you would not think I design to give rules to the Press, *as some of our Tribe have done to the* Stage; *or that I find fault with their Dedications in Complement to my own: No, that's a trick I do not pretend to.*

This passage was considered by Dryden as a personal insult; and, feeling strongly the recent failure of his own play, *The Assignation,* he decided to reprove the impudent poet. The fact that Settle's tragedy had been acted twice at Whitehall by "great personages of the court" and that it had been printed with "sculptures" and sold for two shillings, twice the usual price for a play, probably further aroused the animosity of the laureate, who was not slow to persuade Shadwell and Crowne to collaborate with him in a reply.[2]

Shadwell's dislike for the type of play which Settle was writing may account for his willingness to join in the attack. John Crowne, who had yet to win his spurs as a playwright, was doubtless glad of the opportunity to be associated with two successful dramatists.[3] The *Notes and Observations On the Empress of Morocco, Or, Some few ERRATA'S to be Printed instead of the SCULPTURES with the Second Edition of that PLAY* was published anonymously in 1674. It is impossible to determine exactly which parts of the pamphlet were written by each of the three authors; but it is likely that Dryden had much to do with the entire work. Many years later, Crowne said that he himself wrote "above three parts of four" of the notes;[4] and Settle attributed the criticism of the fourth act to Shadwell.[5]

The pamphlet is full of abuse. In the preface, Settle is called

[2] Settle's statement is the sole authority for attributing to Shadwell a share in the *Notes and Observations on the Empress of Morocco.* That statement, however, seems to me to be sufficient since Shadwell, when he attacked Settle in the preface to *The Libertine,* did not deny the charge. For accounts of this quarrel, see the Scott-Saintsbury edition of Dryden, XV, 393-396; F. C. Brown, *Elkanah Settle, His Life and Works* (Chicago, 1910), pp. 51-61; and A. F. White, *John Crowne, His Life and Dramatic Works* (Cleveland, 1922), pp. 32-34.

[3] John Dennis, in the preface to his *Remarks upon Mr. Pope's Translation of Homer* (London, 1717), attributes the writing of the *Notes and Observations* to jealousy on the part of the three coauthors.

[4] John Crowne, *Caligula* (London, 1698), "To the Reader."

[5] Elkanah Settle, *Ibrahim, the Illustrious Bassa* (London, 1677), "To the Reader."

an *"upstart illiterate Scribler"* and a *"contemptible . . . Wretch"* who should be made an example *"to the discouragement of all such petulant Ill Writers."* The plot of *The Empress of Morocco* is described as *"incoherent and full of absurdities,"* and the characters are *"so ill chosen, that they are all either Knaves or Fools."* In the observations *"one half of the faults and absurdities are not shown"*; what is presented *"is only Selected Fustian, Impertinence, and false Grammar."* Shadwell's "examinations on the fourth Act" were thought by Settle to be "more malicious" than the commentaries of the two other writers.[6] An example or two will suffice: "if *Elkanah* had had as little Gall as Brains, he had not shewn all Malice in his Epistle, and no Wit"; "never was any man so unlucky at sentences, similes, or descriptions as this Fumbler in poetry by name *Elkanah* Settle." In commenting upon the lines

> Kings that want Armes, do not want Majesty.
> Heav'n is still Heav'n, though't lays its thunder by,

Shadwell remarks, "if it wanted Thunder as he Arms, or could be rob'd of it, it were no Heaven as certainly as Mr. *Settle* is no Poet."[7]

The author of *The Empress of Morocco,* who was not the sort of person to allow such a pamphlet as this to lie ignored, replied shortly afterwards in his *Notes and Observations on the Empress of Morocco Revised. With Some few Errata's to be Printed instead of the Postscript, with the next Edition of the Conquest of Granada.* After mentioning, in his preface, that no author's name had been attached to the work he was answering, Settle wrote:

> *by those three remarkable Qualities of* Railing, Boasting *and* Thieving *I found a* Dryden *in the Frontispiece. Then going through the Preface, I observ'd the drawing of a Fools Picture to be the design of the whole piece, and reflecting on the Painter I consider'd, that probably his Pamphlet might be like his Plays, not to be written without help. And according to expectation I discovered the Author of* Epsome-Wells, *and the Author of* Pandion *and* Amphigenia *lent their assistance. How! Three to One thought I? and Three Gentlemen of such disagreeing Qualifications in one Club: The First a Man that has had wit, but is past it; the Second that has it, if he can keep it, and the Third that*

[6] *Ibid.*

[7] *Notes and Observations on the Empress of Morocco* (London, 1674), pp. 35, 49, 37.

neither has, nor is ever like to have it. Then boldly on I went, and fortified with patience (as I found it requir'd) for a full perusal, I wonderd the less at the Deformity of the piece, when such different hands went to the composure. The first of these is the only person that pretends an injury receivd from a Satyrick Line or two in the Epistle *to* Morocco: *Such as the Author never design'd for a particular reflection, and such as I am sure* Elkanah *would have thank'd him for, provided like them, as they had been true, they had been harmless too. And consequently I conclude him the promoter of so Ill-natur'd, and so scurrulous a retort. The Second I suppose only putting his Comical hand to the Work, to help forward with the mirth of so ridiculous a Libel: and the Third perhaps out of a Vain Glory of being in Print, knowing himself to be so little a Reptile in Poetry, that hee's beholding to a Lampoon for giving the World to know, that there is such a writer in being. Some have advised me in answering these* Notes, *to retort upon all Three: But that would be a tedious work, besides the inconvenience of it. The two last had not the same ends in writing, nor are they so fair marks as the First, One having no Heroicks in Print, and the other such as cannot well be Attacqued; his Plays being fortified against Objections.*

Surely there was nothing in this pamphlet directed against Dryden that could have offended Shadwell; and the matter might very well have been allowed to drop here. Dryden and Crowne did withdraw from the field; but Shadwell—if a statement in the preface to *Ibrahim* may be believed—elbowed his way into further controversy by inserting a scene ridiculing Settle in Newcastle's *The Triumphant Widow,* produced in November, 1674. This passage is one in which "a silly Heroick Poet . . . speak[s] the very words [Shadwell] had heard [Settle] say, and [makes] reflexions on some of the very Lines he had so sencelessly prated on before in his *Notes.*"[8] It is impossible to identify the "very words"; and specific lines from *The Empress of Morocco* do not occur in *The Triumphant Widow.* But, as Mr. Perry has pointed out, the entire character of Crambo, the heroic poet, suggests satire, and was very likely intended to represent Settle.[9]

This attack stirred the other dramatist to action; and, in the postscript appended to *Love and Revenge,* published in 1675, Settle refers slurringly to the boasts frequently made by Shadwell that his plays are written rapidly:

[8] Settle, *Ibrahim,* "To the Reader."

[9] H. T. E. Perry, *The First Duchess of Newcastle and Her Husband as Figures in Literary History,* p. 163.

I could make Excuses for putting an ill Head upon Worse Shoulders; Or tell you as some of our Impertinent Tribe do, that 'twas Written in three Weeks, or a Months time, if I thought any Reasonable Man, would be more Favorable to the Defects of the Play for such an Apology. But as I am Sensible, that that Excuse to a Play, would be much like that of a Builder, that after the fall of a House, shall tell you, truly he Built slightly, and chose an ill Foundation; I will not urge that Plea for the Plays Defence; which in the best Interpretation must render an Author Lazy, if not Dull: In the first of which, he shews himself Impudent, when he dares be so Disrespectful to an Audience, as to obtrude such incorrect Stuff upon 'em, as he is, or ought to be ashamed of: Or else proves himself a Blockhead, and makes that Excuse, when really he wanted Abilities, not Leisure to write better.

These words, as well as others in the epistle to *The Conquest of China*,[10] invited an insulting reply, which Shadwell readily furnished in his preface to *The Libertine*, published in 1676. Here he calls Settle "*a rough hobling Rhymer*," one who "*ought not to have measured any Man's Abilities, who writes for the Stage, with his own; for some may write that in three Weeks, which he cannot in three Years.*" He also upbraids his adversary for placing himself among the poets: "*they are all Gentlemen, that will not own him, or keep him Company.*" He finally dismisses his opponent by saying:

I shall never trouble my self to take Notice of him hereafter, since all Men of Wit will think, that he can do the Poets no greater Injury, than pretending to be one. Nor had I said so much in answer to his coarse Railing, but to reprehend his Arrogance, and lead him to a little better Knowledge of himself; nor does his base Language in his Postscript deserve a better Return.

The last word was said by Settle, who, in the "Preface to the Reader" prefixed to *Ibrahim*, published in 1677, penned a scorching rejoinder. He describes Shadwell as "the ingenious Translater of three French Plays that calls himself the *Author* of the *Libertine*" and as "a wretched Dabler in Verse, [who] put Heroicks quite out of countenance, when he spoil'd an old Womans Tale, and call'd it *Psyche.*" He wonders why his adversary, if he knows so much about gentility, makes such coxcombs of the gentlemen

[10] Printed in 1676.

he portrays. He accuses Shadwell of plagiarism, ridicules his pretensions to learning, and laughs at the title-page of *Epsom-Wells.* The fact that the author had there called himself *"Student of the Middle Temple"*[10a] causes Settle to become sarcastic: "The proficiency in so crabbed a study as the *Law*, with the Toil and Trouble of *Practice* and *Clients* might easily be prejudicial to an Authour's progress in Poetry, Poetry being a study, which we all know requires a great deal of freedom, and moves but heavily and dully, when clogg'd with such weighty Fetters. And indeed I expect to see the Muses in mourning, for the loss of so considerable a Pillar; since he is so unkind to them, as to do that honour to the *Gown* which he robs the Theater of." Settle goes on to say that Shadwell had tried to "ruine [him] in the esteem" of the family of the Duke of Newcastle and that he had also made a consistent practice of damning plays:

> For no sooner comes a Play upon the Stage, but the first day 'tis Acted, he wallows into the Pit like a Porpoise before a Storm, with the very Prognosticks of ill luck in his Face, and uses all his interest and spight right or wrong to damn it. Yet *I* have a little more reason than my Fellow sufferers to complain: For he makes it his business before he sees a Line of any of my Plays, to cry 'em down; and long before they are Acted to make Factions and Cabals to damn them: and in all Companies, he cries *God damme I can't write Sence nor Grammar.*

Enough of this preface has been quoted to indicate the character of Settle's reply. Shadwell kept his promise and ignored the attack. Dryden, who had withdrawn from the contest after the publication of the *Notes and Observations*, did not again take up cudgels against the heroic dramatist until he coupled Settle and Shadwell in the supreme abuse of the second part of *Absalom and Achitophel.*

Shortly after writing his last lines against Settle, Shadwell returned to the question of humour and, in the dedicatory epistle to *The Virtuoso,* intimated that, if he had a pension, he might compose "as correct a Comedy as any of [his] Contemporaries." These words—undoubtedly directed against the poet-laureate—and a passage in the epilogue, which has been interpreted as a slur at *Aurengzebe*, did not, however, deter Dryden from contributing a pro-

[10a] The copies of the 1673 quarto of *Epsom-Wells* which I have seen do not have these words upon the title-page.

logue to *A True Widow,* produced in 1678. In that same year, he took occasion, in the preface to *All for Love,* to mention Rochester's allusion to "hasty Shadwell and slow Wycherley":[11] "The sharpness of [Rochester's] satire . . . falls most heavily on his friends, and they ought never to forgive him for commending them perpetually the wrong way, and sometimes by contraries. If he have a friend, whose hastiness in writing is his greatest fault, Horace would have taught him to have minced the matter, and to have called it readiness of thought and a flowing fancy. . . . But he would never have allowed him to have called a slow man hasty, or a hasty writer a slow drudge." These words criticizing Rochester's method in satire exhibit no animus towards either of the dramatists referred to.

But Dryden's next mention of Shadwell was characterized by marked hostility. When and why did the laureate write *MacFlecknoe?* As a result of recent investigations,[12] the old explanation of this satire as Dryden's answer to Shadwell's *The Medal of John Bayes* is no longer sound. Dryden's poem was in circulation —possibly only in manuscript—as early as November, 1681, or four months before the publication of *The Medal,* to which Shadwell replied in the poem mentioned above. The time of composition was doubtless between the production of *A True Widow,* late in 1678, and November, 1681. Since *MacFlecknoe* was di-

[11] See p. 94.

[12] For a summary of the discussion occasioned by the discovery of a manuscript copy of a portion of *MacFlecknoe* dated "1678" and said to be in the handwriting of John Oldham, see Mark Van Doren, *The Poetry of John Dryden* (New York, 1920), pp. 339-350. G. Thorn-Drury in his note, "The Date of MacFlecknoe" (*Review of English Studies,* I, 187-190) suggests "that if October 4, 1682, was the actual date of publication of *MacFlecknoe,* it had been written and circulated in MS. some considerable time before." He thinks that "two pieces of evidence . . . found in the poem itself . . . point to 1678 rather than a later year as more probably the date of its composition." The satire contains no reference to Shadwell's political leanings, which would have been mentioned if Dryden had written the poem in 1682. Also, it seems unlikely that Dryden would wait four years before making the slurring allusion to Herringman, who ceased being his publisher in 1678. Even if we are unwilling to accept these facts as conclusive evidence that *MacFlecknoe* belongs to 1678, we cannot help being convinced by two other quotations cited by Mr. Thorn-Drury that Dryden's poem was known nearly a year before the date usually assigned for its publication. The expression, *"a MacFlecknoe,"* appears in *The Loyal Protestant* of February 9, 1681/2. In *Sir Barnaby Whigg* (acted not later than November, 1681) Shadwell is ridiculed in a song containing the line, "Thersites *my Humour, and* Fleckno *my Wit."* It is possible that Dryden may have taken the idea from D'Urfey of joining Shadwell's name with Flecknoe's, but it is more likely that D'Urfey had seen Dryden's poem in manuscript.

rected against Shadwell the dramatic poet, and not Shadwell the political pamphleteer, it seems proper to believe that it was written before either author or victim became enmeshed in the controversies between Whig and Tory.

MacFlecknoe is allied in purpose to the *Notes and Observations On the Empress of Morocco.* In each work, Dryden attempted to render ridiculous a dramatist who had aroused his ire. With the information at present available, it is impossible to state definitely what caused the laureate to turn against Shadwell. Had he wearied of the younger writer's repeated boasts of friendship with the wits? Had he become disgusted with the other dramatist's arrogant treatment of those who did not applaud the humours in *The Virtuoso* and *A True Widow?* Had he tired of seeing Shadwell "wallow into the pit" and condemn plays? Or did some word or act bring to his mind the former controversy and the threat then made of condemning dulness?

The poem itself is too well known to require detailed treatment here. It is enough to recall that Dryden represents Flecknoe, who he elsewhere implies is a "bad poet,"[13] as seeking a successor to rule in the realms of nonsense. From his numerous progeny he selects Shadwell who has been "mature in dulness from his tender years." At the Nursery, Shadwell swears that he will maintain "true dulness" to death and never "have peace with wit nor truce with sense." After being given a "mighty mug of potent ale" and a copy of *Love's Kingdom* for ball and scepter, he is crowned with a garland of poppies. The crowd then acclaims the new leader with enthusiasm, and Flecknoe tells his son to advance "in new impudence, new ignorance." Instead of writing plays, he should compose anagrams and acrostics or set his own songs and sing them to the lute. These words of advice are brought to a close by the sinking of the trap upon which Flecknoe is standing; and Shadwell is left with the mantle of the former ruler. In addition to stressing the dulness of his victim, Dryden refers to Shadwell's "mountain belly," his slowness at composition, his assistance from Sedley, his stealing from Etherege, and his "northern dedications" to Newcastle, and also introduces—either by title, allu-

[13] In Dedicatory Epistle to *Limberham.*

sion, or paraphrase—*The Humourists, The Miser, The Hypocrite, Epsom-Wells, The Tempest, Psyche,* and *The Virtuoso.*[14]

When Shadwell taxed Dryden with the authorship of this satire, the laureate "denyed it with all the Execrations he could think of."[15] But this disavowal should not have been taken seriously; the poet was merely continuing the jest by not satisfying the curiosity of his victim. In an essay written many years later,[16] Dryden refers to *MacFlecknoe* as his own work and calls it an example of Varronian satire, or that type which diverts rather than teaches. This description could not be more apt. Because it diverts, the poem is still alive, with the result that most readers are inclined to rate Shadwell at Dryden's valuation.

[14] Editors of Dryden's poems have noted the allusions to all the plays mentioned except *The Hypocrite* and *The Tempest.* For *The Hypocrite* see p. 23. Among Shadwell's contributions to the operatic *Tempest* is a song entitled "Arise, ye subterranean winds." In *MacFlecknoe* the "drugget robe" of the luckless poet is borne "upwards by a subterranean wind."

[15] Epistle to *Tenth Satyr of Juvenal* (London, 1687).

[16] "Discourse concerning the Original and Progress of Satire," published in 1693.

CHAPTER IV

POLITICAL CONTROVERSIES, 1680-1687

IN his next controversy Shadwell was not glorifying Jonson or attacking Settle, but upholding the cause of the Whigs and vilifying the Church of Rome. Not later than November, 1681, his comedy, *The Lancashire Witches, and Tegue O'Divelly, The Irish Priest,* was produced at the Duke's Theatre.[1] With the exception of Tony Leigh, who acted Tegue, and Mrs. Barry, who with him spoke the epilogue and probably took the part of Isabella, the names of the players in the first performance have not been preserved. Although this play, which was "well perform'd," may have "prov'd beyond Expectation; very Beneficial to the Poet and *Actors,*"[2] it seems not at first to have been received with acclaim. The author of *Rome's Follies, or the Amorous Friars* (published in 1681) writes in the epistle dedicatory that his play "would be far more difficult to get play'd than *Cæsar Borgia* was: or if it should chance to have been played, might have found a colder entertainment than *Tegue O'Divelly,* The Irish Priest, at the Duke's Theatre, merely for the Subjects sake."

In his statement to the reader, Shadwell writes that he had been informed a month before the acting of *The Lancashire Witches* that his work was strongly opposed by a party who accused him of satirizing the Church of England in the character of Smerk. The complaints of these alarmists reached the ears of the Master of the Revels, Charles Killigrew, who had at first licensed the play with little alteration, but who now acted upon the report that the work was "full of dangerous Reflections" and expunged a considerable amount of material. Despite these omissions, the author's opponents, when the play was performed, determined to hiss his work "Right or Wrong; and had gotten mercenary Fellows, who were such Fools, they did not know when to hiss." Shadwell, on his part, "had so numerous an Assembly of the best sort of Men,

[1] Advertised in the catalogue for Michaelmas Term, 1681 (Arber, *Term Catalogues,* I, 463).

[2] Downes, pp. 38-39.

who stood so generously in [his] Defence, for the three first Days, that they quash'd all the vain Attempts of [his] Enemies; the inconsiderable Party of Hissers yielded, and the Play lived in spight of them."[3] "Some of the worsted Party of Hissers were so malicious to make People believe (because [he] had laid the Scene in *Lancashire*) that [he] had reflected personally on some in that, and in an adjoyning County." Another party reported that he had "written Sedition and Treason, had reflected upon His Majesty, and that the Scope of the Play was against the Government of *England*."

The Lancashire Witches came upon the stage when the spirit of faction ran high. The "Popish Plot," which three years before had brought to a head the growing distrust of Catholics, was still a cause of fear to many Englishmen. Because of the report by Titus Oates of the details of this conspiracy by which Charles was to be killed and Protestantism wiped out of England, and because of the murder of the magistrate to whom Oates had made his deposition, many Catholics were put to death. A bill with the purpose of preventing the Romanist Duke of York from succession to the throne was advocated by the Earl of Shaftesbury, who strongly urged the right of the Protestant Duke of Monmouth to become the next king. Charles, who remained throughout loyal to his brother James, dissolved Parliament in May, 1679, but refused to summon the new Parliament, which was elected shortly afterwards. Shaftesbury's followers, who were soon to be known as Whigs, petitioned the king; whereupon another group, the Abhorrers or Tories, sent in counter-petitions expressing abhorrence at this attempt to force their ruler's will. As a result of the efforts of the Whigs, however, Parliament was assembled in October, 1680. The Exclusion Bill, which was again stoutly championed, passed the Commons, but was rejected by the Lords. In January, 1680/1, the king once more dissolved Parliament; and, in March, he summoned a new body to meet at Oxford. The House of Commons, predominantly Whig, supported Shaftesbury who again

[3] Dryden in his *Vindication of the Duke of Guise* refers to the "bustle that was made" to uphold *The Lancashire Witches:* "Upon the first day, the whole faction (in a manner) appeared; but after one sight of it, they sent their proxies of serving-men and porters, to clap in the right of their patrons" (*Works,* ed. Scott-Saintsbury, VII, 152).

pressed the claims of Monmouth. After a session of one week, Charles dissolved this Parliament. Beginning to distrust the Whigs, who they believed were fast hastening the return of civil war, the people rallied to the support of the king. A Tory reaction set in with the result that Shaftesbury was accused of high treason and sent to the tower on July 2, 1681.

The drama of the time echoed the sympathies of the opposing factions. Shadwell's comedy, which ridiculed the Church of Rome in the person of Tegue O'Divelly, had been preceded by Settle's ribald attack upon the papacy, *The Female Prelate*. More numerous, however, were the plays written against the Whigs. During the two years following the Oxford parliament, the theatres presented works of a decided Tory bias by Dryden, D'Urfey, Crowne, Southerne, Otway, and Mrs. Behn.[4] Not the least effective of the comedies produced about the time of *The Lancashire Witches* was *Sir Barnaby Whigg*. The character who gives the name to this play was probably intended to be a satirical portrait of Shadwell. Certainly the song he sings in the third act could refer to no other than the victim of Dryden's satire:

Farewell my Lov'd Science, my former delight,
Molière *is quite rifled, then how should I write?*
My fancy's grown sleepy, my quibling is done;
And design or invention, alas! I have none.
But still let the Town never doubt my condition;
Though I fall a damn'd Poet, I'll Mount a Musician.

I got Fame by filching from Poems and Plays,
But my Fidling and Drinking has lost me the Bays;
Like a Fury I rail'd, like a Satyr I writ,
Thersites *my Humour, and* Fleckno *my Wit.*
But to make some amends for my snarling and lashing,
I divert all the Town with my Thrumming and Thrashing.[5]

About the time of the performance of *The Lancashire Witches* Shadwell was named with three other Whigs in a "new Song on the Death of *Colledge* the *Protestant Joyner*":

[4] For the entire subject, see Rose A. Wright, *The Political Play of the Restoration* (Yale dissertation, n.d.).

[5] Thomas D'Urfey, *Sir Barnaby Whigg: or, No Wit Like a Womans* (London, 1681), p. 28. The song was identified as referring to Shadwell by R. S. Forsythe in *A Study of the Plays of Thomas D'Urfey* (Cleveland, 1916), p. 38.

Our *Cause* t' th' *Character-men*, we must refer
To *Shadwell*, and *Settle*, to *Curtis* and *Care*.
To know who succeeds, our late Captain the *Joyner* . . .[6]

Possibly the author thought that Shadwell, Curtis, and Care had assisted Settle in the composition of *The Character of a Popish Successor*, a pamphlet written for the purpose of influencing the Oxford Parliament to favor the Exclusion Bill. Or possibly he wished merely to imply that the ideas held by these persons were similar to those expressed in the *Character*.

Shadwell's three associates in the "new Song" were actively opposed to Roman Catholicism. Before writing the *Character*, Settle had directed the elaborate pope-burning pageant of November 17, 1680. Numerous attacks upon the Church of Rome had been printed for the bookseller, Langley Curtis, who was responsible also for the *True Protestant Mercury*.[7] Since December, 1678, Henry Care had published a paper with the self-explanatory title, *The Weekly Pacquet of Advice from Rome, or the History of Popery; A Deduction of the Usurpations of the Bishops of Rome, and the Errors and Superstitions by them from time to time brought into the Church.* The joining of Shadwell to these three writers may indicate that the dramatist had done more in opposition to Catholicism than to write *The Lancashire Witches*. Possibly some of the many anonymous anti-Romish pamphlets should be attributed to his authorship.

During January and February, 1681/2, Shadwell's character and actions were discussed in certain news-sheets. Nat Thompson, described by Luttrell as "printer and publisher frequently of popish news and pamphlets,"[8] printed this brief item in *The Loyal Protestant and True Domestick Intelligence* under date of January 11:

[6] In Nat Thompson's *A Choice Collection of 180 Loyal Songs* (1685), p. 66. Stephen College was executed at Oxford on August 31, 1681.

[7] Two of the books printed for Curtis were *The Character of a Turbulent, Pragmatical Jesuit and Factious Romish Priest* (1678) and *New News from Bedlam* (1682). The latter was published "at the Sign of Sir *Edmund Bury Godfrey's* Head near *Fleet-Bridge*."

[8] Narcissus Luttrell, *Brief Historical Relation* (Oxford, 1857), I, 175. *An Answer to . . . A Character of a Popish Successor* (1681) was sold at Thompson's "House next the *Cross-Keys* in *Fetter-Lane*." On August 31, 1681, the London grand-jury described the "Loyall Protestant domestick Intelligence" as a pamphlet that designed "to divide his majesties true protestant subjects." On June 20, 1682, Thompson and two others were declared guilty of "writing, printing, and publishing two scandalous libells

Near Epsom *in the County of* Surry, *the* Sham-Protestant-Poet *was discover'd by a Person of Quality, & told to his face, that he was a* Papist, *married by a* Popish Priest; *And that all his Writings and Railings against the Church of* England, *was to promote the Church of* Rome's: *To which he Atheistically reply'd:* Come, Dam Religion, Let's Drink aboet; *And said not one word to excuse Himself. Therefore shun an Atheist as you would a Papist, or a worse thing.*

The person whom Thompson terms the "Sham-Protestant-Poet" is Shadwell. By "Writings . . . against the Church of England" are probably meant those scenes in *The Lancashire Witches* in which Smerk appears.

Two weeks later, Richard Janeway, the Whig publisher who, in May, was to bring out *The Medal of John Bayes,* came to Shadwell's defense.[9] In *The Impartial Protestant Mercury* of January 24-27, he reports that a certain Mr. S. had asked Shadwell "Why he was *so Violent against Popery,* since a certain Person told him, he had owned himself formerly to him *to be a Papist,* and to have been *Married by a Popish Priest?*" This accusation was denied by Shadwell, who admitted that he had leaned "toward *Popery* for about eight Months. (19 or 20 Years since) but upon more Mature Inquiry, he found out those absurd Follies and Pernitious Villanies in their Doctrines and Practices, which a Man must search throughly into, to *abhor sufficiently,* as he does." Upon this story, Janeway continues, Thompson grounds his lie, "though there was not a word spoken of Writing or *Railing against the Church of* England, (which this Gentleman was never guilty of) nor of serving the ends of *Popery,* which if he did, he should not have been so often *way-laid* and set upon, as he has been by *Popish Ruffians,* within four Months last past, coming home in the Night." The person *"who could make such a Story publick"* is told that *"he will be very* Unwelcome" to *"a Worthy Family where he was a Guest, and nobly entertain'd"* or *"to the* Society

entituled Letters to Mr. Miles Prance, insinuating that sir Edmondbury Godfrey killed himself, thereby defaming the justice of the whole nation." Luttrell, I, 119-120, 195.

[9] Roger L'Estrange, in *A Word Concerning Libels and Libellers* (London, 1681), p. 5, asserts that Care and Janeway are "both one in the *Impartial.*" Among the anti-Catholic pamphlets printed for Janeway in Queens-Head Alley, near Pater-Noster Row, were *The Anatomy of Transubstantiation* (1680), *Popery and Hypocrisy Detected and Opened from the Holy Scriptures* (1680), and *The Case of Protestants in England under a Popish Prince* (1681).

of any Gentlemen." Finally, John Morehouse, "*Minister of* Ebisham, *alias* Epsam [*sic*],"[10] certifies under date of January 23: "*I was by*, when Mr. *S*. told the Person seemed to be reflected on in *Thompson*'s *Intelligence*, (Numb. 102.) by the Name of the *Sham-Protestant Poet near* Epsom), that one had told him, he had formerly been a *Papist*, &c. And whereas *Thompson* says, he Atheistically replied, *Come, damn Religion, let's Drink about;* I do testifie, That there was no such words spoken, nor any tending that way, nor any thing *Atheistical* or *Prophane*, nor was *any Drink* in the Company at that time."

Through the medium of Langley Curtis's *True Protestant Mercury* of February 1-4, Mr. S. answers that "*he never acquainted the said* Thompson" with the story he tells and is "*wholly ignorant how it came abroad*." But

for satisfaction of the World, he thinks fit to give this true Atcount of the same. That in Christmas *last, the said Mr.* S. *being in company with a Gentleman that was an old acquaintance of Poet* S. *and then discoursing of the high Whiggism of the said Poet, the Gentleman said he wondred to hear the said Poet was so violent against the Papists, since he had frequently to him owned himself to be a Papist and that he was Marryed by a Popish Priest, and that during the time of his professing himself such, he brought the Gentleman acquainted with Sir* George Wakeman, *with whom the said Poet had an intimate acquaintance and was beholding to him for many friendly kindnesses, and farther said, He had reason by the said Poets Conversation to conclude him of no Religion, but never knew he professed himself to be other than a* Roman *Catholick till the Plot broke out, That it was his Interest made him disown it, the greatest part thereof the said* Mr. S. *acquainted the said Poet near* Epsom *with, and then named the Author to him, and told him he would justify the same, which the said Mr.* S. *upon Discourse with him since, finds him ready to do in every Circumstance that is here set down, with advantage; Mr.* S. *conceives the Poet hath not dealt ingeniously with him, to charge the matter upon him, without acquainting him first therewith, from whom he should have had all satisfaction, and as advantagious a Certificate as from the Minister of* Epsom, *that there was no such thing said, as* Damn Religion, lets Drink about, *as* Thompson *in his Intelligence hath falsely suggested.*

In the *Loyal Protestant* for February 9, Thompson denies that

[10] John Morehouse, B.A., was instituted vicar of St. Martin's Church, Epsom, on March 11, 1669. *Some Particulars Relating to the History of Epsom . . . By an Inhabitant* (Epsom, 1825), p. 32.

he received the account of the conversation from Mr. S.; and, after joking considerably at Shadwell's expense, he concludes the affair with these words:

Since our Poet *hath owned himself to have been formerly leaning to* Popery, *and* was married by a Popish Priest, *(for which very reason it is possible he hates the Order, as well as the Religion) it would be a great confirmation to his party, that he would satisfie the world when he conformed to the* Protestant Religion, *which will give him an opportunity to own God; in which point he has been formerly very nice to declare himself, as appears by the following story.*

Our quondam Atheist (*but now* Protestant-Poet, *since the Reformation of the* Plot) *being wounded in the Tripes in a Fray, and apprehending the matter to be mortal, sent for an Eminent Divine, and (declaring his contrition for his former Heathen Life) made a Recantation under his hand of his former Atheistical Opinions; but upon his Recovery, relapsed into his former Errors and Practice; A certain Gentleman meeting in Company, saluted him by the title of* Christian Shad. *whereupon our* Poet *replied,* He denied the name; *and said,* He hoped no man would suspect him for such a Rogue as to deny his Principles. *The Gentleman said, that* He was satisfied our *Poet* had done it, and if he insisted upon it, he would send him his Recantation next morning, with a *MacFlecknoe,* and a brace of Lobsters for his Breakfast; *All which he knew he had a singular aversion for: Therefore (by this circumstance) our* Poet *is a Sham Atheist, as well as a* Sham Protestant-Poet.

Shadwell's "high Whiggism" was in a short time again to be called into play by *The Medal,* Dryden's second attack on Shaftesbury. *Absalom and Achitophel,* which had been published on or shortly before November 17, 1681, had been written for the purpose of exciting public feeling against the Whig leader, who was at that time in the Tower awaiting trial on the charge of high treason. The poem was unsuccessful in its purpose; for, on November 24, the bill of indictment of Shaftesbury was rejected by the London grand jury. This act was considered a triumph by the Whigs, who thereupon had a medal struck in honor of the event. According to the familiar story told by Spence, the king suggested writing a poem on this subject to his laureate, who took the hint and, by the middle of the following March, was able to see his work in circulation.

The Medal, A Satire Against Sedition, to which was prefixed a prose "Epistle to the Whigs," immediately excited the wrath of

Shaftesbury's adherents.[11] The latter were not slow to reply; and, in their answers, they were as ready to insult Dryden as to praise their leader. The first retort was *The Mushroom: Or, A Satyr Against Libelling Tories and Prelatical Tantivies*, said by its author, Edmund Hickeringell, to have been written on March 17. Its eight pages of stumbling couplets are concerned almost entirely with abuse of Dryden. A milder rejoinder was that of Samuel Pordage, which appeared on or before March 31 with the title, *The Medal Revers'd. A Satyre Against Persecution.* Although Dryden is censured in this poem, the author is more interested in emphasizing the danger from Rome than in heaping up reproach. Somewhat harsher than Pordage's effort was *The Loyal Medal Vindicated*, which came off the press of Richard Janeway about April 8. The opening verses exhibit considerable animus against Dryden; but this is soon forgotten and the poem closes with laudation of Shaftesbury.

More abusive than these three replies was *The Medal of John Bayes. A Satyr against Folly and Knavery*, published by Janeway on or before May 15.[12] In the prose "Epistle to the Tories" and in

[11] The dates of the poems are given by Malone on the authority of manuscript notes by Luttrell. Thus *The Medal* "was published on or before the 16th of March." See Malone, *Critical and Miscellaneous Prose Works of John Dryden*, I, pt. 1, 163-165.

[12] Luttrell ascribes this poem to Shadwell. Malone, *op. cit.*, I, pt. 1, 165. G. Thorn-Drury (in *Review of English Studies*, I, 190-192) questions Shadwell's authorship on the ground that Janeway, the publisher of *The Medal of John Bayes*, "had not been concerned in the issue of any single scrap of Shadwell's identified work," that references to Shadwell's authorship are not found in the exchange of abuse provoked by the religious and political differences of the period, that Dryden makes no reference to Shadwell's attack in the *Vindication of the Duke of Guise*, and that, had Shadwell been the author, he would not have made the claim, in his reply to Dryden in the preface to his translation of the tenth satire of Juvenal, that he has been neither base nor dishonest. Coming from Mr. Thorn-Drury, these arguments cannot be ignored. However, I am not convinced that they prove Luttrell to be incorrect. Even if Janeway was not the publisher of other works by Shadwell, he was undoubtedly favorably disposed towards the dramatist; otherwise he would not have allowed his newssheet, *The Impartial Protestant Mercury*, to defend Shadwell in January, 1681/2. As a publisher of Whig pamphlets and of one verse attack on Dryden's poems, his press would be a natural choice for the author of *The Medal of John Bayes*. Lack of references to Shadwell's authorship in the numerous religious and political pamphlets seems to me to prove nothing. I also feel that there is no particular significance in Dryden's failure to mention *The Medal of John Bayes*. In his *Vindication*, Dryden states that he has hitherto contented himself with the "ridiculous part" of Shadwell, and in the passage which he devotes to the dramatist he adds further details to his ludicrous portrait. He apparently did not think it necessary, in replying to a prose pamphlet, to refer to Shadwell's political verse. A short time before, in the second

the poem itself, Shadwell pours upon Dryden all his pent-up animosity. Here he is not only coming to the defense of Shaftesbury; but he is also returning blows for the earlier attack upon himself as a dull poet in *MacFlecknoe.* In the introductory epistle, the conversation of the laureate, who is termed a "meer Poet," is described as "*lumpish and flegmatick, or arrogant and silly.*" He is called a great plagiary of "Spanish, Italian, French, *and* Classick *Authors.*" "*His* Panegyricks *are full of such nauseous flattery, that they are* Libels; *and he is now become so infamous, that his* Libels *will be thought* Panegyricks." His lack of sophistication as a young man is illustrated by the story that a coffee-house woman "*put Coffee upon him for Chocolate, and made him pay three pence a dish for two years together: till at length . . . he discovered the Cheat.*" His present employment is designated as "*that of a Hired Libeller, an Executioner of mens Reputations.*" Certain statements made by Dryden in the epistle to *The Medal* anger Shadwell, particularly the one in which the jury that acquitted Shaftesbury is compared to a "*Jury taken out of* Newgate." In the opinion of the Whig writer, the spirit that actuates the Tories "*seems . . . to breath forth nothing but Ruine, Murther, and Massacre.*" Their understanding is shown by their belief in a Protestant Plot on the circumstance of a "*Joyner riding with Sword and Pistols to* Oxford, *who had used to ride so armed many years before*" and by their denial of a Popish Plot after being acquainted with all the convincing evidence. He then bids the Tories farewell and concludes his epistle with the threat: "*let your Poet know, that the first occasion he gives, he shall hear from us farther.*"

The verses continue in a similar vein. They begin with an attack upon Dryden:

> How long shall I endure, without reply,
> To hear this *Bayes*, this Hackney-rayler lie?

part of *Absalom and Achitophel,* he had mentioned the "clumsy verse, unlick'd, unpointed," in which Og had "shamefully defied the Lord's anointed." These words may refer to the lines in *The Medal of John Bayes* in which Shaftesbury is glorified. And finally, may not some significance be attached to the fact that Shadwell, when answering Dryden's charge of dulness, uses an idea which had appeared earlier in *The Medal of John Bayes?* Compare "indeed he gives his own *dullness* a civiller term, and calls it being *Saturnine*" (Preface to tenth satire) with

"For thou art *Saturnine,* thou dost confess;
A civil word thy Dulness to express"
(*Medal of John Bayes,* p. 3).

The fool uncudgell'd, for one Libel swells,
Where not his Wit, but Sawciness excels;
Whilst with foul Words and Names which he lets flie,
He quite defiles the *Satyr's* Dignity.
For Libel and true *Satyr* different be;
This must have *Truth*, and *Salt*, with *Modesty*.
Sparing the Persons, this does tax the Crimes,
Gall's not great Men, but Vices of the Times,
With Witty and Sharp, not blunt and bitter rimes.
Methinks the Ghost of *Horace* there I see,
Lashing this *Cherry-cheek'd Dunce* of Fifty three;
Who, at that age, so boldly durst profane,
With base hir'd Libel, the free *Satyr's* Vein.

On three occasions, Shadwell, following the example of *Mac-Flecknoe*, refers to the dulness of his adversary.

For thou art *Saturnine*, thou dost confess;
A civil word thy Dulness to express. . . .
How low thy Farce! and thy blank Verse how mean!
How poor, how naked did appear each Scene!
Even thou didst blush at thy insipid stuff,
And laid thy dulness on poor harmless Snuff. . . .
Thou deserv'st whipping, thou'rt so dull, this time
Thou'st turned the *Observator* into Rime.

Several lines are marked by unquotable vulgarity; others contain eulogies of Monmouth, Shaftesbury, and the city of London, called the "Bulwark to the Peoples Liberty." Those who "would dissolve that Sacred knot" binding king and people are "curst"; those "who hate a *Parliament*" and who would "gladly sell the Land to *France*, or *Rome*" are termed "Miscreants" and "*Slaves*." Shadwell does not conclude his poem with the lines asking Heaven to "*preserve our Legal Monarchy*" or damning those who "would the best of Governments deface," but returns to Dryden:

Now farewel wretched Mercenary *Bayes*,
Who the *King* Libell'd, and did *Cromwel* praise.
Farewel, abandon'd Rascal! only fit
To be abus'd by thy own scurrilous Wit.
Which thou wouldst do, and for a Moderate Sum,
Answer thy Medal, and thy *Absolom*.
Thy piteous Hackney-Pen shall never fright us,
Tho'rt dwindl'd down to *Hodge*, and *Heraclitus*.

Go, *Ignoramus* cry, and *Forty One*,
And by *Sam Parsons* be thou prais'd alone.
Pied thing! half Wit! half Fool! and for a Knave,
Few Men, than this, a better mixture have:
But thou canst add to that, Coward and Slave.

Shortly after the publication of *The Medal of John Bayes*, Shadwell was singled out for special mention in a poem directed against Shaftesbury. These verses were occasioned by the action of *scandalum magnatum* brought by the leader of the Whigs against one Cradock, a mercer of Paternoster Row, for £5000 damages. When, on May 10, the counsel for the defense moved the Court of King's Bench for trial in another county, the application was unanimously granted on the ground that an unprejudiced jury could not be found in London or Middlesex since Shaftesbury had constantly resided in the city, had been concerned in trade there, and was on terms of intimacy with the two sheriffs. Shaftesbury then told the Court he "would rather let his action fall than try it elsewhere." The Court acted in a similar manner on May 16 when Shaftesbury's charge of conspiracy against Graham, principal of Clifford's Inn, came up for debate.[13]

In the poem attributed to Tom D'Urfey called *Scandalum Magnatum: Or, Potapski's Case. A Satyr Against Polish Oppression,*[14] Shaftesbury, under the name of Potapski, is represented as singling two offenders from the "Loyal Rout" for damages. After the jury, which he has picked, swear to give him a favorable verdict, he goes to the court confident. But his case is spoiled with too much zeal. The pleadings of the witty Jaffier persuade the Judge Solon of the defendant's right. Then Potapski

Vext to a Feavour, cries in eager Passion,
Justice is fled to Heaven, no Law is in the Nation.
But streight his train of *Parasites* appear,
Insects that riggle in their Patrons Ear,
And with the *News-Intelligences* swell,
Publisht by Fiends not to be matcht in Hell;
Base crawling Worms, that hourly Venome shed,
Slaves, to whom Treason's natural as Bread;

[13] Luttrell, *Brief Historical Relation,* I, 183, 185-186.

[14] Advertised in catalogue for Trinity Term (i.e., June), 1682. The passage dealing with Shadwell has been heretofore unnoticed.

That with dull Lies their sinking Cause advance,
And Damn to get a wretched Maintenance.
Yet these are the lewd Towns Sedition-Tools:
But amongst all the Factious scribling Fools,
Shad——l's the worst, an unform'd shapeless thing,
That Nature never thought worth finishing;
But from Creations secret Store-house kickt,
Into the World a wallowing Cub unlickt.
Nature no Form has given, nor Heaven no Grace,
The Man must needs be in a blessed Case.
And when he Writes a Tale to please the Town,
Should every witty Friend but take his own,
How the laborious Nothing would be maul'd,
No Winter *Cuckoo* e're was half so bald.
From any Figure that his Fancy draws,
From such a Poet, propping such a Cause,
'Mongst all Earths dilatory Plagues, let me,
(Heaven I beseech thee) be for ever free.
Sick-men use Quacks, because they sometimes please,
But trust 'em not to cure a grand Disease;
So these *Potapski* us'd, and thought 'em fit
For mischief, but durst never trust their wit.

To 1682 belong two other poems which have been ascribed to Shadwell: *Satyr to His Muse. By the Author of Absalom and Achitophel* and *The Tory Poets.* They are the sort of verses he was capable of penning, and it is not unlikely that he was here fulfilling the threat made in the final words of the epistle to *The Medal of John Bayes. Satyr to His Muse,* which has also been attributed to Lord Somers, is assigned to Shadwell by William Oldys in his annotated copy of Langbaine. *The Tory Poets,* published on or before September 4, 1682, has always been attributed to Shadwell, says Malone,[15] writing in the latter part of the eighteenth century, but he cites no contemporary evidence. Both poems are largely concerned with coarse ridicule of Dryden. In *The Tory Poets* the author also takes the opportunity to sneer at Otway, who "never writes a Verse but when he is drunk," and at D'Urfey, who is described as a "*Debauchee, Buffoon,* a *Knave,* a *Dunce.*" Shadwell had reason to consider that he was justified in attacking

[15] *Op. cit.,* I, pt. 1, 165. There is a copy of *The Tory Poets* in the library of Harvard University. Another poem directed against Dryden, *A Lenten Prologue Refus'd by the Players,* has been attributed to Shadwell.

these political rivals. Otway, in *The Poet's Complaint of his Muse,* had referred, in a passage describing the companions of his early days in London, to "Bullies of o're grown Bulks, and little Souls," undoubtedly a slur at Shadwell.[16] D'Urfey's abuse in *Sir Barnaby Whigg* and *Scandalum Magnatum* would amply account for the lines in *The Tory Poets.* Another passage is of interest because it couples the writers who were soon to be derided as Og and Doeg:

> *Shadwel* and *Settle* are both Fools to *Bays,*
> They have no bawdy Prologues to their Plays;
> These silly Villains under a pretence
> Of wit, deceive us and like men write sence.

In October appeared *MacFlecknoe, or, a Satire upon the True-Blew-Protestant Poet, T. S.,* printed not for Dryden's usual publisher, Jacob Tonson, but for D. Green, who wrote in an advertisement following the poem, "*A Gentleman having a curious Colection of Poetry by the most Ingenious of the Age, Intends to oblige the World with a Poem every* Wednesday *Morning, and with all New ones as they come to his hand.*" This satire, as we have seen, had been in circulation—probably in manuscript—at least as early as the previous November and so could not have been written as a reply to *The Medal of John Bayes.* The text of this "pirated" edition of 1682 contains many careless errors which were corrected by the author for the reprint of the piece in the *Miscellany Poems* of 1684.

Dryden's direct reply to Shadwell's scurrilous lines is found in the second part of *Absalom and Achitophel.* This poem, which is largely the work of Nahum Tate, contains some 250 lines by the laureate. The most important passage among Dryden's contributions is that in which are described the Whig pamphleteers, the "troop of busy spirits . . . of little fortunes, and of conscience less." After disposing of Ferguson, Forbes, Johnson, Burnet, and Pordage, the author turns to Settle and Shadwell and, under the names of Doeg and Og, holds them up to everlasting ridicule. The unforgettable lines on Shadwell—as powerful as those in

[16] Roswell G. Ham, "Shadwell and 'The Tory Poets'" (*Notes and Queries,* CLII, 6-8).

MacFlecknoe—do not refer by title to any specific works of the dramatist; but they emphasize his corpulence and his habits, his pamphlets and his bad poetry.[17]

In November, the month of the publication of the second part of *Absalom and Achitophel*, Dryden poked fun at Shadwell on two other occasions. In "A Prologue to the King and Queen, upon the Union of the two Companies," recited by Betterton on November 16, the audience is told what they may expect in the theatre:

We'll take no blund'ring verse, no fustian tumor,
No dribbling love, from this or that presumer;
No dull fat fool shamm'd on the stage for humor.

The last line is an obvious reference to Shadwell. In the conclusion of the *Religio Laici*, mention is also made of the Whig poet:

And this unpolish'd, rugged verse, I chose,
As fittest for discourse, and nearest prose;
For while from sacred truth I do not swerve,
Tom Sternhold's, or Tom Sha——ll's rhymes will serve.

Richard Duke followed Dryden's lead in uniting Shadwell and Settle as mediocre poets. In his lines "To Mr. Creech on His Translation of *Lucretius*," he penned words which were partly responsible for Shadwell's version of the tenth satire of Juvenal

Thou only for this Noble task wert fit,
To shame thy Age to a Just Sense of Wit,
By shewing how the Learned *Romans* writ.
To teach fat heavy Clowns to know their Trade,
And not turn Wits, who were for Porters made,
But quit false Claims to the Poetick Rage,
For Squibs and Crackers, and a *Smithfield* Stage,
Had Providence e're meant that in despight,
Of Art and Nature, such dull Clods shou'd write,
Bavius and *Maevius* had been sav'd by fate
For *Settle* and for *Shadwel* to translate,

[17] An echo of Dryden's line, "Rhyme is the rock on which thou art to wreck," is found in the words of Charles Shadwell in the Dedicatory Epistle to his *Works* (Dublin, 1720): "Poetry is a Science I do not, nor dare not Value myself upon; I may say with my Father, 'It was not a Harbour I chose, but a Rock I split upon.' "

> As it so many Ages has for Thee
> Preserv'd the mighty Work that now we see.[18]

Duke also mentioned these writers in a poetical epistle addressed to Otway:

> Thou see'st I'm dull as *Shadwell's* Men of Wit,
> Or the Top Scene that *Settle* ever writ.[19]

Shadwell was not frightened from the field by the derogatory verses of the poet-laureate. As soon as a fitting occasion presented itself, he was ready to strike back at his foe. The opportunity came when the United Companies produced *The Duke of Guise*, a tragedy written in collaboration by Dryden and Lee. This play, which the Lord Chamberlain had banned on July 18, 1682, was acted with success in the early part of December.[20] Although Dryden professed that he and Lee had intended a parallel between "the Holy League, plotted by the house of Guise and its adherents" and "the Covenant plotted by the rebels in the time of King Charles I," the Whigs discerned in the play more marked resemblances to the situation then prevailing in England. In the presentation of the échevins, they saw a fling at the sheriffs of London; in the assembly of the States General at Blois, a parallel to the parliament at Oxford; and, in the murder of the Duke of Guise, an encouragement to assassinate the Duke of Monmouth.

Protests soon appeared. Thomas Hunt, a lawyer who two years before had written a tract in favor of the Exclusion Bill, devoted some pages[21] to *The Duke of Guise* in his *Defence of the Charter, and Municipal Rights of the City of London.* In anger, he accuses Dryden of corrupting the manners of the nation and of uttering public blasphemies against religion. More violent than Hunt's pamphlet, however, was the remonstrance entitled *Some Reflections upon the Pretended Parallel in the Play called The Duke*

[18] Printed in [T. Creech], *Titus Lucretius Carus His Six Books of Epicurean Philosophy, Done into English Verse: with Notes,* 3d edition (London, 1683). These verses by Duke are dated, "*Cambridge,* Decemb. 18, 1682."

[19] *Poems by the Earl of Roscomon . . . Together with Poems by Mr. Richard Duke* (London, 1717), p. 515.

[20] Nicoll, *History of Restoration Drama,* pp. 10 n., 311.

[21] Pp. 24-31. This pamphlet was "censured as a libell" in the latter part of January, 1682/3.

of Guise. In this work, the authors, said by Dryden to be a "poet" (i.e., Shadwell) and a "Whig gentleman of the Temple,"[22] charge the poet-laureate with persuading Lee to turn from his original intention of exposing "that unparallel'd Villany of the *Papists* in the most horrid *Parisian Massacre*" and to write instead this diabolical incentive to murder. As they comment upon the various parallels, they give their opponent such epithets as "*old Serpent Bays*," "Mercenary Varlet," and "loose and infamous *Scribler.*" They question whether "this Villain [does not] deserve to be hang'd, drawn, and quartered." They also do not neglect to mention the "Good and Great" king, whom they would like to see "punish all that Work Evil against him." Among the latter are to be numbered those "Licentious Poets" who publish "foolish and impious Works."

Although a friend urged him in verse to ignore these "two malicious Pamphlets," Dryden wrote a vigorous reply. In *The Vindication of The Duke of Guise,*[23] he avers that his contributions to the tragedy were made at the "earnest desire" of Lee. He also proves to his own satisfaction that the parallel is due not to the intention of the dramatists but to the malicious ingenuity of the Whig writers, the "sputtering triumvirate" as he terms them. Of greatest interest to us, however, are not the pages in which Dryden refutes the charges of his adversaries, but those in which he indulges in ridicule of his old enemy, Shadwell. In commenting upon the fact that the play has been called a "dull entertainment," he confesses that "that is a dangerous word . . . from one of the greatest masters in human nature, of that faculty." In another passage he adds further details to the portrait of his corpulent foe:[24]

> . . . their celebrated writer [i.e., Thomas Hunt] knows no more of style and English than the Northern dedicator; as if dulness and clumsiness were fatal to the name of *Tom.* It is true, he is a fool in three languages more than the poet; for they say, "he understands Latin, Greek, and Hebrew," from all which, to my certain knowledge I acquit the other. Og may write against the king, if he pleases, so long as he drinks for him, and his writings will never do the government so much harm

[22] I am unable to identify Shadwell's co-worker.

[23] Licensed April 2, 1683.

[24] *Works,* ed. Scott-Saintsbury, VII, 180-181.

as his drinking does it good; for true subjects will not be much perverted by his libels; but the wine-duties rise considerably by his claret. He has often called me an atheist in print; I would believe more charitably of him, and that he only goes the broad way, because the other is too narrow for him. He may see, by this, I do not delight to meddle with his course of life, and his immoralities, though I have a long bead-roll of them. I have hitherto contented myself with the ridiculous part of him, which is enough, in all conscience, to employ one man; even without the story of his late fall at the Old Devil, where he broke no ribs, because the hardness of the stairs could reach no bones; and, for my part, I do not wonder how he came to fall, for I have always known him heavy; the miracle is, how he got up again. I have heard of a sea captain as fat as he, who, to scape arrests, would lay himself flat upon the ground, and let the bailiffs carry him to prison, if they could. If a messenger or two, nay, we may put in three or four, should come, he has friendly advertisement how to escape them. But to leave him, who is not worth any further consideration, now I have done laughing at him,—would every man knew his own talent, and that they, who are only born for drinking, would let both poetry and prose alone.

After the publication of Dryden's pamphlet, Shadwell seems to have withdrawn from the arena of political controversy. He was evidently willing to return to his first love, the stage; but the doors of the theatre were closed to him. No new play under his name had been produced for a year and a half; and five more years were to pass before he was again given a hearing. In 1689, he wrote that he had been "*silenc'd for a* Non-conformist *Poet*" and that "for near ten years [he had been] kept from the Exercise of that Profession which had afforded [him] a competent Subsistence."[25] If an anecdote published in *The Muse's Mercury* for January, 1707, be true, Dryden was influential in keeping Shadwell from the stage. According to the story, Shadwell threatened to "*put a stop*" to the prologue which Dryden had written for Betterton's alteration of *The Prophetess* (produced in 1690) on the ground that certain lines contained a reflection on the Revolution. When a gentleman in the audience asked why he would do the author such a disservice, Shadwell "said, *Because while Mr.* Dryden *was Poet Laureat, he wou'd never let any Play of his be Acted.*"[26]

[25] Prologue and Epistle Dedicatory to *Bury-Fair*. Shadwell is doctoring the facts somewhat here. "For near seven years" would be more accurate.

[26] R. P. McCutcheon, "Dryden's Prologue to the *Prophetess*," in *Modern Language Notes*, XXXIX (1924), 123-124.

That Shadwell was in financial straits during these years of silence is plausibly attested by contemporary versifiers. Two poems addressed to Julian, who acted as a copyer and distributor of lampoons at Will's Coffee-House, refer to this fact. George Villiers, Duke of Buckingham, in "*A Consolatory Epistle to Captain* Julian *the* Muses *News-Monger in his Confinement*," writes:

> *Shadwell* and *Settle* both with Rhimes are fraught,
> But can't between 'em muster up a Groat.[27]

The anonymous author of a similarly named poem states

> *Shadwell*, and *Settle*, who pretend to Reason,
> Tho paid so well for scribling Doggrel Treason,
> Must now expect a very barren Season.[28]

Matt Prior, in "*A* Satire *upon the* Poets, *in Imitation of the* Seventh Satire *of* Juvenal," urges his readers not to envy the poets whom "the Stage has fed":

> Much rather starve in *Shadwel's* silent Fate,
> Then new vamp Farces, and be damn'd with Tate.[29]

In 1685 was published anonymously *The Laurel, A Poem On the Poet-Laureat.* The author, after telling how Dryden and his "*Sheva*" [i.e., Sir Roger L'Estrange] had "crusht . . . Dead in Loyal Verse and Prose" the "*Baxt . . rs, Sh . . wlls, Owens, Hunts,* and *Cares*," continues in a much coarser vein the laureate's characterization of Shadwell:

> But let thy stubborn *Ogg* be ne're forgot,
> Whose drowsie Verse lurks deep, as still their Plot
> In something's understood, in something's not.
> He from Wits Empire, and his Princes flew,
> Or rather, Wit asham'd from him withdrew.
> Hail Mighty *Gutts!* for Drink the Standard made,
> Thou swilling Pensioner to the Brewers Trade.

[27] *Works of . . . George Villiers, Late Duke of Buckingham* (London, 1715), I, 141.

[28] *Poems on Affairs of State* (London, 1716), II, 132.

[29] Prior, *Dialogues of the Dead and Other Works in Prose and Verse* (Cambridge, 1907), p. 57. Tate's farces, *A Duke and No Duke* (1684) and *Cuckolds-Haven* (1685), are based respectively upon *Trapolin suppos'd a Prince* and *Eastward-Ho.*

Go with thy Masters Horses, feed on Grains,
As theirs thy Massy Gutts, as theirs thy Brains.
We envy not thy Greatness; still drink on,
'Till two-legg'd Hogshead swell up to a Tun,
And famous *Heidelberg* it self out-done.
Go then invoke thy rotting Patrons Tap,
Instead of Muse, to vent the flowing sap.
Thy better Midwife, and with lesser Pain,
Brings forth both Excrements, of Gutts and Brain;
You wou'd swear to see him sordid Satyr write.
The Poet Rhym'd, but Doctor did indite,
Tom, and his *Titus*, both one Province chose,
This Rascals it in Verse, and that in Prose.
If not to both disabled, Whore and Fight,
Or any thing wee'll grant him but to write.
Let him sing well his Dogrells, play them too;
Wee'll give to him, as to the Devil his due.
But who with docile Beasts would Art dispute,
The Bear and Fiddle, *Sh——ll* and his Lute.
Such rugged Monsters in a *Smithfield* Booth,
(Where ought to be the Poets Stage in Truth.)
Act, show at every Fair, for usual price,
And Tuneful *Sh——lls* seen for Pence a piece.
But as in every kind we something see,
Grac't with Perfection in more high Degree.
His frighten'd Dam, ran trembling from her kind,
And left the shapeless Lump unlickt behind:
The forc't Neglect beyond all natural Care,
Made him the more compleat, and better Bear;
To Dulness damn'd, and Faction since he fell,
To perfect all the Punishment of Hell,
His stubborn Error, is incurable.
His spungy, sappy Soul, would yield to thee,
But's body'd up by Trunk of sturdy Tree.
Your Loyal Pen attempts with fruitless stroke,
With Spriggs of Bays, for to chastise an Oak.
Your too keen Satyr, does oblige your Foe,
As harmless *Tom*'s kind dulness still does you.
Your *Fleckno*'s kind, (tho' still severe enough)
It Arms him Cap-a-pe with Nonsense Proof.
He fears no more, of harden'd dulness full,
He is not, will not, can't be made more dull.[30]

It is not improbable that Shadwell had a hand in the farce, *The*

[30] Pp. 20-22.

Devil of a Wife, or A Comical Transformation, printed as the work of Thomas Jevon and produced before March 1, 1685/6.[31] Thomas Whincop, who died in 1730, in writing of this play, said that "some People doubted if [it], at the Time it first came out, was not partly wrote by [Jevon's] Brother-in-law, *Shadwell.*"[32] Jevon, who had been a member of the Duke's Company since 1673 and who for ten years had been an actor of low-comedy parts, was without experience as a playwright. Nothing was more natural than that he should seek advice from a practiced writer. Since Shadwell was unable to gain a hearing for a play of his own, he would probably be willing to help a novice in his first attempt at dramatic composition. It is, of course, impossible to determine accurately the extent of his contributions; but that Shadwell had something to do with the play is more than likely. The general setting of *The Devil of a Wife* is not dissimilar to that of *The Lancashire Witches,* and some of the verbal resemblances to Shadwell's undoubted work are striking.[33]

At the time of the production of *The Devil of a Wife,* Shadwell was still living in the parish of St. Bride's. On October 27, 1686, the register of that church lists the burial of William Shadwell and the christening of "Anne Dau. of Thomas Shadwell by Anne his wife." Near the latter entry is written in another hand "Crown Alley by the Playhouse," presumably the dramatist's place of residence.

In the following year, Shadwell was aided financially by Sir Charles Sedley. The latter, who wrote but infrequently for the

[31] "Jobson *the* Cobler's *Wife,*" a character in *The Devil of a Wife,* is mentioned in the epistle to D'Urfey's *The Banditti,* which was licensed on March 1, 1685/6.

[32] *Scanderbeg . . . to which are added A List of all the Dramatic Authors,* etc., (London, 1747), p. 199.

[33] For a discussion of the relationship of this farce to Shadwell's plays, see Alfred E. Richards, "A Literary Link Between Thomas Shadwell and Christian Felix Weisse" (*Publications of the Modern Language Association of America,* XXI, 808-830). In *The Lancashire Witches* is Sir Edward Hartfort, "a worthy, hospitable, true English Gentleman, of good understanding and honest Principles"; in *The Devil of a Wife* is "Sir *Rich. Lovemore,* an honest country Gentleman belov'd for good old *Engl.* Housekeeping." Each man is the soul of hospitality. In each household is a chaplain with whom the master is not in sympathy. Mr. Richards cites several similarities in phraseology between *The Devil of a Wife* and *The Lancashire Witches, the Squire of Alsatia,* and *Bury-Fair.* Among these, he notes that Noddy (*Devil of a Wife,* Act III) and Hackum (*Squire of Alsatia,* Act I) sing a snatch of song beginning, "He that wears a brave Soul." These words, with a slight variation, are also sung by Sir Christopher Swash (*The Woman-Captain,* Act II).

theatre, was one day engaged upon the first act of an adaptation of Terence's *Eunuchus*. A friend came to his chamber and "seem'd to approve [the] design"; whereupon, in Sedley's own words, "I told him I found it extream easie to go through with: And that if he cou'd get it Acted under his own or anothers Name, I wou'd finish it for him: But for I know not what reasons he cou'd not do it; and I was oblidg'd to own it my self, or my friend had lost his third day."[34] The play, which was produced in May, 1687, "found . . . success." The friend was Thomas Shadwell, who later in the month took the opportunity to thank Sedley for his "Favour and Bounty" extending over many years and especially for the "late great obligation in giving me the advantage of your Comedy, call'd *Bellamira*, or the *Mistress*."

On May 25 was licensed *The Tenth Satyr of Juvenal, English and Latin, The English by Tho. Shadwell. With Illustrations upon it*, from the dedicatory epistle of which the words just quoted are taken. In this epistle, Shadwell expresses his sense of the honor done him in being allowed from his youth to live "in the *favour* of the *wittiest men of England*, [Sedley's] familiar *friends and acquaintance*, who have encouraged [his] Writings; and suffer'd [his] Conversation." After mentioning two of "the *greatest wits* of the *age*, . . . the *Earl of Rochester*, and the *Duke of Buckingham*," with whom he "had the honour to be acquainted," he turns to Dryden and with moderation, if not with force, replies to some of the statements in *MacFlecknoe*:[35]

After all this I may think I hope without *vanity*, that the Author of *Mack-Fleckno* reflects more upon himself than me; where he makes *Fleckno* commend *Dulness*, and chuse me for the *Dullest* that ever writ; and repeats *dull*, *dull*, *&c.* over and over: indeed he gives his own *dull-*

[34] Sedley, *Bellamira, or The Mistress* (London, 1687), "The Preface to the Reader."

[35] This preface contains Shadwell's last words in reference to his famous adversary unless *The Address of John Dryden, Laureat To His Highness The Prince of Orange* is Shadwell's work. This poem, printed and sold by Randal Taylor in 1689, was reprinted in *Poems on Affairs of State . . . Part III* (1698), p. 295; and, in the Table of Contents of that volume, it is ascribed to Shadwell. Dryden makes brief mention of Shadwell on two occasions after 1687. In his translation of the first satire of Juvenal (1693), he refers to such "woful stuff as I or S——ll write"; and in the verses "To my Dear Friend Mr. Congreve, on His Comedy called the Double-Dealer" (1694) is the line "For Tom the Second [i.e., Thomas Rymer, Shadwell's successor as historiographer royal] reigns like Tom the First."

ness a civiller term, and calls it being *Saturnine.* But sure he goes a little too far in calling me the *Dullest*, and has no more reason for that, than for giving me the *Irish* name of *Mack*, when he knows I never saw *Ireland* till I was three and twenty years old, and was there but four Months.

Besides as I have heard you observe the foundation of that *Libel* is *false* and *unnatural*; for tho some may have mistaken *dulness* for *wit*, and commended it as such; yet no man ever commended *Dullness* as *dulness.* Had he staid till he had supplied the *Stage* with more new *humour* then I have done, or till he had written a better *Comedy* than *Epsom Wells*, or the *Virtuoso* (neither of which by the way are taken from a *Novel*, or stollen from a *Romance*) he might with a better *Grace*, and more *Authority* have pronounced me *dull.* But he is not content with that, but has another fling at me for playing upon the *Lute.* I must confess that that and all other Gentleman-like Exercises, which I was capable of Learning, my Father was at the charge of, and let the Libeller make his best of it. . . .

It is hard to believe that the supposed *Author* of *Mack Fleckno* is the real one, because when I taxed him with it, he denyed it with all the Execrations he could think of. However my *Dullness* admits of an excuse, because I endeavour to avoid it all I can. But had I been base or dishonest, I could have made none, yet if he pleases to let my *Reputation* alone, I shall not envy him the *Fame* he has.

Although he has always looked upon translating as "a difficult, and irksom piece of Drudgery, and below any man who had a genius of his own," he "was provoked" to attempt this version of the Latin satirist because of Dryden's statement that he understood "neither Greek nor Latin" and also because of Richard Duke's lines to the effect that "*Bavius* and *Maevius* ought to have been reserved by Fate to be Translated by [Shadwell] and *Settle.*" In his translation he has endeavored "to come as near the words and thoughts of [his] Author, as [his] skill in both Languages could enable [him]." "In keeping close to [his] *Author*, [he has been] forced to make [his] *Periods* sometimes in the middle of Lines; . . . and [he has] alwaies chosen rather to make a rough Verse, than to loose the sense of *Juvenal.*" "If [he finds] this *Essay* to be favourably received, [he] will go on with the rest of the *Author*, in which [he has] already made some progress." He "can only do [this] by way of diversion," since he has "more material business upon [his] hands at this time."

Shadwell's translation was the cause of some justifiable sarcasm on the part of Henry Higden, who had made a version of the same satire. That gentleman's "*Modish and Familiar*" rendering was licensed on June 2, 1686, but its printing at that time "*was by some Accident prevented.*" During the following vacation Shadwell "*did* [Higden] *the Favour to peruse it.*" After keeping the manuscript for a considerable time, he returned it, saying that he had determined to make a translation of his own. He kept his resolution and was able to see his version off the press before the publication of the earlier rendering. When Higden's *A Modern Essay on the Tenth Satyr of Juvenal* was printed later in 1687, it was preceded by a preface directed against Shadwell and his translation. The author does not bewail the fact that the "Younger Brother *has by the* Common-Mother *the* Press *outstript* the Elder, *and lurch'd him of the* Blessing"; nor does he blame Shadwell's "*Haste to Christen his Own Child first, which is but the way of the World.*" He does, however, think it very hard that the other writer's "*Fondness to his own way, should make him (in crying up his own) fall so severely upon all others; proclaiming his own for an Exact and Standard Translation,* close *to the* Words *and* Sence *of the* Author." Then after ridiculing four of Shadwell's verses, which he shows are not exact renderings of the Latin lines, Higden makes a final suggestion: "*Let* Milo *in the Satyr be an Example to him, not to presume too much on his own strength, despising others, lest being wedged in a trap of his own making, he become a Prey to the merciless Criticks.*"[36]

Not much need be said about Shadwell's translation. It is just another of those tiresome renderings of classic poetry in heroic couplets of which the late seventeenth and eighteenth centuries were so fond. It doubtless satisfied the author since it proved that he understood Latin; but it apparently did not create enough interest to make him wish to continue his translation of the other satires. A comparison of this version with Dryden's shows again that Shadwell's special talent did not lie in poetry. Comedy was his forte. The authorities at the theatre had not forgotten that fact, and within a twelvemonth they were ready to throw open their doors for *The Squire of Alsatia.*

[36] Higden attributes to Shadwell's son the translation of Cato's speech from Lucan, which was printed with the dramatist's version of the tenth satire.

CHAPTER V

DRAMATIC WORK, 1688-1692

IN 1688, after seven years of silence, Shadwell made his reappearance as a writer for the London stage. On the fifth of May, Lord Granville wrote, in a letter to Sir William Leveson: "We are promised this week another new play of Shadwell's, called the Alsatia Bully, which is very much commended by those who have had the private perusal of it."[1] On the twelfth, Peregrine Bertie, corresponding with the Countess of Rutland, informed her: "We have had since my last another new play, a comedy writ by Shadwell, called the *Esquire of Alsatia.* It has been acted nine days successively, and on the third day the poet got 16 *l.* more than any other poet ever did. When all this is granted, there is nothing in it extraordinary—except it is a Latin song[2]—but the thin reason why it takes soe well is, because it brings severall of the cant words uppon the stage which some in towne have invented, and turns them into ridicule."[3] Although these letters do not corroborate each other in exact detail, they indicate that *The Squire of Alsatia* was produced for the first time in the early part of May, 1688.[4]

Since the production of *The Lancashire Witches,* numerous changes had taken place in the theatre. The two rival companies had joined forces. Many of the favorites of an earlier day—Hart and Nell Gwyn, Mohun and Harris, Smith[5] and Mrs. Shadwell —had either retired or died. Of the dramatists who were active in 1680, Otway was now dead, Dryden had not written a play for three years, Lee had been silent for more than four years, and

[1] *Hist. MSS. Comm. Fifth Report,* pp. 197-198.

[2] Shadwell, IV, 35. Truman sings Horace's ode, "Integer vitae."

[3] *Hist. MSS. Comm. Twelfth Report, Pt. V,* p. 119.

[4] In the concluding line of the epilogue, the author informs the audience that "Monday's his visiting Day" [i.e., the third day]. The first performance must then have been on a Friday. The most plausible Friday, it seems, would be May 4. Apparently Lord Granville did not know on the fifth that Shadwell's play had been presented. Sir George Etherege, writing in the early part of March, 1687/8, asks that Will Richards send him Shadwell's new play "as soon as it is printed, that I may know what follies are in fashion."

[5] Smith returned to the stage in 1695.

Settle for six. It seems that the only "new" plays produced in 1686 and 1687 were the three farces, Jevon's *The Devil of a Wife*, Mountfort's *Doctor Faustus*, and Mrs. Behn's *The Emperor of the Moon;* three comedies, D'Urfey's *The Banditti*, Mrs. Behn's *The Lucky Chance*, and Sedley's *Bellamira, or the Mistress;* and Tate's alteration of Beaumont and Fletcher's *The Island Princess*. Certainly the time was ripe for a new play by the author who had pleased the court as well as the city with *The Sullen Lovers*, *Epsom-Wells*, and *The Virtuoso*.

The list of actors, although it lacked the names of Kynaston, Mrs. Barry, and the two Bettertons, would have assured the success of a much poorer play than *The Squire of Alsatia*. Leigh, remembered as Sir Formal, Gripe, and Tegue, was Sir William Belfond, a part in which he was commended by Downes and Cibber. The latter attests that he "shew'd a more spirited variety than ever [he] saw any actor, in any one character, come up to: the poet, 'tis true, had here exactly chalked for him the out-lines of nature; but the high colouring, the strong lights and shades of humour that enliven'd the whole and struck our admiration with surprize and delight, were wholly owing to the actor. The easy reader might, perhaps, have been pleased with the author without discomposing a feature, but the spectator must have heartily held his sides, or the actor would have heartily made them ach for it."[6] Cibber also singles out Underhill's Lolpoop for special mention: "in the boobily heaviness [of that character], he seem'd the immoveable log he stood for!"[7] The other comic rôle, that of the Elder Belfond, the Squire of Alsatia, was taken first by Nokes and later by Jevon.[8] Sandford quite properly was cast as the rascal Cheatly. Other former members of the Duke's Company to appear were Bowman as Truman, Bright as the Alsatian Captain Hackum, and Freeman as the hypocritical Scrapeall.

Griffin, whom Downes mentions as so excelling in the part of Sir Edward Belfond that "*none succeeding . . . have Equall'd him*,"[9] had been a member of the King's Company, as had Martin Powell, now cast for the minor rôle of the Attorney. Four of the women had also received their early dramatic training under

[6] *Colley Cibber. Written by Himself*, I, 208.
[7] Cibber, I, 214.
[8] Downes, p. 41.
[9] P. 40.

Killigrew's charge. Mrs. Corey, who excelled in character parts—such as Dol Common in *The Alchemist*, the Widow Blackacre in *The Plain Dealer*, and Dame Dobson in Ravenscroft's play of that name—was the "Precise Governess" Ruth. Mrs. Mountfort, formerly Mrs. Susannah Percival, and Mrs. Knight were the young women, Isabella and Teresia. Mrs. Boutell, who had "created" such varied rôles as Mrs. Margery Pinchwife in *The Country Wife*, Fidelia in *The Plain Dealer*, Melantha in *Marriage à la Mode*, and Statira in *The Rival Queens*, was the "furious, malicious, and revengeful" Mrs. Termagant.

Of the actors who had become eminent since the union of the companies, the most important at that time was William Mountfort, who played the rôle of the Younger Belfond. Tall, well-made, and fair, with a "clear, full, and melodious" voice, he gave, says Cibber, "the truest life to what we call the fine gentleman; his spirit shone the brighter for being polish'd with decency. . . . He had a particular talent in giving life to bons mots and repartees: the wit of the poet seem'd always to come from him extempore, and sharpen'd into more wit from his brilliant manner of delivering it; he had himself a good share of it, or what is equal to it, so lively a pleasantness of humour, that when either of these fell into his hands upon the stage, he wantoned with them to the highest delight of his auditors."[10] George Powell, who had joined the company the preceding year, and who was later to appear in many of the parts acted by Betterton, was the decoy-duck Shamwell. The minor rôle of the sharper Termagant was taken by Alexander;[11] and Lucia, the attorney's daughter, was acted by Mrs. Bracegirdle, who was destined to be "the darling of the theatre" and to perform the same service for the plays of Congreve that Mrs. Barry had performed for those of Otway.

By reason of the excellent acting, *The Squire of Alsatia* had an "Uninterrupted run of 13 Days together"; it was "often Honour'd with the presence of Chancellour *Jefferies*, and other great Persons."[12] Its success surpassed the expectation of the author, who wrote in his epistle dedicatory: "I had the great Honour to

[10] I, 186-187.

[11] Alexander is usually identified with Verbruggen. Mr. G. Thorn-Drury, however, suggests that "Alexander and Verbruggen were two distinct individuals." See *Works of Congreve* (ed. Montague Summers, 1923), I, 246-248.

[12] Downes, p. 41.

find so many Friends, that the House was never so full since it was built, as upon the third Day of this Play; and vast Numbers went away, that could not be admitted." Downes confirms this statement when he notes, "*The Poet receiv'd for his third Day in the House in* Drury-Lane *at single Prizes* 130 *l. which was the greatest Receipt they ever had at that House at single Prizes.*" In fact, Shadwell's return to the theatre was a triumph; and, from 1688 to the time of his death, he stood at the head of the dramatists actively engaged in writing plays for the English stage.

The first act of *The Squire of Alsatia* had been written at Copt Hall, the seat of Shadwell's old friend, the Earl of Dorset and Middlesex.[13] Here the author had been received as one of the family, and had enjoyed "not only the Excellence of the Air, and Regularity of living," but also "the Conversation which in all the World [he] would chuse." Dorset's approval of the beginning of this play encouraged him to proceed and finish it "in a Month's time."[14] But Dorset was soon to do something for Shadwell more tangible than merely to express approbation.

In 1688, James II, who had become extremely unpopular because of his arbitrary methods, was sitting unsteadily upon his throne. Finally, some of the most prominent members of both the political parties sent a letter in cipher to the king's son-in-law, William of Orange, inviting him to come to England in order to protect their constitutional liberties. William landed on November 5; and, on December 23, James fled to France. After William and Mary had been proclaimed king and queen on February 13, a readjustment of offices took place. Dorset became Lord Chamberlain; and, seeing that it was no longer possible for Dryden to continue in the post of Poet-Laureate, suggested Shadwell as his successor. It is said that when he was asked why he did not give the office to a better poet, he replied, "I do not pretend to say how great a poet Shadwell may be, but I am sure he is an honest man."

[13] Copped-Hall or Copt-Hall was left by Lionel Cranfield, Earl of Middlesex, to his nephew Charles Sackville, Lord Buckhurst, upon his death in 1674. Sackville was created Earl of Middlesex on April 4, 1675. In 1700, he sold this seat and estate to Thomas Webster. Philip Morant, *The History and Antiquities of the County of Essex* (London, 1768), I, 48.

[14] Epistle Dedicatory.

Shadwell had shown his satisfaction with the Revolution in two effusions published in 1689: *A Congratulatory Poem On His Highness the Prince of Orange His Coming into England. Written by T. S. A True Lover of his Countrey*, and *A Congratulatory Poem to the Most Illustrious Queen Mary Upon her Arrival In England*, signed "*The Humblest of Your Majesties Subjects*, THO. SHADWELL." What sort of complimentary poetry this author was capable of writing will appear from the final passage in each of these poems. The first, after describing the happy conditions "under the great *Eliza*," the destruction of this happiness through "*haughty Priests*," and the coming of the "*Glorious Orange*" to dispense new life to their "*drooping Lands*," concludes thus:

> Let there be light, th' *Almighty fiat* Run,
> No sooner 'twas pronounc'd, but it was done:
> *Inspir'd* by *Heav'n*, thus the *Great Orange said*,
> Let there be *liberty*, and was obey'd.
> Vast wonders *Heaven*'s great *Minister* h'as wrought,
> From our *dark Chaos*, *Beauteous order* brought:
> H' *Invaded* us with *Force*, to make us *free*,
> And in *anothers Realm*, could *meet no Enemy*.
> Hail *Great Assertor*, of the *Greatest Cause;*
> *Mans Liberty*, and the *Almighty's Laws:*
> *Heav'n Greater Wonders* has for *thee* design'd,
> *Thou Glorious deliv'rer of Mankind!*

The second also contains some superlative compliments and is brought to a close with these lines:

> What *Land* can boast of such a *matchless Pair*,
> Like him so *wise*, so *brave;* like You so *wise*, so *fair?*
> Where e'er so many *sacred Virtues* joyn,
> They to a *Scepter* shew a *Right Divine.*
> Who are approv'd so *Valiant*, *Wise*, and *Just*,
> Have the best *Titles* to the *highest Trust*,
> Tho from the *Loins* of *greatest Kings* deriv'd,
> That *Title*'s not so strong nor so long liv'd;
> For *Princes* more of *solid Glory* gain
> Who are *thought fit*, than who are *born* to *Reign.*

The author of these panegyrics, if he is undeserving of praise as a poet, was at least well qualified for political office under the new king and queen. Although "A Warrant to sware Thomas Shadwell Esqr into the place and quality of poet-Laureat to His Matie" was dated "March 9, 1688/9,"[15] the actual patent confirming his appointment to this position and to that of Historiographer Royal was not drawn up until August 29, 1689. In the latter document, it is stated that the appointment, which carried a pension of three hundred pounds and "one Butt or Pype of the best Canary Wyne yearly," was made "in consideration of the many good and acceptable services . . . and taking notice of the Learning and Eminent Abilities of . . . Tho. Shadwell."[16] The gratitude of the recipient was expressed in the epistle dedicatory to his next play, where he thanks Dorset for making him the "King's Servant."

Contemporary versifiers did not neglect the possibilities lurking in Shadwell's elevation to the laureateship. The active pen of Tom Brown was ready with *"The Fable of the* Bat *and the* Birds, *In Imitation of that of the* Buzzard *in the* Hind and Panther, *In the Year* 1689."[17] In this poem, the beasts and their ally, the bat (i.e., Dryden), are in warfare with the birds, who attack and rout them. The bat is forced to take shelter in a cellar; but his place of hiding is soon discovered and he is haled before the bar. Here, in the presence of parrot Settle, cuckoo Rymer, peacock Chetwood, owl D'Urfey, and others, the eagle pronounces judgment:

> From all our Diets be thou first expell'd
> Or those in flow'ry Groves, or those in Steeples held,
> When our gay Tribes in youthful Pomp appear,
> To join in Nuptial Bands, and meet the smiling Year:
> Nay more, to make thee mortify and grieve,
> To Buzzard *Shadwell* we thy Places give;
> Him we appoint Historian of our State,
> And Poet-Laureat of the Woods create.

[15] D. M. Walmsley, "New Light on Thomas Shadwell" (London *Times Literary Supplement,* April 16, 1925).

[16] Edmund K. Broadus, *The Laureateship* (Oxford, 1921), p. 79 n. The Accounts Commissioners, in their report for the period from November 5, 1688, to September 29, 1691, record "Thomas Shadwell, Esq., Poet Laureate, 2 years' salary . . . £600" (*Hist. MSS. Comm. 13th Report, Pt. V,* p. 373), and in their report for the year ending September 29, 1692, "Thomas Shadwell, Poet Laureate . . . £300" (*Hist. MSS. Comm. 14th Report, Pt. V,* p. 166). In the year ending with the Feast of St. Michael, 1693, the "Executors of Thomas Shadwell, Poet Laureate" were paid £150 (*MSS. of House of Lords, 1693-1695,* p. 90).

[17] *Works of Mr. Thomas Brown* (London, 1720), IV, 36 ff.

Out-law'd our Realms, and banish'd from the Light,
Be thou forever damn'd to steal Abroad by Night.

On May 14, 1689, Matthew Prior addressed "An Epistle to Fleetwood Shephard, Esq., *Burleigh*," which concludes with a reference to the new poet-laureate:

Thus, without much Delight, or Grief,
I fool away an idle Life;
'Till *Shadwell* from the Town retires
(Choak'd up with Fame and Sea-coal Fires)
To bless the Wood with peaceful *Lyric;*
Then hey for Praise and Panegyric,
Justice restor'd, and Nations freed,
And wreaths round *William's* glorious Head.[18]

Shadwell's first effusion as laureate represents the nadir of his poetic efforts. *An Ode on the Queen's Birth-Day, Sang before their Majesties at Whitehal*, was written for performance on April 30, 1689,[19] with music by Henry Purcell. The praise of the sovereign is ridiculously superlative. According to the author, her zeal to God and benevolence to man must raise her above all former monarchs; the great name of Elizabeth will be lost in the greater name of Mary. The second stanza is enough to quote:

It was a work of full as great a weight,
And require the self-same Power,
Which did frail Humane kind Create,
When they were lost them to restore,
For a like Act, Fate gave our Princes Birth,
Which adding to the Saints, made Joy in Heaven,
As well as Triumphs upon Earth,
To which so great, so good a Queen was given.

[18] Prior, *Poems on Several Occasions* (ed. A. R. Waller, Cambridge, 1905), p. 15. Other references to Shadwell as laureate are found in *The Late Converts Exposed: or the Reasons of Mr. Bays's Changing his Religion . . . Part the Second* (London, 1690), p. 51; *"A Congratulatory Poem to the Right Honourable Sir* E. S. &c." in *A New Collection of Poems Relating to State Affairs* (London, 1705), p. 538.

[19] Broadus, *op. cit.*, p. 79. The earliest printing of this ode that I have been able to find is in *The Muses Farewel to Popery & Slavery, Or, A Collection of Miscellany Poems, Satyrs, Songs, &c. Made by the Most Eminent Wits of the Nation, . . . the Second Edition, with Large Additions, most of them never before Printed . . . 1690.* Mr. Broadus suggests (p. 80) that the ode on the queen's birthday for 1691 "is probably but not certainly by Shadwell." It is printed in the *Works of Henry Purcell*, XI, pt. 1.

About the time of the performance of Shadwell's first ode, *Bury-Fair* was produced.[20] This comedy, the author states, was "written during eight Months painful Sickness wherein all the several Days in which [he] was able to write any part of a Scene amounted not to one Month, except some few which were employ'd in indispensable Business." It met "with a kind Reception from all, . . . but some of the late Loyal Poets, . . . and from some who are still so fond of the Doctrine of *Passive Obedience* and *Non-resistance*, that they think it a Profanation to bring the very Words into a Comedy." In the epilogue, Mrs. Mountfort bemoaned the fact that most of the constant friends of the theatre had left the town to serve king and country.

Those who remained behind and attended performances at Drury Lane could not have been dissatisfied with the cast provided for *Bury-Fair.* Leigh again had an excellent opportunity in the part of the French barber La Roch, who masquerades as a count. Underhill and Nokes had congenial rôles in Mr. Oldwit and his "witty" friend, Sir Humphrey Noddy. Mountfort was once more cast for a gay young man, Wildish, in love with Gertrude, played by his wife. Betterton was the tiresome and moralistic Bellamy; Bowman played Trim, the rejected suitor of Mrs. Fantast; while Bowen had the slight rôle of the Valet to Wildish. Mrs. Corey was chosen to act the affected Lady Fantast. Mrs. Boutell had a similar part in that of her daughter. The girl who goes disguised as the page Charles was played by Mrs. Butler, "allow'd in those days to sing and dance to great perfection," and further described by Cibber as having "a sweet-ton'd voice, which, with her naturally genteel air and sensible pronunciation, render'd her wholly mistress of the amiable in many serious characters."[21]

Bury-Fair was followed by a decidedly inferior piece, *The Amorous Bigot: with the Second Part of Tegue O'Divelly*, produced not later than May 5, 1690.[22] In his epistle dedicatory, addressed to Charles, Earl of Shrewsbury, Shadwell again alludes to the "long Sickness," which made him unfit for playwriting. Nevertheless he had "no Reason to complain of the Reception of this Play." This comedy was doubtless written to enable Leigh

[20] Advertised in *London Gazette*, May 23-27, 1689.

[21] I, 223.

[22] Date of the Epistle Dedicatory.

to appear once more in the rôle of the Irish priest, which he had acted in *The Lancashire Witches.* Underhill had the important part of Colonel Bernardo, a "vapouring blustring Soldier"; Nokes, who on five other occasions had acted female rôles,[23] was cast for the bawd Gremia. Williams, Bowman, and Alexander were the gentlemen Luscindo, Doristeo, and Finardo. The parts of the young ladies, Rosania and Elvira, were taken by Mrs. Bracegirdle and Mrs. Jordan. Mrs. Butler, remembered as the woman in disguise in *Bury-Fair,* again had an opportunity to wear male attire as the jealous Levia. Mrs. Corey, the Lady Fantast of the previous year, was the "amorous bigot," Belliza. The minor rôles of the waiting gentlemen Hernando and the servant Diego were given to Bowen and Michael Leigh. The "old Governante" Grycia was allotted to Mrs. Osborne.

Two of Shadwell's tributes to William III were published in 1690. *The Ode on the Anniversary of the King's Birth* had, however, been written for performance at court on November 4 of the preceding year.[24] In this poem, the author, after praising the race from which William had sprung, assures the monarch that Europe depends for freedom on his sword, that he is destined to tumble down the "Savage Monster from the *Gallick* Throne," and that there will be an increase of arts and industry during the peace which is to follow his victories.

> Then shall the Vile Ungrateful Murm'ring Band,
> Whom our great *Moses* has set free
> From *Egypts* Bondage, and Idolatry,
> Glad to submit to his Command;
> For Shame their guilty Heads hang down,
> Owning the best of Kings that ever fill'd the Throne.
>
> Thus the Prophetick Muses say,
> And all the Wise and Good will pray,
> That they long, long, may Celebrate this Day.
> Soon Haughty *France* shall bow, and Coz'ning *Rome,*
> And *Britain* Mistress of the World become;

[23] Menanthe (Stapylton's *The Slighted Maid,* produced 1662/3), Nurse to Caelia (Payne's *The Fatal Jealousie,* produced August, 1672), Lady Beardly (D'Urfey's *The Virtuous Wife,* published 1680), Nurse (Otway's *Caius Marius,* published 1680), Megaera (D'Urfey's *The Banditti,* published 1686).

[24] Broadus, p. 80. Luttrell records that there was "a great ball at court" on that day (*Brief Historical Relation,* I, 600).

And from thy Wise, thy Godlike Sway,
Kings learn to Reign, and Subjects to Obey.

The *Ode to the King, On his Return from Ireland*[25] celebrates in lifeless verse William's courage at the Battle of the Boyne, his wound—the "*Royal Breach*"—and the fear he had been able to instill into the French king. It concludes with these uninspired lines:

Now, since so many, and so great Affairs
Employ your *Royal Mind* with Cares;
And you the mighty Weight *alone* Sustain,
Your happy *Subjects* you with *Arms defend*,
Instruct with *Manners*, and with *Laws amend*;
I, from *Mankind*, cou'd no Indulgence gain
If, from the *Public Good*, you longer I detain.
Welcome, *Great Prince!* from Toils, and Arms,
To soft *Maria's* Beauteous Charms:
Who in your Absence *Reign'd* so well,
And did so much the *Virgin Queen* excel,
No more shall we old Tales of our *Eliza* tell.
Welcome, *Great Sir!* to fill your *Brittish* Throne:
Brittain, with Justice, you may call your own;
Which to a Mighty Kingdom you advance,
From a poor Province, to Insulting *France*.

In this year, 1690, Shadwell provided the ode[26] to be sung at the annual celebration of the Feast of St. Cecilia on November 22. From a notice in the *Gentleman's Journal* of January, 1691/2, referring specifically to the celebration of 1691, one may gain some idea of what the ceremony was like. On that day "most of the Lovers of Music, whereof many are persons of the first Rank, meet at *Stationers-Hall* in *London*, not thro a Principle of Superstition, but to propagate the advancement of that divine Science. A splendid Entertainment is provided, and before it is always a performance of Music by the best Voices and Hands in Town; the Words, which are always in the Patronesses praise, are set by some of the greatest Masters in town. . . . 6 Stewards are chosen for each ensuing year, four of which are either Persons of Quality or Gen-

[25] The king landed on September 6. He arrived at Windsor on the ninth and was at Kensington on the tenth.

[26] The music was by Robert King.

tlemen of Note, and the two last, either Gentlemen of their Majesties Music, or some of the chief Masters in town. . . . This Feast is one of the genteelest in the world; there are no formalities nor gatherings like as at others, and the appearance there is always very splendid. Whilst the Company is at Table, the Hautboys and Trumpets play successively." Shadwell's poem, although it flows smoothly and is in places rather spirited, suffers in comparison with Dryden's *Song for St. Cecilia's Day, 1687,* and his masterly *Alexander's Feast* (1697). It is, however, not inferior to the odes of D'Urfey and Brady, which were sung in the years 1691 and 1692.

Probably in December, 1690, or January, 1690/1—certainly not later than February, 1690/1[27]—Shadwell's *The Scowrers* was acted by the United Companies. In this comedy, the author returns to London, which he had deserted for Bury St. Edmunds and Madrid in his two previous plays, and moralizes on the practice, engaged in by some of the young bloods, of destroying property and fighting the watch. Again the cast was excellent. Mountfort was the chief scourer, Sir William Rant; Williams and Leigh were his comrades in rioting, Wildfire and Tope. Bright, who had been Captain Hackum in *The Squire of Alsatia,* appeared as the foolish Jacobite alderman, Sir Humphrey Maggot; and Bowman, who had acted Truman, Trim, and Doristeo in plays by Shadwell, was Whachum, the "City-Wit" with the ambition of equalling Sir William as a scourer. The less important parts of the "Scoundrels," Bluster and Dingboy, were taken by Freeman and Cudworth; of the valets, Ralph and Jasper, by Bowen and Will Peer. Mrs. Bracegirdle and Mrs. Barry were the young ladies, Clara and Eugenia; Mrs. Corey, but recently the "amorous bigot," was their governess Priscilla; Mrs. Osborne again appeared as an old woman in the rôle of Sir William's housekeeper Abigal; and Mrs. Richardson, a newcomer, was the maid Lettice.[28]

Two members of the cast, who were apparently in a play by Shadwell for the first time, deserve special mention. Edward Kynaston, who had been on the stage since 1660, acted the much-vexed father Mr. Rant, who is finally able to make his son mend

[27] Advertised in *London Gazette,* February 19-23, 1690/1. There it is called "the last new Comedy."

[28] Spelled "Richeson" in the quarto of 1691.

his ways. In this part, Kynaston may have shown some of the "masterly strokes of nature," which Cibber attributes to him in the scene between the King and his son in *Henry IV*. There he expressed "all the various motions of the heart with the same force, dignity, and feeling they are written, adding to the whole that peculiar and becoming grace which the best writer cannot inspire into any actor that is not born with it."[29] Mrs. Leigh, for twenty years an actress, Cibber also describes as at this time having "a very droll way of dressing the pretty foibles of superannuated beauties," and as being able to infuse a good deal of humor "into the affected mothers, aunts, and modest stale maids that had miss'd their market."[30] As Lady Maggot in *The Scowrers*, she acted just such a part.

This was the last of Shadwell's plays to be produced during his lifetime. The gout, of which he complains in the prologue, evidently made composition difficult. He apparently did little writing during the year 1691. On New Year's Day, 1692, he presented to the king *Votum Perenne*, in form and substance not unlike his other poetical addresses to William. In this, he assures the monarch that, because of the great wonders he has performed in subjugating Ireland, France avoids battle, but that the present year has been designed by Fate for him to "*Quiet* the *Disturber* of *Mankind*" and thus usher in a "*firm* and *glorious* Peace."

In January, 1691/2, Shadwell interested himself in a tragedy by Nicholas Brady, minister of St. Catherine Cree Church and somewhat of a dabbler in poetry. This divine, then in his thirty-third year, had doubtless commended himself to the laureate because, while living in Ireland, he had been "no inconsiderable sufferer" in the cause of King William.[31] At that time, he was also chaplain to the Duke of Ormond, whose grandfather some years before had "specially recommended" that John Shadwell "be elected and continued" in one of his offices.[32] Shadwell's efforts at intercession in behalf of Brady's play, *The Rape; or, The Innocent Impostors*, were at first in vain. After being "turned off" with "a great slight" and told by Thomas Davenant that he would

[29] I, 185.
[30] I, 222.
[31] Epistle Dedicatory to *The Rape, or The Innocent Impostors* (1692).
[32] *Cal. State Papers, Dom. Ser.*, 1673, p. 504.

"trouble himself no more about the Play," the laureate, on January 19, wrote a letter to the Lord Chamberlain, Dorset, begging him to order this tragedy "to be the next new play to be acted."[33]

This plea evidently met with some success; for Brady's play with epilogue by Shadwell was soon performed. *The Gentleman's Journal* of March, 1691/2, printed this brief item: "We have had lately a new Play, called, *The Innocent Impostors*. It hath been acted four times. Mr. *Shadwell*, Poet-Laureat, usher'd it into the Stage. It is said that the Author of it is not one of the Laity; therefore since he desires not to be known, I shall not presume to let you know his Name, tho the Play being Historical, and altogether of the Tragick kind, and withal treated with all the decency imaginable, can never be inglorious to its ingenious Author." On May 2, Shadwell sent this play to Dorset; and, in the accompanying letter, complained again of being troubled with the gout.[34]

In a communication, dated May 14, 1692, in the *Gentleman's Journal* Peter Motteux promised "before the long Vacation . . . a comedy by Mr. *Shadwell*, whose *Genius* for that sort of Poetry, is sufficiently known to the Ingenious." But the play did not come forth; and, in October, the still hopeful Motteux reported: "We are promis'd a Comedy by Mr. *Shadwell* in a short time, and two or three new Plays after that; which will be a pleasing Entertainment for us this Winter." These words represent the last reference made to Shadwell during his lifetime.

The end came on the nineteenth or twentieth of November.[35] Troubled by painful illness for at least four years, Shadwell had formed the habit of taking opium, an overdose of which is believed to have caused his death. The funeral was held on November 24 at the old Church of St. Luke, Chelsea, where the sermon was preached by the friend whom he had assisted but a short time before, Nicholas Brady.[36]

Those who were present at the funeral listened to a sermon on

[33] *Hist. MSS. Comm. Fourth Report*, p. 280.

[34] *Ibid.*, p. 281.

[35] One of the lines of the inscription intended for Shadwell's monument in the Poets' Corner was "*Ob. Nov.* 19. *Æt. suae* 52." On the monument which was actually erected these words were changed to "Ob. Nov. 20 1692 Ætat. Suae 55."

[36] The "Register book of the Parish of Chelsey for Mariages Births and Burialls," 1653-1704, records on November 24, 1692, the burial of "Thomas Shadwell Esqr Poet Laureat."

the text, "*Blessed are the dead, which die in the Lord.*" In his discourse, Brady insisted that he "who is always conversant in the Duties of his Profession, always employed in the Exercises of Devotion, and keeps a *Conscience void of offence towards God, and towards man:* he is the Man who, let Death come when it will, is never found dejected or unprovided: . . . he takes the surest and most infallible way, to secure to himself, whenever he shall die, *the Blessedness of those dead which die in the Lord.*" Then the preacher went on "to prove the thing affirmed in [his] text" by showing it to be true when Death is considered "as a Passage out of this World" and also "as the entrance into another World." After the argumentative portion came the concluding sentences, which, because they contain specific reference to Shadwell, are worth quoting in their entirety here:

> Into this happy State and Condition, I hope, our deceased Brother is already enter'd; with whom my Acquaintance was so intimate, during my short Familiarity with him, that it qualified me to know him as well, as those who had conversed with him much longer: and I cannot but do his memory that Justice, to declare, that during the time of my Acquaintance with him, I found in him a most zealous Affection to the present Government, a great deal of Honesty and Integrity, a real Love of Truth and Sincerity, an inviolable Fidelity and Strictness to his Word, an unalterable Friendship wheresoever he professed it, (and however the World may be mistaken in him) a much deeper Sense of Religion, than many others have, who pretend to it more openly: His natural and acquired Abilities made him sufficiently remarkable to all that he conversed with, and cannot be unknown to any here present, very few being equal to him, in all the becoming Qualities and Accomplishments, which adorn and set off a complete Gentleman: His very Enemies (if he have left any behind him) will give him this Character, at least if they knew him so throughly as I did; and therefore it is but cold Justice in a Friend, who received from him, during his Life, all the Marks of a true Affection, which shall make his Memory dear to me, when he is nothing else but Dust and Ashes. His Death seized him suddenly, but could not unprepared, since (to my own certain knowledge) he never took his Dose of *Opium*, but he solemnly recommended himself to God by Prayer, as if he were then about to *resign up his Soul into the Hands of his faithful Creator.* These Considerations give me good Grounds to hope, that *this dead man is blessed;* because from thence I have reason to believe that *he died in the Lord.* I should enlarge farther upon his Character, but that he always in his life time disapproved of that Custom upon these Occasions, and most especially in relation to himself, nor should

I thus far have infringed his Will in this particular, but that I was willing to inform the World, how much some People have erred in their Opinion of him.

Let us then, in the Name God, so manage our selves, during the Course of this Life, that we may be qualified for the Enjoyment of a better; that when we shall *go hence and be no more seen*, we may *rest from our labours*, not enter upon greater Miseries, and that *our works which shall follow us*, may recommend, and not impeach us: that so we may have a just Title to *that Blessedness*, which is the portion of those *dead which die in the Lord. To which, God, of his infinite Mercy, bring us all through the Merits and Mediation of our Blessed Saviour: to whom with the Father, and the Holy Spirit, be ascribed all Honour, Power, Might, Majesty, and Dominion, henceforth, and for evermore.* Amen.[37]

Shadwell's will, which had been "declared, signed, and sealed" in 1690 at his house in Chelsea, is also deserving of quotation in its entirety:[38]

KNOW ALL MEN BY THESE PRESENTS That revoakeing all other Wills and Testaments whatsoever by mee formerly made I doe declare and appoynt this to bee my last Will and Testament in manner and forme following. Imprimis I desire to bee buryed in Flannel with the least charge that may bee. Item I give and bequeath to the Earle of Dorsett Sr Charles Sedley William Jephson Esqre[39] and Coll Edmund Ashton[40] my most deare freinds by whome I have beene extreamely obliged and to each of them one Ring of gold weighing twenty shillings with

[37] Nicholas Brady, *A Sermon Preached at the Funeral of Thomas Shadwell, Esq., . . . Published at the Earnest Request of the Friends of the Deceased* (London, 1693).

[38] The text of the will as here printed is "extracted from the Principal Registry of the Probate Divorce and Admiralty Division of the High Court of Justice. In the Prerogative Court of Canterbury." In spelling, punctuation, and capitalization it differs somewhat from the original will, a photograph of which appears in volume I of Summers' edition of Shadwell. The phraseology is, however, the same in both texts.

[39] On June 7, 1691, "William Jepthson, esq., secretary to the lords of the treasury, died" (Luttrell, II, 242).

[40] Edmund Ashton, gentleman of the bed-chamber to the Duke of York and lieutenant-colonel of the horse guards, had been a friend of Shadwell's since at least 1671. In that year he was visited by the dramatist at his seat, Chadderton Hall, near Oldham market-place, Lancashire. On May 25, Shadwell wrote a letter to the Duchess of Newcastle from "a place called *Chaddeston*, near *Manchester*." See p. 19n. During the visit he may have written his verse "Letter from Mr. Shadwell to Mr. Wicherley" (printed in *Complete Works of William Wycherley*, ed. Montague Summers, 1924, II, 243-245), in which appear these lines:

"In Rhyme I greet my Friend in Town,
From *Hall* yclepped *Chaderton*."

Nahum Tate dedicated his *Cuckolds-Haven; or, An Alderman no Conjuror* (London, 1686) to Ashton, whom he describes as an "accomplisht Courtier, Souldier, and Scholar."

this Motto Memor esto tui. Item I give one ring to my brother[41] at the discretion of my executrix as to the price with the same Motto Item I give to my sonne John five pounds for mourning and my Latine and philosophicall bookes with Mr. Hobbes his workes warning him to have a care of some ill opinions of his concerning government but hee may make excellent vse of what is good in him I doe alsoe charge and command my said sonne to bee obedient to his mother Item I doe by these presents constitute and appoynt my dearely beloved wife Anne the daughter of Tho. Gibbs late of Norwich deceased Proctor and Publick Notary my EXECUTRIX of my last Will and Testament above declared to whom I give and bequeath my Lease of two tenements holden by mee in Dorsett Garden als Salisbury Court in London by the Theatre as alsoe the Rent I purchased of the Lady Davenant and Mr. Cave Vnderhill issueing out of the dayly proffitts of the said Theatre vizt out of the said Lady Davenants and Cave Vnderhills severall proportions of Rent for the said Theatre Item I give and bequeath to my said executrix all money and sumes of money whatsoever put out vpon mortgage bond or any other way and all my interest in anuall rents or houses whatsoever Item I give and bequeath to my said executrix all my plate and household stuffe and all my goods and chattells whatsoever as I have declared in a Deed in Trust for her Sr Charles Sedley and William Jephson Esqre being her Trustees in that Deed mentioned Lastly I give my said executrix all the money goods and chattells which I shall dye possessed of or which shall bee due to mee at the time of my death intreating her to reserve all for my children after her death as I doubt not but shee will haveing beene a dilligent carefull and provident woeman and very indulgent to her children as ever I knew, for which reason I intrust her with the disposall of what I shall leave behind mee to my children in what proportions shall please her, but principally I recomend my poore little daughter Ann[42] the greatest comfort to mee of all my children to her particular care which I doubt not but shee will imploy to the vtmost in her education I desire her to pay my just debts and performe this my last Will to which I have sett my hand and seale this

— THOMAS SHADWELL —

Declared signed and sealed in the presence of — ANTHONY LEIGH — RICHARD GUILFORD — ELLENOR LEIGH.

13 December 1692.

WHICH DAY APPEARED PERSONALLY Ellianor Leigh (wife of

[41] Probably Edward Shadwell who was commissioned captain-lieutenant to the Duke of Bolton's company in his regiment of foot on March 1, 1694 (*Cal. State Papers,* Dom. Series, 1694-1695, p. 47). On June 8, 1704, he petitioned Queen Anne for "the grant of letters patent for erecting an office of insurance in the Kingdom of Ireland for the support of widows and orphans" (*MSS. of Duke of Portland,* IV, 93). The petition was approved by the Duke of Ormonde on August 23, 1704 (*MSS. of Duke of Portland,* IV, 112). See p. 16n.

[42] See p. 71.

Anthony Leigh of the parish of St Bridgett als Brides London gent) and deposed vpon the holy Evangelists That shee was present when Mr. Thomas Shadwell did seale and execute his last will and testament in his owne house at Chelsea beginning thus Know all men by these presents that, and ending thus, To which I have sett my hand and seale this, which was Betweene Bartholomew Tide and Michaelmas 1690, and this shee doth the better remember because that shee tooke lodgeings at Chelsea some few dayes before Bartholomew Tide in the said yeare 1690, and left the said lodgings at Michaelmas following And she further deposed that the said deceased was at such his sealeing and publishing his said Will of perfect mind and memory and did soe execute his said Will in the presence of this Deponent her said husband Anthony Leigh and Richard Guilford who all subscribed their names as witnesses to the said Will in the presence of the said Thomas Shadwell deceased — —
ELLENOR LEIGH — Eodem die dicta — ELLIANORA LEIGH
Jurata fuit Coram me THO PINFOLD Surr.
Proved
13th December 1692

Two of the three witnesses to the signature on the will appeared in Shadwell's last play, *The Volunteers, or The Stock Jobbers,* presented within the month following his death. Leigh, who had played the principal humorous rôles in Shadwell's six preceding comedies and who was himself to die before the end of the year, acted in this play what was probably his last new part, that of Major-General Blunt, the old Cavalier officer.[43] Mrs. Leigh was cast for Mrs. Hackwell, described in the dramatis personae as a "most devilish imperious Wife." Colonel Hackwell Senior, a former member of Cromwell's army, was played by Thomas Doggett, then at the beginning of his career as an actor, but "vegetating fast." The younger Powell and Hodgson were the soldiers who had won honor in the recent wars, Colonel Hackwell Junior and Welford. Bowman, who had more than once appeared as a beau, had a part of that nature in Sir Nicholas Dainty. Bowen, promoted since his appearance in *The Scowrers* from acting servants, was the other beau, Sir Timothy Kastril. Alexander and Freeman played the rogues, Nickum and Dingboy. The affected young ladies, Teresia and Winifred, were acted by Mrs. Knight and Mrs. Rogers, the latter a newcomer to the company; whereas Mrs.

[43] The names of the actors do not appear in the 1720 edition of Shadwell's plays, but are given in the quarto of 1693.

Mountfort and Mrs. Bracegirdle were the sensible Eugenia and Clara. The very minor part of the tailor was taken by Pinkethman, who was destined in the next century to please countless times in comic rôles.

The only contemporary report concerning the fate of *The Volunteers* is that found in *The Gentleman's Journal* of November, 1692: "Though that Orphan wanted its Parent to support it, yet it came off with reasonable success." Tom D'Urfey supplied a prologue. The epilogue "Spoken by one in deep Mourning" contains lines in praise of the author and his type of comedy. Although some of the sentiments may impress a modern reader as hyperbolic, they doubtless represented the opinions of many of the theatregoers of 1692, and are therefore not at all unfitting to come at the end of Shadwell's last play.

> *Enough of Mirth; the* Sportive Scene *is done,*
> *And a new doleful* Theme *is coming on:*
> *These Sable Robes, at* Plays *so seldom worn,*
> *Do silently express the Loss we mourn:*
> S H A D W E L L, *the great Support o' th'* Comick Stage,
> *Born to expose the Follies of the Age,*
> *To whip prevailing Vices, and unite*
> Mirth *with* Instruction, Profit *with* Delight;
> *For large* Idea's, *and a flowing* Pen,
> *First of our* Times, *and second but to* Ben;
> *Whose mighty* Genius *and discerning* Mind
> *Trac'd all the various* Humours *of Mankind,*
> *Dressing them up with such successful Care,*
> *That ev'ry* Fop *found his own* Picture *there,*
> *And blush'd for Shame at the surprising Skill,*
> *Which made his lov'd Resemblance look so ill:*
> S H A D W E L L, *who all his* Lines *from Nature drew,*
> *Copy'd her out, and kept her still in View;*
> *Who never sunk in* Prose, *nor soar'd in* Verse,
> *So high as* Bombast, *or so low as* Farce;
> *Who ne'er was brib'd, by* Title *or* Estate,
> *To fawn and flatter with the* Rich *or* Great,
> *To let a gilded* Vice *or* Folly *pass,*
> *But always lash'd the* Villain *and the* Ass.
> *Many within this crowded Pit I see,*
> *Friends to our* Author *and his* Memory:
> *To them he leaves, to cherish and maintain*
> *The last and youngest Off-spring of his Brain:*

By your just Care of this, you best will show
The kind Respect you to its Parent *owe.*
Crown you his last Performance with Applause,
Who love, like him, our Liberties *and* Laws.
Let but the honest *Party do him Right,*
And their loud Claps will give him Fame, in spight
Of the faint Hiss *of grumbling* Jacobite.

CHAPTER VI

REPUTATION

WITH the exception of the Italian poem by Reggio, the conclusion of the funeral sermon, and the epilogue to *The Volunteers*, most of the comments on Shadwell quoted in the preceding pages have been uncomplimentary. Coming from his opponents in pamphlet warfare or their adherents, these estimates of his character and works are naturally far from generous. The verses of Dryden and the Tories, however, give but an incomplete idea of the attitude of his contemporaries. During Shadwell's lifetime were written lines which showed that many persons well-acquainted with the theatre did not confirm the charge of dulness.

Among the latter was the brilliant and dissolute John Wilmot, Earl of Rochester, who is reported to have said that if Shadwell "had burnt all he wrote, and printed all he spoke, he would have had more Wit and Humour than any other Poet."[1] In his *Allusion to the Tenth Satyr of the First Book of Horace*,[2] Rochester, while reviewing the dramatists whose works were popular on the London stage of the 1670's, writes thus of Shadwell:

> Of all our Modern Wits, none seems to me
> Once to have toucht upon true Comedy,
> But hasty *Shadwell*, and slow *Wycherley*.
> *Shadwell's* unfinish'd works do yet impart
> Great proofs of force of Nature, none of Art;
> With just bold strokes he dashes here and there,
> Shewing great Mastery, with little Care;
> And scorns to varnish his good touches o're,
> To make the Fools and Women praise 'em more.

Near the end of the same poem, he shows in what high estimation he holds the judgment of Shadwell:

[1] Thomas Whincop, *Scanderbeg. . . . To which are added a List of all the Dramatic Authors, with some Account of their Lives* (London, 1747), p. 284.

[2] In *Critical Essays of the Seventeenth Century*, ed. J. E. Spingarn (Oxford, 1908), II, 282-285. In his *First Epistle of the Second Book of Horace*, l. 85, Pope follows Rochester in his characterization of Shadwell and Wycherley.

I loath the rabble; 'tis enough for me
If *Sidley*, *Shadwell*, *Shephard*, *Wycherley*,
Godolphin, *Butler*, *Buckhurst*, *Buckingham*,
And some few more whom I omit to name,
Approve my sense: I count their censure Fame.

Aubrey, in his "Life of Shakespeare," writes that Shadwell "is counted the best comoedian we have now."[3] Phillips calls him "a noted Dramatic Writer of the present Age; happy especially in several witty and ingenuous Comedies,"[4] while Winstanley designates him as one "whose Pen hath deserved well of the Stage, not only for the number of the Plays which he hath writ; but also for the sweet Language and Contrivance of them."[5] Langbaine, the detector of plagiarisms, prefers Shadwell to Dryden as a writer of comedies. In 1691, he describes the dramatist in the following words:

A Gentleman, whose Dramatick Works are sufficiently known to the World; but especially his Excellent Comedies; which in the Judgment of some Persons, have very deservedly advanced him to the Honour he now enjoys, under the Title of *Poet Laureat* to their present Majesties. . . . Mr. *Dryden*, I dare presume little imagined, when he writ that Satyr of *Mack-Flecknoe*, that the Subject he *there* so much exposes and ridicules, should have ever lived to have succeeded him in wearing the *Bays*.

But I am willing to say the less of Mr. *Shadwell*, because I have publickly professed a Friendship for him: and tho' it be not of so long date, as some former Intimacy with others; so neither is it blemished with some unhandsome Dealings, I have met with from Persons, where I least expected it. I shall therefore speak of him with the Impartiality that becomes a Critick; and own I like *His* Comedies better than Mr. *Dryden*'s; as having more Variety of Characters, and those drawn from the Life; I mean Men's Converse and Manners, and not from other Mens Ideas, copyed out of their publick Writings: tho' indeed I cannot wholly acquit our *Present Laureat* from borrowing; his Plagiaries being in some places too bold and open to be disguised. . . . So far only give me leave to premise in our Laureat's Defence, that the Reader is not to measure his Merit by Mr. *Dryden*'s Standard; since *Socrates* never was more per-

[3] John Aubrey, *Brief Lives,* ed. Andrew Clark (Oxford, 1898), II, 226.

[4] Edward Phillips, *Theatrum Poetarum, or a Compleat Collection of the Poets* (London, 1675), p. 183.

[5] William Winstanley, *The Lives of the Most Famous English Poets, or The Honour of Parnassus* (London, 1687), p. 216.

secuted by the Inhumane *Aristophanes*, than Mr. Shadwell by Mr. *Dryden*'s pen; and with the same injustice; tho' I think, whoever shall peruse the Modest Defence of the former, in his Epistle to the tenth Satyr of *Juvenal*, will not only acquit him, but love him for his good Humour and gentle Temper, to One who endeavour'd to destroy his *Reputation*, so dear to *All Men*, but the very *Darling* of Poets.[6] . . .

I must do Mr. *Dryden* so much Justice, as to acknowledge, that in *Epick Poetry*, he far exceeds not only Mr. *Shadwell*, but most, if not all the Poets of our Age: and I could wish our present Laureat, would not give his predecessor such frequent Advantages over him; but rather confine himself within his own Sphere of Comedy.[7]

In the *Athenian Gazette* of December 5, 1691, John Dunton attempted to answer the question, "*Whom do you think the best Dramatick Professor in this Age?*" After eliminating D'Avenant, Cowley, Rochester, Otway, Mrs. Behn, and Mrs. Phillips from the discussion, he turns to "those still living who have deserv'd very well of the Drama" and writes:

if *true Comedy*, and perhaps the best that comes on our Stage, cou'd justly entitle to the *Laurel*, he may be said to merit it best who now wears it, for which we have not only his Testimony who is held *Infallible* among our *English* Writers, but that of our own *Sences*, in many or most of his Plays that might be named:—tho' the truth is, we find few of 'em too full of *Virtuous Characters*, which are now almost confin'd to Tragedy, and there seldom or never appear, unless to be *miserable*. As for his *Predecessor*, we doubt not but Mr. *Laureat* himself has the justice to own him his *Master* in many parts of *Poetry*, and the *numerousness* of his Verse among other things, we suppose hee'l scarce dispute with him, since 'tis really almost Musick but to hear a page of him read, and Mr. *Drydens* Heroick Verse is undoubtedly the sweetest in the World.[8]

Of those who "approv'd"[9] Shadwell's writings, none was more eminent as a wit than George Villiers, Duke of Buckingham. His words in commendation of the dramatist have unfortunately not been preserved. In his "*Tryal of the Poets for the Bays, In Imitation of a Satyr in* Boileau,"[10] Buckingham represents Apollo as

[6] Gerard Langbaine, *An Account of the English Dramatick Poets* (Oxford, 1691), pp. 442-444.

[7] *Ibid.*, p. 452.

[8] *The Athenian Gazette: or Casuistical Mercury Resolving All the Most Nice and Curious Questions. Proposed by the Ingenious of Either Sex*, Vol. 5, Numb. 2.

[9] See epistle dedicatory to *Timon of Athens*.

[10] In *Works of George Villiers, Late Duke of Buckingham* (London, 1715),

calling the poets together and giving each an opportunity to plead his cause. After Dryden, Etherege, and Wycherley appear,

> Next into the Crowd, *Tom Shadwell* does wallow,
> And swears by his Guts, his Paunch, and his Tallow,
> That 'tis he alone best pleases the Age,
> Himself, and his Wife, have supported the Stage:
> *Apollo* well pleas'd with so bony a Lad,
> T'oblige him, he told him, he should be huge glad,
> Had he Half so much wit, as he fansi'd he had.

The laurel is finally bestowed upon Betterton. Another uncomplimentary reference to Shadwell occurs in a poem attributed to Buckingham, "Timon, *a* Satyr, *in Imitation of Monsieur* Boleau, *upon several Passages in some new Plays then acted upon the Stage.*"[11] Here "a dull dining Sot" seizes Timon as he is walking in the Mall.

> He takes me in his *Coach*, and as we go,
> Pulls out a *Libel* of a Sheet or two;
> Insipid as *the Praise of Pious Queens*,
> Or *Shadwell*'s unassisted former Scenes.

Buckingham was not alone in depicting Shadwell at meetings of the poets. In some verses of anonymous authorship, "*The Session of the* Poets, *to the Tune of* Cook Lawrel,"[12] Apollo is forced to adjourn the court and leave the unruly poets "together by th' Ears for the *Bayes*." One of the reasons why he resorted to this measure is explained in the stanza:

> *Ethridge* and *Shadwell*, and the Rabble appeal'd
> To *Apollo* himself in a very great rage;
> Because their best Friends so freely had deal'd,
> As to tell them their Plays were not fit for the Stage.

Matthew Prior, in *A Session of the Poets*, which he never revised for publication, again shows the dramatists contending for the laurel:

I, 151-155. The poem is there attributed to "*the Duke of* Buckingham, *and the Earl of* Rochester."

[11] *Ibid.*, I, 159-166. Also attributed to Buckingham *and* Rochester.

[12] Printed in *Poems on Affairs of State: From the time of Oliver Cromwell, to the Abdication of K. James the Second. Written by the greatest Wits of the Age* (1697), pp. 217-223.

The next that put in for't was little Jo Crown
He swore his Sir Courtly had ravish'd the Town.
Then Shadwel too sweated amain in the Praise
Of the language and Plot of his Squire of Alsace
They both were put by, So were two or three more
That fell short of the Laurel the Session before
For they cou'd no more their Pretensions repeat
Than a horse thats once distanc'd may run second heat.[13]

The passages which I have just quoted were written during Shadwell's lifetime. The first notice to appear after his death was that by Peter Motteux in *The Gentleman's Journal* of November, 1692:

We have lately lost *Thomas Shadwell* Esquire, Poet Laureat and Historiographer Royal. His Works are so universally known, particularly his Comedies, that none can be a Stranger to his Merit; and all those that love to see the Image of humane Nature, lively drawn in all the various Colours and Shapes with which it is diversifyed in our age, must own that few living have equall'd that admirable Master in his Draughts of Humours and Characters. 'Tis true that his greatest excellence lay in treating Comic Subjects; yet none ought to wonder either at the Reputation or Honours it gained him: Since, that a Painter may deserve the name of Famous, it is not always necessary he should paint Lofty Palaces, and only employ his Pencil to draw the Pictures of Princes and Monarchs: A homely Shed well drawn is sometimes more esteem'd, if by the hand of a good Artist, than a Marble Palace by that of a bad one; and the Picture of a King which hath nothing to recommend it, but the Name of the Person it represents, is less admired than that of a Clown, when it wants nothing of what may cause it to be look'd upon as a good Piece. The most animated Figures of our Painters are only dumb Pictures, if compar'd with those in the Works of that Author. His Genius was inexhaustible on those sorts of matters; Neither were its Productions less usefull than diverting; since the best way to reform us is, to lay before us our Faults; thus observing *Horace*'s Rule; which the Comic Glass doth often: And so, even those whose Characters he hath wrote are oblig'd to him; for by showing the Picture of Avarice he hath sham'd Misers into Liberality; by exposing Bullying Sparks and Prodigal Squires, he hath made the first tamer and the other wiser; how many contented Cuckolds has he not hindred from taking their Gloves, and going out, when their Wives Gallants came in to visit them? how many Maids hath he not sav'd from ruin by the Picture of that in others? how many Hypo-

[13] *Dialogues of the Dead and Other Works in Prose and Verse,* ed. A. R. Waller (Cambridge, 1907), p. 301.

crites, Coquetts, Fops, Gamesters, has he not reclaim'd? and in short what store of Fools and Madmen did he not reform? [14]

Shortly after Shadwell's death, Tom Brown wrote two mock-epitaphs. In one of these, "In Obitum *Tho. Shadwell,* pinguis memoriae. 1693,"[15] the laureate is given the stock name for a bad poet, Bavius:

I

Conditur hoc tumulo Bavius, *gravis esse memento*
Terra tuo Bavio, *nam fuit ille tibi.*

II

Tam citò miraris Bavii *foetere cadaver?*
Non erat in toto corpore mica salis.

III

Mors uni Bavio *lucrum: nam jugera Vates*
Qui vivens habuit nulla, sepultus habet.

IV

Porrigitur novus hic Tityus *per jugera septem,*
Nec quae tondebit viscera deerit Avis.

V

Dicite, (nam benè vos nostis) gens Critica, Vates
An fuerit Bavius *pejor, an Historicus.*

VI

Militiam sicco Wilhelmus *Marte peregit,*
O Clemens Caesar! consulis historico.

VII

Tom writ, his Readers still slept o'er his Book,
For *Tom* took *Opium,* and they Opiates took.

The other, "*An* Impromptu *to* Shadwell's *Memory, by Dr.* B—,"[16] is brief and caustic:

And must our glorious Laureat then depart!
Heav'n, if it please, may take his loyal Heart;
As for the rest, sweet devil, fetch a Cart.

[14] *The Gentleman's Journal: or the Monthly Miscellany* for November, 1692, p. 21.

[15] *Works of Mr. Thomas Brown* (London, 1720), IV, 104-105.

[16] *Ibid.,* IV, 105.

Because of his corpulence, Brown elsewhere couples Shadwell with Falstaff. In one of the *Letters from the Dead to the Living*, Seignior Guisippe Hanesio [i.e., the actor, Joseph Haines] describes how he has become a physician and astrologer. On the day when he was to make his public appearance, the streets were crowded with interested spectators. "*Tom Shadwell* . . . began the Entertainment with thrumming upon an old broken Theorbo, and merry Sir *John Falstaff* sung to him, and afterwards both of them walk'd upon the slack Rope, in a pair of Jack-Boots, to the Admiration of all the Beholders."[17]

Reference is made to Shadwell and *The Squire of Alsatia* in an anonymous letter in verse addressed "To *T*—— *W*——, Esq.; *May* the 19th, 93."

> *Was not Sage* Terence *at adventure,*
> *By oily* Shadwell *turn'd to banter?*
> *And taught, for duller Sence of's own,*
> *The brisk gay Nonsense of the Town?*
> *And his insipid Tale improv'd,*
> *By what the Town and* Sh——ll *lov'd?*
> Sh——ll, *whose whole Stock is, a Bully,*
> *A Wench, a Usurer, a Cully,*
> *From whence, with little pains, straightway;*
> *Or Wit, he oft does launch a Play;*
> *As Cits, with Blew, secure from staining,*
> *A Heroe fit on Days of Training.*[18]

Shadwell fares no better in a discourse "Of the Modern Comedies," appearing in a volume by James Wright called *Country Conversations*, which was licensed on January 17, 1693/4. In this dialogue,[19] three friends are represented as riding in a coach from London to the country and discussing the drama. Julio and Lisander are sick of the present comedies, which are "nothing comparable to those Writ before the Civil War, and some in the Reign of King *Charles* the Second." Mitis, on the other hand, would defend them and wants details when Lisander calls "most of our New Comedies . . . the very Pictures of Immorality." Julio then

[17] *Ibid.*, II, 165.

[18] *Familiar Letters . . . By . . . John Late Earl of Rochester . . . and Letters by several Eminent Hands* (London, 1697), II, 176.

[19] [James Wright], *Country Conversations: Being an Account of some Discourses That Happen'd in a Visit to the Country last Summer,* (London, 1694), pp. 1-18.

replies in a speech levelled at modern comedies in general, but in particular at the plays of Shadwell:

First I must observe, that the Common Parts and Characters in our Modern Comedies, are two young Debauchees whom the Author calls Men of Wit and Pleasure, and sometimes Men of Wit and Sense (but that is when they admire the Name of *Lucretius*, and seem to have a Judgment above the Common Doctrines of Religion) these two Sparks are mightily addicted to Whoring and Drinking. The Bottle and the Miss (as they Phrase it) twisted together make their *Summum Bonum;* all their Songs and Discourse is on that Subject. But at last, partly for Variety of Faces, and partly in Consideration of improving their Estate (shatter'd with Keeping) they Marry two young Ladies, one of which is as wild as possibly can be, so as to scape the Main Chance, the other more reserved, but really as forward to be Marry'd as her Sister. Another necessary Ingredient of a Comedy, is a foolish Kt. (sometimes a Rich Country Squire, but most commonly the Poet Dubs him) and his Fortune is always in the 5th Act to Marry a Cast Whore of one of those fine Gentlemen before mentioned, who like a Man of Honour (such as the Poet makes him) pretends that she is a Person of Quality, and his near Kinswoman. Add to these a Wife somewhat Elderly; but insatiably Liquorish after a fresh Gallant; with a Husband continually exclaiming against the intolerable Labour of a Marry'd Life, and the restless importunities of his Spouse (and yet this unconscionable Cuckold keeps a Whore, *incognita*). These are the Fundamentals of a Modern Comedy; These you have continually over and over again, the Names only vary'd, and some little Alteration in the Writing (most commonly for the worse) till the Humours are become Naucious. For instance, a Lewd Wife pretending Honour (like my Lady *Corkwood* [*sic*], in *she wou'd if she cou'd*) but Lasciviously coveting the two Sparks that are Suiters to her Nieces, and all that Run; was New, well contrived, and very diverting at first; and to have it a second time under other Names, in *Epsom Wells*, was tolerable; but to have the very same again in the *Virtuoso*, and ten years after that in the *Scourers*.

Occidit Miseros Crambe repetita.

When, later, the discussion becomes a debate as to whether diversion or instruction should be the purpose of comedy, Lisander upholds the latter view and, after emphasizing the bad influence of the attitude towards marriage presented by the dramatists, he refers briefly to *The Lancashire Witches:* "I will pass over the disrespect that has been shewn to the Clergy of all Opinions (thereby insinuating Religion to be but a meer Trade at best) tho' some Scenes have been so gross, that they have been refused to be Acted, and cut out as Undecent for a Publick Representation (and yet the Poet has been so fond of them, as to Print 'em with the Rest, in a different Character)." Finally, Julio resumes his discourse and proves to his own satisfaction the superiority of the plays of "*Ben. Johnson*, *Shakespear*, *Beaumont* and *Fletcher*, *Messenger* [*sic*], *Shirley*, and Sir *William Davenant*, before the Wars, and some Comedies of Mr. *Drydens*, since the Restauration" to the comedies of a later date. His speech is brought to an end by the arrival of the coach at Lisander's village.

This passage from *Country Conversations* did not lead to other essays upon the immorality of Shadwell's plays. In fact, no reference is made to Shadwell or to his writings in Jeremy Collier's *Short View of the Immorality and Profaneness of the English Stage.* But four of the replies to that attack—all published in 1698—mention plays by Shadwell in proof of their statements. John Dennis holds that the business of ancient tragedy was "to exhort men to Piety and the worship of the Gods; to perswade them to Justice, to Humility, and to Fidelity, and to incline them to moderation and temperance. And 'tis for the omission of one of these duties that the persons of the modern Tragedy are shewn unfortunate in their Catastrophes." The first example he cites is from Shadwell: "Thus *Don John* is destroy'd for his libertinism and his impiety."[20] The didactic value of two of Shadwell's works is pointed out by the unknown author of a pamphlet on the usefulness of plays:

> And who that sees a Vitous Person severely Punish'd, will not tremble at Vice? I think the *Libertine Destroy'd* cannot fail to put serious thoughts into the most hardened and profligate Atheist, and rouze him from his Diabolical Lethargy, as powerfully as the loudest Denunciations from the Pulpit. . . . The *Squire* of *Alsatia* gives more effectual Instruction to the Country Gentleman, for the avoiding his Ruin both in Person and Estate by the Town-Sharpers, by exposing their Shifts and Cheats, that [*sic*] the best Advice of the ablest Divines.[21]

Edward Filmer also uses Shadwell's plays in his two essays defending dramatic poetry. He cites the actions of Timon and

[20] John Dennis, *The Usefulness of the Stage, To the Happiness of Mankind, To Government, and To Religion* (London, 1698), pp. 116-117.

[21] *A Vindication of the Stage, with the Usefulness and Advantages of Dramatick Representations. . . . In a Letter to a Friend* (London, 1698), p. 26.

Evandra to prove that it is "not the *Criminal* but the *Penitent,* the *Virtue* not *Vice* in the Character moves the Compassion."[22] He answers Collier's objection to Sir Tunbelly Clumsey in *The Relapse* by saying:

> For 'tis not *One* Fool that sits for the Picture; but the Imagery in one single Character sometimes may include a whole Sect of *Fools* or *Knaves.* How many excellent Dramatick pieces would otherwise be lost, such as a *Morose* in the *Silent Woman*, Sir *Nicholas Jimcrack*, in the *Virtuoso*, and indeed most of the Characters of Fools or Humorists, if their Authors had no Poetical grains for a little stretch in the Pencil work? [23]

And, in disposing of the idea that the words spoken by the characters in a play actually represent the thoughts of the writer, Filmer refers to *The Libertine:*

> The *Fool* in the *Psalmist*, says *in his Heart, there is no God;* but I hope Mr. *Collier* will not tell us the *Psalmist* himself says so. If the Poet was accountable for every Excursion, Levity, Loosness or Atheism it self from every Character in his Play, The Author of the *Libertine Destroy'd*, if he were alive, would have a long Black Scroll to answer for; in his *Don John* and his two wicked Companions: at least if Mr. *Collier* had the handling of him.[24]

Some years after writing the lines just quoted, Dr. Filmer again made use of *The Libertine.* In a work published in 1707, he questions whether Collier was really convinced "that no Punishment, no Stage Discipline, could attone for the Representation of any thing smutty or prophane." As a matter of fact, the author of the *Short View*

> seems industriously to avoid all those Plays, how lewd, or how prophane soever they may be, where that one necessary Rule, of rewarding the Good and punishing the Bad, is anything tolerably observ'd. Otherwise, how came the *Libertine* to escape his Censure? A Play, whose very Title promis'd him work enough; and where he might have met with as great Variety, of Smut, Prophaness, Blasphemy, and Atheism, as in any three of those Plays he has taken so much Pains to expose. But the

[22] Edward Filmer, *A Defence of Dramatick Poetry* (London, 1698), pp. 73-74.

[23] Edward Filmer, *A Farther Defence of Dramatick Poetry* (London, 1698), p. 23.

[24] *Ibid.*, p. 41.

Catastrophe was there too exemplary, too terrible, and too amazing for his Purpose; he cared not to meddle with it. There, after Don *John* had for a long time triumph'd in his Lewdness, the Earth at last opens; and sending forth vast Flashes of terrifying Flames, receives the trembling Atheist into her gaping, flaming Bowels. For there indeed the Poet did well, and wisely stretch the Law of Comedy, rather than suffer so much Wickedness to go off with a less remarkable Punishment.

But, instead of rallying all his forces against those plays where stage-discipline "had been religiously observ'd" and thus striking at the "Root of the Play-house," Collier had chosen to attack "those few of our modern Writers, who had unwarily enough neglected that Discipline." He had "too deep a Design against the Stage, to hazard all his Hopes upon such an Uncertainty."[25]

The reply to Filmer appeared in the following year. By references to passages in two of his earlier pamphlets, Collier feels justified in affirming that he has "already perform'd what the Doctor requires." He has "shewn in general, that no Stage Discipline, though never so severe, will justifie the representation of *Smut* and Profaneness." Then, by quoting lines from Filmer, among them being some dealing with *The Libertine*, he concludes that "No Gun-powder could blow up the *Theatre* more effectually than these Concessions and Maxims laid down by this Gentleman."[26]

So much for the use of Shadwell's plays by the authors engaged in the Collier controversy! In 1699, the year after the publication of the *Short View*, Gildon, who in his *Lives and Characters of the English Dramatick Poets* disagrees more than once with Langbaine's estimates of the playwrights, had to concede that Shadwell's "Comedies, at least some of them, shew him to understand Humour; and if he cou'd have drawn the Character of a Man of Wit, as well as that of a Coxcomb, there wou'd have been nothing wanting to the Perfection of his Dramatick Fables."[27] In a dia-

[25] Edward Filmer, *A Defence of Plays: Or, The Stage vindicated. . . . Wherein is offer'd the most Probable Method of Reforming our Plays. With a Consideration How Far Vicious Characters may be allow'd on the Stage* (London, 1707), pp. 43-45.

[26] Jeremy Collier, *A Farther Vindication of the Short View of the Profaneness and Immorality of the English Stage* (London, 1708), pp. 23-24.

[27] [Charles Gildon], *The Lives and Characters of the English Dramatick Poets. . . . First begun by Mr. Langbain, improv'd and continued down to this Time, by a Careful Hand* (London, 1699?), p. 124.

logue attributed to Gildon, "A Comparison Between the Two Stages," Shadwell's comedies are called "true copies of Nature, but generally low and aukward; his Tragedies are a mixture of Mirth and Melancholy, and those of his own making good for little."[28]

In *The Muses Mercury, for the Month of July, 1707,* appeared "The *Stage* Vindicated: A Satyr—By I. H. Esq." The author of these pedestrian verses singles out for special mention episodes or characters from three of Shadwell's plays, *Epsom-Wells, Timon of Athens,* and *The Libertine.*

> Sir Clodpate too is in a mortal Rage,
> To see his Dogs insulted on the Stage;
> And when the Justice fills the drunken Scene,
> He cries the Magistracy's made too mean;
> Hard Hap! If such as are to keep the Peace
> Uncensur'd, may not break it when they please.
> The Jest their Worships tell us is unjust,
> And dare not our impartial Satyr trust.
> Let 'em be still offended, is it fit
> That Wit shou'd yield to them, or they to Wit?
> Shou'd Bards, to humour 'em, transgress their Rules,
> And err against their Art to flatter Fools;
> What Pow'r superior to the Force of Sense,
> Can silence 'em, or with their Laws dispense;
> Both Knaves and Fools must stand the Poet's Test,
> And either be a Nusance or a Jest.
>
> Our Poets, faulty as they are, have shown,
> Severe Examples to this erring Town;
> The Prodigal in *Timon's* Fate may see
> The sad effects of Vice and Vanity;
> How those who crowd the treating Cully's Door
> Court when he's rich, and curse him when he's poor.
> The powder'd Fop an empty Fool appears,
> And blushes at his own affected Airs;
> The gay Coquet may in this Mirror view,
> How false Accomplishments belie the true;
> The fickle Fair her error may perceive,
> And Women not be false, or Men believe;
> The Ways of Life are suited to each Kind,
> And Manners in the School of Wit refin'd;
> Men learn to live, and Women to appear,

[28] [Charles Gildon], *A Comparison Between the Two Stages* (London, 1702), pp. 57-58.

> The Good to pity, and the Bad to fear;
> For change the Tale of Joy to that of Woe,
> And let the Tragick Muse her Terrors show:
> Can you in *K——gs* empty Lessons find,
> Such moving Truths to work upon the Mind.
> The Libertine who burns with lawless Fires,
> Sinks in the Scene, and in blue Flames expires.
> How oft has Vice been follow'd to the throne,
> And tyrant Kings in bloody Colours shown.

Shadwell's works are subjected to rather ignominious use in one of the poems of Thomas Parnell. Here the author represents himself as catching a book-worm,[29] which he determines to sacrifice. He makes a sacred altar by piling high the works of Homer, Virgil, and Tasso. Then he kills the worm, opens the entrails to "see what Dangers threat the Year," and finds sonnets and translations from the French among the contents.

> But hold, before I close the Scene,
> The sacred Altar shou'd be clean.
> Oh had I *Sh——ll's* Second Bays,
> Or *T——!* thy pert and humble Lays!
> (Ye Pair, forgive me, when I vow
> I never miss'd your Works till now)
> I'd tear the Leaves to wipe the Shrine,
> (That only way you please the *Nine*)
> But since I chance to want these two,
> I'll make the Songs of *D——y* do.

Shadwell and Tate appear together also in a clever parody of Dryden's "Epigram on Milton."[30] Their names are here united with that of their successor in the office of poet-laureate:

> Three English Laureats in one Age were born,
> Whom Want made Poets in Apollo's Scorn.
> The First in Barrenness of Art surpast,
> The Next, of Genius; and of both the last.
> The Curse of Nature cou'd no further go,
> Shadwell and Tate she join'd to form a ROWE.

[29] "The Book-Worm" is printed on pp. 134-140 of Thomas Parnell's *Poems on Several Occasions* (London, 1722).

[30] In Mist's *Weekly-Journal; or Saturday's Post. With fresh Advices Foreign and Domestick* of Saturday, February 8, 1718.

The words of Parnell and the parodist do not express the prevailing opinion concerning Shadwell during the first quarter of the eighteenth century. Both Addison and Steele recognized the dramatist's "most excellent Talent of Humour."[31] Less judicious than the estimate given by the guiding spirits of *The Spectator* was that of the authoress who used the pen-name of "Corinna, a Country-Parson's Wife." In her discussion of Charles Johnson's *The Masquerade,* she writes "that there is nothing of a Comic Genius to be found in it, nothing of that Humour which has distinguish'd *Ben Johnson, Shadwell, Wycherly, Congreve* and some others, from all those who have writ *Comedy* in any other Nation."[32]

In 1720 was published a collected edition of Shadwell's plays dedicated to the king by the laureate's son, Sir John Shadwell, who seems also to have furnished the material for the "Account of the Author and his Writings" prefixed to the first volume. The evaluation of the dramatist's character and works is brief and, with one or two exceptions, free from over-praise:

> His Principles were very Loyal and firm to the Interest and Laws of his Country, and to such good Princes as govern'd by their Authority; at once approving himself a good Patriot and a good Subject.
>
> He was allow'd by all who knew him to be an accomplish'd Gentleman; he had a great deal of ready Wit, and very quick Parts, improv'd by the best Advantages of Learning, the best Conversation and other Acquisitions; amongst which I might mention his Great Skill in Musick.
>
> He had not only a strict Sense of Honour and Morality, but likewise (particularly in his latter Days) a true Sense of Religion too.
>
> As to his Writings, *Langbain* has endeavour'd to do him Justice, in his View of the Stage; wherein he shews how free he is from the Barrenness of some other Poets, which made them turn Plagiaries, and copy from other Authors, what he, like a skillful Observer, drew to the Life from Nature. His writing thus his own unborrow'd Thoughts, what he had himself collected immediately from the World, (the most instructive Library for a Man of Genius and Observation,) accounts for that easie Turn of Conception and Language that graced every Thing he said or wrote. He is universally allow'd to have excell'd in Humour, which is a Talent almost peculiar to the *English* Nation. The famous Earl of *Rochester* has given him a Character, which, tho' seemingly alloy'd by

[31] The *Spectator,* Nos. 35 and 141.

[32] *Critical Remarks On the Four Taking Plays of this Season, . . . Dedicated to the Wits at Button's Coffee-House. By Corinna, a Country Parson's Wife* (London, 1719), p. 50.

the Frankness of the Expression, is not only less liable to the Suspicion of Flattery, but plainly allows him that known Commendation of *Horace*, such an easie Turn of thought and Language,

—Ut sibi quivis
Speret idem: Sudet multùm, frustràque laboret,
Ausus Idem. —

The "Account" concludes with the lengthy inscription which Sir John Shadwell intended for the monument he erected to his father's memory in the Poet's Corner of Westminster Abbey.

Upon the Pyramid was Engrav'd

ΣΚΗΝΗ
ΠΑΣ ‘Ο ΒΙΟΣ
ΚΑΙ ΠΑΙΓΝΙΟΝ.

Upon the Stone the following inscription.

P. M. S.
Thomae Shadwell Armigeri,
Antiquâ Stirpe in Comitatu Staffordiae
Oriundi:
Qui, inter caeteras Eruditionis dotes,
Animum feliciter ad scribendum appulit.
At hoc Poeseos proposuit munus,
Ut quas fecisset Fabulas
Populares deriderent Ineptias
Morésque corrigerent profligatos,
Ut delectarent simul & prodessent;
Majori enim sibi laudi duxit
Bonus Civis haberi
Quam Principibus Poetis inseri.
Inde, Imperante Gulielmo Tertio,
Poetae Laureati & Historiographi Regii
Titulos meruit & exornavit.
Ob. Nov. 19. *Æt. suae* 52.
H. M. P. C.
In perpetuam Pietatis Memoriam,
Johannes Shadwell, M. D. Thomae **F.**

After these words had been engraved upon the stone, certain of the clergy made exception to them "as being too great an Encomium upon Plays to be set up in a Church"; and, at the desire of the Bishop of Rochester, Thomas Sprat, they were altered to this unembellished statement:

M. S.
Thomae Shadwell, Armigeri
Antiqua Stirpe in Agro Staffordiae
Oriundi,
Qui, Regnantibus Gulielmo Tertio & Maria
Poetae Laureati
Et
Historiographi Regii
Titulos Meruit
Ob. Nov. 20, 1692 *Ætat. Suae* 55
Charissimo Parenti
Johannes Shadwell M. D.
P. P.[33]

Three years after Sir John Shadwell brought out the collected edition of his father's plays, John Dennis, whom we have already met as one of the repliers to Collier's *Short View,* boasted that "*no* English *Author of any Note has commended so many* English *Poets, as* [*he has*]." In his list of those whom he has "*occasionally commended*" or in whom he has "*found out Beauties, which every one could not discover*" occurs the name of Shadwell.[34] His first effort in behalf of the dramatist was "*A Dedication designed to the Volunteers. By Mrs.* Shadwell. To the Queen. *Written by Mr.* Dennis."[35] This letter was not used, however, when the play was published. Some years later, in commenting upon *The Spectator* of April 16, 1711, he mentions that "*Shadwell* is of Opinion that your Bully with his Box and his false Dice is an honester Fellow than the Rhetorical Author, who makes use of his Tropes and Figures, which are his High and his Low-runners, to cheat us at once of our Money and of our Intellectuals."[36] On another occasion, Dennis counts Shadwell among the "Eight Gen-

[33] An inscription differing from these two appears in [Giles Jacob], *The Poetical Register* (London, 1723), I, 225-226.

[34] Preface to *Remarks on a Play, call'd The Conscious Lovers* (London, 1723).

[35] *Letters upon several Occasions: Written by and between Mr. Dryden, Mr. Wycherly, Mr. . . . , Mr. Congreve, and Mr. Dennis* (London, 1696), pp. 129-133.

[36] *Original Letters, Familiar, Moral, and Critical* (London, 1721), II, 407. The reference is to a passage in *The Virtuoso* (Shadwell, I, 320).

tlemen alive at a Time who have writ good and diverting Comedies."[37] And, in his "Remarks on the Preface to the *Conscious Lovers*," he refers to *The Squire of Alsatia:* "when Shadwell undertook to write a Comedy upon the Plan of the *Adelphi*, he, who very well knew the Nature of his Art, and by consequence knew what was defective in the *Roman* Comedy, took particular Care to supply from his own Invention the Ridicule that was wanting in that; and it was by using that Method that he made the *Squire of Alsatia* a very good and very entertaining Comedy."[38]

The claims of Shadwell were not overlooked by Lewis Crusius when he attempted, in his "Life of Terence," to determine the comparative merits of the English comic dramatists:

> If I might dare to offer my opinion of our own comic writers on this occasion, I should think Mr. *Congreve's* Plays excel in wit, purity of stile, and polite language, unless the Author of the *Careless Husband* should dispute the first place with him. *Wicherley* and *Farquhar* will come next, unless disputed by Sir *John Vanbrugh* or *Shadwell.* Mr. *Addison's Drummer* is beyond any of that kind in our language, and comes nearest to the manner of *Plautus* without his faults.[39]

During the second quarter of the eighteenth century, unfavorable comments on Shadwell are found twice in *The Gentleman's Magazine.* In "The Apotheosis of Milton," the author dreams he is locked in Westminster Abbey. An old man approaches him and conducts him to the place of assembly of those poets who are buried or have monuments within the Church. They are gathering for the purpose of admitting Milton to their number. Chaucer, Drayton, Spenser, Jonson, many "sons of Ben," and Beaumont appear. Then comes Dryden with a garland of laurel in his hand; but, instead of placing it upon his head, he lays it on the table. In his eye is a "noble Indignation, mix'd with a deep Concern." The entire company become angry as they look towards the door.

> Soon I perceiv'd a bloated Figure enter, who seemed rather to be fit for a Midnight Revel than to be a Member of that august Body. He

[37] *Remarks Upon Mr. Pope's Translation of Homer* (London, 1717), p. 4. The seven other dramatists are Wycherley, Dryden, Etherege, Buckingham, Crowne, Otway, and Sir Robert Howard.

[38] *Remarks on . . . The Conscious Lovers*, p. 11.

[39] L. Crusius, *The Lives of the Roman Poets*, 3d edition (London, 1753), II, 256.

used a thousand ridiculous Gestures, sometimes he affected a polite, easy Air, sometimes he appeared to aim at the *French* Grimace; but all was forced, unnatural, and ungraceful, soon he relapsed into his *Bacchanalian* Fits, and it appeared that the nauseous Part cost him nothing; He wore on his Brow a Branch of withered Ivy, bound up in form of a Garland, which seemed to be pulled down from the Door of an Alehouse: When he came up to take his Seat, all the Assembly looked at him with a contemptuous Eye, especially when, with an Air of Triumph, he seated himself opposite to *Dryden. That person so unlike the other awful Form,* said my Guide, *is* Shadwell; *he has a Seat here by the Indulgence of a Tasteless Court, who bestowed on him the laurel in prejudice of the Great* Dryden.

To Shadwell goes a young man, Otway, who affects the same airs, but "that abandoned Deportment seemed as unnatural in him, as the Airs of Wit and Politeness appeared in the other."[40]

The other reference in the *Gentleman's Magazine* appears in a communication *"On the Poets and Actors in King* Charles II's *Reign"*[41] submitted in 1745 by a gentleman who professed to be eighty-seven years of age. He gives pen pictures of Dryden, Settle, Otway, and other Restoration playwrights. He is briefest and harshest in his characterization of Shadwell, who is described in these words: *"Shadwell* in conversation was a brute."

Even the gentle Goldsmith becomes caustic when writing of Shadwell. In "A Poetical Scale" printed in the *Literary Magazine* for January, 1758, he dismisses the dramatist as being "below all criticism."[42] His introductory remarks to "Mac Flecknoe" in *The Beauties of English Poesy*, published in 1767, also show the influence of Dryden's satire:

At present, an ordinary reader would scarce suppose that Shadwell, who is here meant by MacFlecknoe, was worth being chastised; and that Dryden, descending to such game, was like an eagle stooping to catch flies. The truth, however, is Shadwell at one time held divided reputation with this great poet. Every age produces its fashionable dunces, who, by following the transient topic, or humour, of the day, supply talkative ignorance with material for conversation.[43]

[40] *The Gentleman's Magazine: and Historical Chronicle,* VIII (1738), 234-235. Otway is called "Tom Shadwell's dear Zany" by Buckingham in his "Tryal of the Poets for the Bays."

[41] *Ibid.,* XV (1745), 99.

[42] Goldsmith, *Works* (London, 1885), IV, 420.

[43] *Ibid.,* V, 157.

More just than Goldsmith in their appraisement of Shadwell were the editors of the *Biographia Britannica* and Charles Dibdin, the author of *A Complete History of the English Stage.* The former, after giving a brief account of Shadwell's life, state:

> Mr. Dryden . . . is generally condemned for treating our author a little too unmercifully, his resentment carrying him even beyond the bounds of truth; for that, though it must be owned he fell vastly short of Jonson, whom he set to himself as a model of excellence, yet it is certain there are high authorities in favour of many of his comedies, and the best judges of that age gave their testimony for them. They have in them fine strokes of humour; the characters are often original, strongly marked, and well sustained.[44]

Dibdin acknowledges that "many of [Shadwell's] plays have considerable merit" and feels that Dryden's ridicule "had less in it of truth and justice, than envy and disappointment."[45]

In 1800 appeared Malone's edition of the critical and prose works of Dryden, in its day a mine of valuable new material on the literary history of the Restoration period. But since Malone is quite ready to see Dryden's enemies through Dryden's eyes, Shadwell fares badly at his hands. Instead of suggesting that Dryden may have used exaggeration in his statements for the purpose of rendering his opponent ridiculous, he writes such sentences as these: "Shadwell lived much in taverns, and was equally noted for his love of eating and drinking, and the coarseness of his manners and conversation"; "Shadwell's conversation is represented by his contemporaries to have been extremely immoral and profane."[46]

These two passages aroused the wrath of Genest, who took their author to task for not bringing "the slightest proof of his assertions." "Malone," he says, "was the more bound to tell us from what source he borrowed his accusation, as Shadwell lived at a time when the spirit of party ran very high, and when it may fairly be presumed, that all which was said against Shadwell was not true."

[44] *Biographia Britannica: Or the Lives of the Most Eminent Persons who have flourished in Great Britain and Ireland, From the earliest Ages, down to the present Times* (London, 1747-63), VI, Pt. I, 3626-3627. The estimate of Shadwell in the *Biographia Dramatica* (London, 1812), I, 644, is drawn almost entirely from this work.

[45] Charles Dibdin, *A Complete History of the English Stage* (London, 1800?), IV, 181, 246.

[46] Edmund Malone, *The Critical and Miscellaneous Prose Works of John Dryden* (London, 1800), III, 106 n., 144 n.

Genest avers that Dorset and Sedley "surely would not have suffered Shadwell to keep company with them, if his manners had been coarse." The charge of profaneness, he thinks, arose from the dramatist's hatred of high-church principles. From the sentiments expressed in the opening scene of *The Lancashire Witches*, he judges that Shadwell "might in conversation speak his mind very freely of the high church party—but it is hardly possible, that if his conversation had been really and habitually profane, he would not, at one time or other, have been profane in his wrintings."[47]

In the notes to his great edition of Dryden, Sir Walter Scott had frequent occasion to comment upon Shadwell's verse and plays. Although he follows Malone in emphasizing the playwright's "coarseness of manners" and "ungentlemanly vulgarity of dialect," he goes beyond his predecessor by stressing as well "that insight into human life, that acquaintance with the foibles and absurdities displayed in individual pursuits, that bold though coarse delineation of character, which gave fame to Shadwell's comedies in the last century, and renders them amusing even at the present day."[48] In another passage, after correctly designating Shadwell's essays in verse as "deplorably bad," he writes:

> But in comedy he was much more successful; and, in that capacity, Dryden does him great injustice, in pronouncing him a dunce. On the contrary, I think most of Shadwell's comedies may be read with great pleasure. They do not, indeed, exhibit any brilliancy of wit, or ingenuity of intrigue; but the characters are truly dramatic, original, and well drawn, and the picture of manners which they exhibit gives us a lively idea of those of the author's age. As Shadwell proposed Jonson for his model, peculiarity of character, or what was then technically called *humour*, was what he chiefly wished to exhibit; and in this it cannot be denied that he has often succeeded admirably.[49]

The characters and the pictures of manners presented in Shadwell's plays were not forgotten when Scott turned novelist. From *The Squire of Alsatia* he "derived some few hints" for his delineation of the dwellers in Whitefriars and of their relationship with "their

[47] [John Genest], *Some Account of the English Stage* (Bath, 1832), II, 40-44. Genest considers *The Squire of Alsatia* and *Epsom-Wells* to be Shadwell's best plays.

[48] *Works of John Dryden. . . . Illustrated with Notes, Historical, Critical and Explanatory . . .* by Sir Walter Scott, 2d edition (Edinburgh, 1821), X, 430.

[49] *Ibid.*, X, 444.

neighbors, the fiery young students of the Temple," which he introduced in *The Fortunes of Nigel.*[50] *The Volunteers*, a play which he characterizes—I think, unjustly—as "dull," furnished some of the suggestions for the contrast of the manners of Cavalier and Puritan found in *Peveril of the Peak.*[51] In *The Pirate*, Scott presents a great admirer of the "immortal John Dryden," Claude Halcro, who tells how he "learned the lute from the same man who taught honest Shadwell—plump Tom, as they used to call him."[52]

Macaulay, like Scott, knew a good source for authentic material on the manners of the latter part of the seventeenth century; and, in his *History of England from the Accession of James the Second*, he more than once drew information from William III's laureate. When he refers to the condition of the clergy, the roistering in the streets of London after dark, Whitefriars as a place of sanctuary, the "valiant fops and epicures" who volunteered for the campaign of 1691 in Flanders, and the "hypocrisy and knavery" of the stock-jobbers, he cites Shadwell's plays as authority.[53]

In June, 1821, a review of Moore's edition of the works of Richard Brinsley Sheridan appeared in *Blackwood's Edinburgh Magazine* with the title, "On the alleged Decline of Dramatic Writing." The author, who signs his article with the initials "T.D.," after discussing Restoration tragedy—incidentally mentioning the ribaldry of Don John—turns to comedy and glances briefly at Shadwell:

> Of Shadwell one does not well know what to think or to say. His pieces, both tragedy and comedy, are duller than a "Concert of Antient Music," and twice as uncouth. He is destitute of wit, but contrives to supply its place with a strange slang, and coarse jog-trot kind of humour. His characters are by no means devoid of originality, but they are inva-

[50] See p. 217n.

[51] See p. 245n.

[52] Chapter XII. Shadwell is also mentioned in Chapter XIV. In Chapter XXXVII of *Rob Roy*, the Justice sings a song beginning "And let her health go round." A foot-note states that "this pithy verse occurs, it is believed, in Shadwell's play of Bury Fair." The belief is not well founded; for no such verse is found in any of Shadwell's plays.

[53] The references cited are found in Chapters III, XVII, and XIX. Macaulay also mentions the fact that Shadwell cleared £130 by a single representation of *The Squire of Alsatia* (Chapter III), that his best comedy was written at Dorset's country seat (Chapter VIII), and that he called Howard Sir Positive Atall (Chapter XIV).

riably heavy, and smack of the vulgar. Perhaps the best description of Shadwell's plays is to say, with Dogberry, "They are most tolerable, and not to be endured." They are precisely the productions to be expected from such a man as Dryden has described "Og" to be.[54]

In 1828 there was printed in the *Retrospective Review*[55] an anonymous article written for the purpose of putting "the reputation of [Shadwell] on its true level" and of vindicating "his memory from that charge of dulness which hangs over it." In the opinion of the author, Shadwell "was an accomplished observer of human nature," one who "had a ready power of seizing the ridiculous in the manners of the times," and one who "possesses and displays in his writings a very considerable fund of humour." He writes that "though Shadwell may resemble the celebrated Ben in his partiality to pourtray extravagance in character, in the desultoriness of his plots, and in his general method and style, he falls far short of his model in his ability to represent passion and that intensity of feeling which Jonson infuses into his characters." He does not deny that the prologues and epilogues are "very dull, very full of pretensions, and excessively abusive and illiberal." The plays, although they "abound in indecency and loose conversation," are important for "the light which they throw on the manners and morals of his age." Then, by well-chosen quotations from eleven of the comedies and by brief comments on the passages, the author amply fulfils his purpose of showing that Shadwell is not dull.

Forty-five years after the publication of the article in the *Retrospective Review*, Dryden's unjust charge called forth another plea in Shadwell's defense. The author of an unsigned essay in *The New Monthly Magazine*[56] feels that "no surer method to damage any reputation could possibly have been devised than to connect the name of him who possessed it with that of Settle" and censures those biographers of Dryden who "seem to convert Shadwell's ungainly presence into a serious charge against him, and are never weary of directing attention to his obesity and slovenliness." Instead of reviewing several of Shadwell's plays, he devotes consid-

[54] IX, 282.

[55] "The Dramatic Works of Thomas Shadwell" in *The Retrospective Review, and Historical and Antiquarian Magazine* (London), Second Series, II, 55-96.

[56] "Thomas Shadwell" in *The New Monthly Magazine* edited by Wm. Francis Ainsworth, III, New Series (London, 1873), 292-297, 353-361.

erable space to a discussion of one, *The Lancashire Witches,* and is then ready to draw the conclusion

> that of all the numerous charges brought against Thomas Shadwell, that of dulness has least of [t]ruth in it. He possessed a fancy as bright, an imagination as lofty, and a humour as subtle, as any dramatist of his time. His style, if less polished than that of Congreve, is more vigorous. His dialogue, if less laden with wit, is more natural. In humour, he approaches Farquhar, the best of the Restoration writers of comedy. He had formed his style on that of earlier masters. In the depicting of character he followed closely in the steps of Ben Jonson. If, notwithstanding all this, no breath of the fame which he achieved in his own days has served to keep his memory sweet in ours, we must lay the blame upon the greater bard, who wrote of him in words that everybody has read, but into the justice of which few have considered it worth while to enquire.

The next essay on Shadwell came from the pen of Professor Saintsbury,[57] who, as biographer of Dryden, had had ample opportunity to consider the shortcomings of Og. But his reflections did not lead him to dismiss "glorious John's" victim with a shrug. Instead, he attributes to Shadwell "a much greater command of comic incident and situation" than Dryden, and "much more direct power of dramatic observation of actual life" than Wycherley. He thinks that to Shadwell rather than to Etherege should be ascribed "the fatherhood of the seventeenth-and-eighteenth-century comedy of manners." He emphasizes this dramatist's greatest fault, "the absence of style," and makes the interesting suggestion that "a collaborator who could have put into terse, witty, and scholarly English Shadwell's exuberant stock of situations, and his accurate observation of manners, would probably have made of the joint work one of the capital things of English literature."

Two other essays on Shadwell—both belonging to the twentieth century—deserve to be mentioned. The first of these to be published is by William Hand Browne and was written to show that "Shadwell was anything but dull."[58] It is eminently readable and serves as a good appreciative estimate of the dramatist. More brilliantly written than this essay are the five pages which Mr. Bonomy

[57] Introduction to the volume of plays by Shadwell in the *Mermaid Series* (London, 1903?).

[58] "Thomas Shadwell" in *The Sewanee Review,* XXI, 257-276 (July, 1913).

Dobrée devotes to Shadwell in his stimulating little book on Restoration comedy.[59] Steeped in the wit of Etherege and Congreve, he can but say that "Shadwell's dullness defeated even laughter" and discern in his style a "kind of pudding-like quality." After charging Shadwell with superficiality in the portrayal of character, he ventures the opinion that *A True Widow* is "possibly his best play."

The historians of the Restoration drama, with the exception of Mr. Allardyce Nicoll, add little to our knowledge of Shadwell. Sir A. W. Ward, although calling him "often original" in the invention of comic characters and "truthful as well as vivid" in his portrayal of manners, declares that "he did little or nothing to advance his art" and that "the artistic pleasure . . . to be derived from [his] comic pictures" is "scant."[60] Mr. Whibley, in the single paragraph which he devotes to Shadwell, avers that the dramatist "had a trick of invention, and was determined to turn the best models to account"; but that, "when he had invented (or adapted) his puppets, he handled them so carelessly, that they long since lost their interest for us."[61] Mr. Nettleton goes no farther in evaluating Shadwell than to say "it would be hard to find more faithful reproduction of the details of fashionable Restoration life than in some of his comedies of manners."[62]

Mr. Nicoll does not deny that Shadwell is coarse, that he is "positively nauseating with his 'humours,'" and that—in *The Squire of Alsatia*, at least—he plays the rôle of "perverted moralist." But he also asserts that the author of *Bury-Fair* "could be almost as witty as Etherege if he chose" and that his plays "have to a large extent that artistic finish and workmanship which characterise the work of a master hand." Although Mr. Nicoll[63] is inclined to doubt the validity of Professor Saintsbury's claim that this dramatist should be considered "a father of the comedy of manners," he feels that "in his old age [Shadwell] was one of the fathers of the comedy of sentiment," and that "for sheer merit,

[59] Bonomy Dobrée, *Restoration Comedy* (Oxford, 1924), pp. 116-120.

[60] A. W. Ward, *A History of English Dramatic Literature* (London, 1899), III, 455-461.

[61] Charles Whibley, "The Restoration Drama, II," in *Cambridge History of English Literature*, VIII, 197-198.

[62] George H. Nettleton, *English Drama of the Restoration and Eighteenth Century* (New York, 1914), pp. 84-86.

[63] Allardyce Nicoll. *A History of Restoration Drama, 1660-1700* (Cambridge, 1923), pp. 189-198. Mr. Nicoll would seem to be in error when he says that "Shadwell . . . in later years came to be

as for historical importance, he stands next to Dryden after the great masters of the manners comedy."

This survey of the reputation of Shadwell throughout a period of two hundred and fifty years, although it makes no pretense at being exhaustive,[64] does contain—I believe—most of the different opinions that have been held concerning the author and his work. And how contradictory they are! His plays are witty; they are dull. They are instructive; they are the "very Pictures of Immorality." They possess "artistic finish" to a large extent; they are lacking in art. Most of his comedies "may be read with great pleasure"; "the artistic pleasure is scant that is to be derived from [his] comic pictures." He shows real insight into human life; he is superficial in his portrayal of character. And so on! Which of these opinions are the more reasonable?

influenced . . . by Congreve"; for Shadwell died before the production of Congreve's first play.

[64] Among references to Shadwell not given in the text, the following are worth mentioning: S. C. in his lines addressed "To Mrs. Jane Barker, On *Her Ingenious Poems*" printed in *Poetical Recreations by Mrs. Jane Barker* (London, 1688); Richard Savage in "An Author to be Let" in *Works* (London, 1775), II, 261-262; Pope in "The Dunciad," bk. I, l. 240, bk. III, l. 22; Defoe in *Captain Singleton* (*Works*, New York, 1907, VI, 261); Fielding in No. 59 of the *Covent Garden Journal;* Theophilus Cibber in *Lives of the Poets* (London, 1753), III, 48-50; Voltaire in No. XIX of *Lettres Philosophiques* (*Oeuvres*, Paris, 1879, XXII, 156 n); Foote in Act II of *The Commissary;* Wordsworth in the "Essay, Supplementary to the Preface" to the 1815 edition of *Lyrical Ballads;* Hazlitt in Lecture III of his *Lectures on the English Comic Writers;* Southey in his *Life of Cowper* (*Works of Cowper*, 1836 ed., II, 112); W. S. Austin and John Ralph in *Lives of the Poets-Laureate* (London, 1853), pp. 183 ff.; and George Gissing in *New Grub Street,* ch. III. Coleridge quotes three passages from *The Libertine* in his "Critique on Bertram" printed in *Biographia Literaria.* A short story in the *Harvard Advocate* for May, 1924, by John Finley, Jr., has the title, "Shadwell, or The Victory of Dullness."

PART II

SHADWELL'S COMEDIES

CHAPTER VII

THE SULLEN LOVERS

IN the following pages, I shall examine Shadwell's thirteen comedies in their relationship to seventeenth-century drama and life. I am not riding any particular hobby nor am I concerned in the impossible task of transforming an ugly duckling into a swan of immaculate whiteness. In my treatment of the subject, I shall have to present summaries of plots and comparisons of Shadwell's plays with their sources—material which even an enthusiastic admirer of the Restoration period would have difficulty in finding interesting. But whether entertaining or dull, the topics discussed here should, I believe, be considered before one makes any generalizations about the position of Thomas Shadwell in the history of English literature.

Shadwell's first play, *The Sullen Lovers, or The Impertinents,* was successful when produced in 1668 because of its apparent satire of Sir Robert Howard in the character of Sir Positive At-all.[1] In fact, it was so pleasing to royalty that it was selected as one of the two comedies, the other being Caryl's *Sir Salomon,* to be presented at Dover in May, 1670, when the king with all the court met his sister, the Duchess of Orléans, there. According to Downes, this play "pleasd Madam the Dutchess, and the whole Court extremely."[2] The records of the Lord Chamberlain indicate a performance on July 28, 1677.[3] *The Sullen Lovers* may have been revived after Shadwell became laureate; for an edition of this comedy, as "Acted at the Theatre Royal. By their Majesties Servants,"

[1] See pp. 17-19.

[2] One of these plays was acted on Thursday, May 19; the other on Friday, May 20. *The London Gazette,* Number 471, "From Thursday, May 19 to Monday, May 23, 1670," reports under date of May 21, "the 19th instant arrived here [i.e., at Dover] Her Majesty and Royal Highness about three in the afternoon, having the night before lodged at *Sittingborn* on their way from *London.* The same evening the Court was entertained with a Comedy, acted by his Royal Highnesses servants, who acted here for their diversion. Yesterday was acted by the said servants, another Comedy in the midst whereof, Madam, and the rest of the Ladies were entertained with an Excellent Banquet."

[3] Nicoll, p. 311.

was published in 1693. The last recorded performance took place on October 5, 1703, at the theatre in Lincoln's Inn Fields when Powell appeared as Sir Positive.[4]

The plot of this play is rather slight. Stanford, who is "tormented beyond Measure with the Impertinence of People," is resolved to leave the world to be rid of them. But the persons who so trouble Stanford merely amuse his friend Lovel, who loves the vivacious Carolina. Carolina, however, has a sister Emilia, who resembles Stanford in her attitude towards life. Since Carolina cannot be married until Emilia is provided with a husband, she and Lovel decide to force the two revilers of the age into each other's arms by causing them to be plagued incessantly by the bores whom they detest,—the omniscient Sir Positive At-all, the talkative Lady Vaine, the "conceited Poet" Ninny, and the "familiar loving Coxcomb" Woodcock. Stanford is also annoyed by the cowardly Huffe, who borrows money; and Emilia is further bothered by a country gentleman, whom her father has chosen for her husband. As a result, the "sullen lovers" agree to wed for self-protection with the proviso that "if either grows a Fop, the other shall have Liberty to part." Carolina and Lovel are married, and Sir Positive presents Lady Vaine as his wife, only to find later that she is another man's mistress.

In his preface to *The Sullen Lovers*, Shadwell writes: "The first Hint I receiv'd was from the Report of a Play of *Moliere*'s of three Acts, called *Les Fascheux*, upon which I wrote a great Part of this before I read that; and after it came to my Hands, I found so little for my Use (having before upon that Hint design'd the fittest Characters I could for my Purpose) that I have made Use of but two short Scenes which I inserted afterwards (*viz.*) the first Scene in the Second Act between *Stanford* and *Roger*, and *Moliere*'s Story of Piquette, which I have translated into Back-gammon, both of them being so vary'd you would not know them." These words have led students of Molière to look for more of *Les Fâcheux* in *The Sullen Lovers* than the author acknowledges having used and then to see whether the English play contains material derived from other works of the French dramatist, the result being that *Le Misanthrope* and *Le Mariage Forcé* are now listed among Shadwell's sources.[5]

[4] Genest, II, 303.

[5] D. H. Miles, *Influence of Molière on Restoration Comedy*, pp. 238-239.

Let us first consider the indebtedness to *Les Fâcheux.* Briefly, this play depicts the troubles of Éraste who is interrupted in his attempts to see his love Orphise by every conceivable type of bore —the composer of a *courante* and dance, the duellist, the unfortunate gamester, the two women who wish him to assist them in their debate as to whether a jealous or a non-jealous person loves more, the huntsman, the pedant, the projector, and the man who insists upon protecting him from an enemy. In *The Sullen Lovers,* Shadwell introduces many similar types: the composer of a "Corrant" (Sir Positive), the improviser of a dance (Woodcock), the duellist (Sir Positive), the gamester (Huffe), the projector (Woodcock), and the person who will protect Stanford from an enemy (Woodcock).

The scene which presents Huffe's ill-fortune at backgammon is, as the preface indicates, considerably altered from Alcippe's story of his game of piquet. Éraste, when informed of Alcippe's fatal play, interrupts the gamester by assuring him that he was justified in feeling enraged, and expresses hope that he will console himself for his misfortune. Shadwell utilizes the losses at backgammon as an excuse for Huffe's attempt to obtain an additional loan from Stanford and for giving Emilia an opportunity to manifest a growing interest in her "sullen" companion. When Huffe sees that a responsive chord cannot be touched by telling of losses at cards, he drops all reference to backgammon and starts another tale of woe in his play for sympathy.[6] The other scene which Shadwell acknowledges taking from Molière follows the original more closely. In *Les Fâcheux,* the breathless La Montagne comes with news from Orphise, but is unable to divulge it rapidly enough to suit his master. Likewise, Roger approaches Stanford and, after a bit of irritating delay, informs him that he is wanted by Lovel. A comparison of the texts of these last two passages will show how Shadwell has utilized several of Molière's expressions, but has added enough of his own to make the scene more than a bare translation.[7]

Other passages in *The Sullen Lovers* were very likely suggested by *Les Fâcheux.* The scene in which Filinte offers Éraste his services in the forthcoming duel was undoubtedly known to Shad-

[6] *Les Fâcheux,* Act II, scene II; Shadwell, I, 53-54.

[7] *Les Fâcheux,* Act II, scene III; Shadwell, I, 36.

well when he depicted similar zeal in Woodcock. Although Éraste is emphatic in the assurance that he has no quarrel, Filinte insists upon aiding him. Just so, Woodcock continues his offers of assistance after Stanford has ordered him to leave. Each of the devoted bores disappears after hearing that there will be no quarrel unless it is one forced by himself.[8] Again, when Ormin tells of his scheme which will bring an enormous income to the king, Éraste attempts to hurry away and is asked for two pistoles. Similarly, Woodcock has a project that will raise 20,000 pounds, and Huffe, in an earlier scene, after trying various methods of interesting Stanford, is finally quieted with a loan of two pieces.[9] It is possible, likewise, that the passage in which Sir Positive insists upon singing his "Corrant" and Woodcock upon dancing was brought to Shadwell's mind by the scene in which Lisandre sings and dances before Éraste,[10] and that the idea of having Sir Positive interrupt Stanford, who is conversing with Emilia, and ask him to be a second in a duel was suggested by the scene in which Alcandre, on a similar errand, disturbs Éraste and Orphise.[11] With the exception of the first scene, to be discussed later, I have been unable to find convincing evidence of other borrowings from *Les Fâcheux* in *The Sullen Lovers.*[12]

It is possible to see a resemblance between the passage at the end of the fourth act of Shadwell's play and the sixth scene of *Le Mariage Forcé.* In the latter, Pancrace, the Aristotleian philosopher, drives Sganarelle, who wishes some advice, almost distracted by a continuous flow of words, concluding with a list of the numerous sciences in which he is versed. Likewise, Sir Positive, when aroused to talk about his accomplishments by Lovel and Carolina, names them at great length and with such rapidity that he drives Emilia and Stanford away.[13]

[8] *Les Fâcheux,* Act III, scene IV; Shadwell, I, 69.

[9] *Les Fâcheux,* Act III, scene III; Shadwell, I, 37, 35.

[10] *Les Fâcheux,* Act I, scene V; Shadwell, I, 25.

[11] *Les Fâcheux,* Act I, scene X; Shadwell, I, 55.

[12] Despite Dr. Erichsen and Mr. Miles, I am unable to see how Dorante's narrative of the stag-hunt (*Les Fâcheux,* Act II, scene VII) could have suggested Huffe's description of his new profession: "I am going into the City, where I shall have the rarest Bubble, that ever Man had; he was sent me by a Renegado-Linnen-Draper, that fail'd last year in his Credit, and has now no other Trade but to start the Game, whilst we pursue the Chase." (Shadwell, I, 67.)

[13] Shadwell, I, 88.

At present, it is customary for writers on the Restoration drama to see in *Le Misanthrope* a source for "the main points in the plot"[14] of *The Sullen Lovers.* An examination of some of the scenes and characters cited as instances will assist us in determining whether this assumption is correct. Both Alceste and Stanford are filled with aversion for the unpleasing surroundings in which they are placed; and each expresses a willingness to remove himself from the haunts of men. *Le Misanthrope* opens with a scene in which Alceste upbraids his friend Philinte for the meaningless way he greets people with whom he is not acquainted, and urges sincerity in every action, even to the extent of informing Dorilas that he is too importunate and of telling Émilie that she should not set up for a beauty. The underlying trait of Alceste's character is a profound disgust for the manifestations of insincerity which he sees about him. Stanford, on the other hand, in the scene with Lovel, complains of the bores who are always tormenting him. He rails against the troublesome wits who infest the coffee-houses, theatres, and court. The roarers in the street and the bellman with his rhymes are not to his liking. He can scarce endure the sight of women. He has been troubled by the impertinences of Ninny, Woodcock, and Sir Positive. But not a word does he utter to indicate that insincerity in any of these persons is the cause of his anger.

It seems to me that the emphasis in this scene from *The Sullen Lovers* is nearer to that in the opening episode of *Les Fâcheux* than to the scene just described from *Le Misanthrope.* Here Éraste unbosoms his troubles to his valet, La Montagne. After some general remarks on the bores who are continually disturbing him, he tells with much detail a specific instance concerning one who fastened to him in the theatre so tenaciously that he had great difficulty in making his escape. The opening speech of *The Sullen Lovers* which gives the keynote of Stanford's character, "In what unlucky Minute was I born, to be Tormented thus where-e'er I go," is quite clearly an adaptation of the first two lines of *Les Fâcheux:*

[14] Miles, p. 238; Nicoll, p. 174; Asmus Erichsen, *Thomas Shadwell's Komödie "The Sullen Lovers" in ihrem Verhältnis zu Molière's Komödien "Le Misanthrope" und "Les Fâcheux"* (Flensburg, 1906). The relation of Shadwell's play to Molière's comedies is also discussed in J. E. Gillet, *Molière en Angleterre, 1660-1670* (Paris, 1913), pp. 70-80.

> Sous quel astre, bon Dieu, faut-il que je sois né,
> Pour être de Fâcheux toujours assassiné.

After deciding to write a play based upon the troubles of a man who is incessantly disturbed by bores, an author would not need to perform a superhuman feat of the imagination to picture his hero as being willing to withdraw from the sight of men. There is no need to assume that the English playwright must have gone to a French source for the idea: there was *Timon of Athens* in his own dramatic literature. In order that the impatience of Stanford may be properly emphasized, the author introduced a foil in Lovel, described as "one that is pleased with, and laughs at the Impertinents." The creation of this figure does not demand a knowledge of Philinte, the friend of Alceste. There is also no reason for finding in Ninny and his heroic verses a reflection of Oronte and his sonnet.[15] There is resemblance between the two scenes; but why need Shadwell have gone to *Le Misanthrope* for the idea? Once he had determined on the central theme of the play, nothing was more natural than to make one of the impertinents a poet who desires to read his verses. There were numerous examples of the foolish poet in English drama. To mention but a few that were doubtless familiar to Shadwell, there were Treedle whose poem compared the various parts of his lady's body to jewels,[16] Matthew who reads some of his verses to Bobadill,[17] and Sir Abraham Ninny[18] who bears the same surname as the poet in *The Sullen Lovers*, as well as Sir Anthony Altalk, the "pretender to Poetry," in Newcastle's *The Humorous Lovers*.[19]

I am not convinced that Shadwell took qualities from the conceited Marquis Acaste, in order to build the boastful Sir Positive.[20] A more obvious "source," if one must be produced, is to be found in Lady Would-be, who, in the play by Shadwell's favorite dramatist, bothers Volpone with her ceaseless talk of music, painting,

[15] *Le Misanthrope*, Act I, scene II; Shadwell, I, 20-24.

[16] Shirley, *The Witty Fair One*, Act III, scene II.

[17] Jonson, *Every Man in His Humour*, Act I, scene IV.

[18] Field, *A Woman is a Weathercock*, Act III, scene III.

[19] Newcastle, *The Humorous Lovers* (London, 1677), p. 6. Acted in 1667.

[20] In *Le Misanthrope*, Act III, scene I, Acaste gives a catalogue of his virtues to Clitandre. There is little in common between this scene and Sir Positive's description of himself as statesman, philosopher, and painter (Shadwell, I, 26-27).

literature, and philosophy.[21] I am also unable to assent to Mr. Miles' statement that "Célimène suggested Emilia, a second Alceste."[22] Did the author have the brilliant, clever, coquettish Célimène in mind when he drew the morose, melancholy, fault-finding Emilia? If so, Hamlet suggested Sir Positive.

Is it necessary to continue further? I have cited enough examples to show why I reject *Le Misanthrope* as a source for *The Sullen Lovers.* I am willing to accept Shadwell's statement that he derived the idea of his play from *Les Fâcheux;* but I would add that he used more incidents from that work than he mentions in his preface. He may also have received a slight hint from *Le Mariage Forcé.* The ideas suggested by *Les Fâcheux* appealed to Shadwell because, in the persons of the bores, he had an opportunity to experiment in the portrayal of "humours," that type of character associated with the work of his favorite dramatist, Ben Jonson.

Respect for Ben Jonson as a theatrical craftsman was not lacking during the early years of the Restoration. In the complimentary stanzas prefixed to the second edition of Sir Samuel Tuke's *Adventures of Five Hours,* James Long writes of "*Learned* Johnson's *Art;*[23] Etherege, in the prologue to *The Comical Revenge,* refers in a similar manner to the "art of Ben."[24] Flecknoe acknowledges that there are "few of our English Playes (excepting onely some few of *Johnsons*) without some faults or other,"[25] while Sir Robert Howard characterizes Jonson's plays as "*never to be equal'd Comedies.*"[26] Dryden, although not denying certain defects in the work of Ben, concedes him to be "the most learned and judicious writer which any theatre ever had."[27]

Although these dramatists of the first decade of the reign of Charles II unite in extolling the practise of Ben, they do not approach the enthusiasm of Shadwell, who, after placing Jonson upon a lofty pedestal, worships him at a distance as "incomparably the best Dramatick Poet that ever was, or . . . ever will be."[28]

[21] Jonson, *Volpone,* Act III, scene II. Cf. with Shadwell, I, 70-73.

[22] Miles, p. 238.

[23] Published London, 1664.

[24] Etherege, *Works* (ed. Verity), p. 4.

[25] Richard Flecknoe, "A Short Discourse of the English Stage" printed with *Love's Kingdom* (London, 1664).

[26] "To the Reader," *Four New Plays* (London, 1665).

[27] "An Essay of Dramatic Poesy." See also J. F. Bradley and J. Q. Adams, *The Jonson Allusion-Book* (Yale University Press, 1922).

[28] Epistle Dedicatory to *The Virtuoso.*

He would rather be the author of one scene of comedy, "*like some of* Ben Johnson'*s, than of all the* [Operas] *that have been, or ever shall be written.*"[29] In his plays, he wishes to follow "the Practice of *Ben. Johnson,* whom . . . all Dramatick Poets ought to imitate, though none are like to come near; he being the onely Person that appears . . . to have made perfect Representations of Human Life."[30] His adulation reaches its height in the epilogue to *The Humourists,* where he thus indulges his enthusiasm:

> *The Mighty Prince of Poets, learned* BEN,
> *Who alone div'd into the Minds of Men,*
> *Saw all their Wandrings, all their Follies knew,*
> *And all their vain fantastick Passions drew*
> *In Images so lively and so true,*
> *That there each Humourist himself might view,*
> *Yet only lash'd the Errors of the Times,*
> *And ne'er expos'd the Persons, but the Crimes;*
> *And never car'd for private Frowns, when he*
> *Did but chastise publick Iniquity:*
> *He fear'd no Pimp, no Pick-pocket, or Drab;*
> *He fear'd no* Bravo, *nor no Ruffian's Stab:*
> *Twas he alone true Humours understood,*
> *And with great Wit and Judgment made them good.* . . . . .
> *Expect not then, since that most flourishing Age*
> *Of* BEN, *to see true Humour on the Stage.*
> *All, that have since been writ, if they be scann'd,*
> *Are but faint Copies from that Master's Hand.*
> *Our Poet now, amongst those petty Things,*
> *Alas! his too weak trifling Humours brings.*
> *As much beneath the worst in* Johnson'*s Plays,*
> *As his great Merit is above our Praise.*
> *For could he imitate that great Author right,*
> *He would with ease all Poets else out-write.*
> *For to out-go all other Men, would be,*
> *O Noble* BEN! *less than to follow thee.*

In his preface to *The Sullen Lovers,* Shadwell sets forth his endeavor of representing a variety of humours in that play. Most authors he has read, with the exception of Jonson, either have wild romantic tales or "in their lower Comedies content themselves with one or two Humours at most, and those not near so perfect Char-

[29] Preface to *Psyche.* [30] Preface to *The Sullen Lovers.*

acters as the admirable *Johnson* always made, who never wrote Comedy without seven or eight excellent Humours."

What Shadwell meant by a "Humour" is described elsewhere:

> *A Humour is the Byass, of the Mind,*
> *By which with Violence 'tis one way inclin'd:*
> *It makes our Actions lean on one side still;*
> *And in all Changes that way bends the Will.*[31]

This definition closely follows that by Jonson, who transfers the term metaphorically

> *Unto the general disposition:*
> *As when some one peculiar quality*
> *Doth so possess a man, that it doth draw*
> *All his affects, his spirits, and his powers,*
> *In their confluctions, all to run one way.*[32]

In another passage, Shadwell further develops his idea, by calling a humour, "such an Affectation, as misguides Men in Knowledge, Art, or Science, or that causes defection in Manners and Morality, or perverts their Minds in the main Actions of their Lives." He does not count "those Humours, which a great many do; that is to say, such as consist in using one or two By-words; or in having a fantastick, extravagant Dress; . . . nor in the Affectation of some *French* Words. . . . Nor is downright silly Folly a Humour."[33] In his classification of those absurdities which are not to be labelled humours, Shadwell again follows his master:

> *But that a rook, by wearing a pyed feather,*
> *The cable hat-band, or the three-piled ruff,*
> *A yard of shoe-tye, or the Switzer's knot*
> *On his French garters, should affect a humour!*
> *O, it is more than most ridiculous.*[34]

In comedies of humours, then, we expect to find characters presented as slaves of various ruling traits or biases. In the portrayal of such figures, Shadwell holds that the author must be absolutely consistent. "In the writing of a Humour, a Man is confin'd not to swerve from the Character, and oblig'd to say nothing but what

[31] Epilogue to *The Humourists*.
[32] *Every Man Out of His Humour.*
[33] Preface to *The Virtuoso*.
[34] *Every Man Out of His Humour.*

is proper to it." In this type of comedy, less "Design" is to be expected than in "Plays of a higher Nature." If he were to fill his comedies with plot, "at the latter End, where the Turns ought to be many, and suddenly following one another, [he] must have let fall the Humour, which [he] thought wou'd be pleasanter than Intrigues could have been without it."[35]

But Shadwell, in addition to delineating humours in his comedies, used other devices found in Jonson's plays. Miss Woodbridge has shown that the earlier dramatist frequently introduces a character who fulfills the functions of "demonstrator." His duty is to comment upon the eccentricities of the figures that are being held up to ridicule. Among the "demonstrators" are Macilente in *Every Man Out of His Humour*, Crites in *Cynthia's Revels*, and Dauphine in *The Silent Woman.* The characters in Jonsonian comedy also fall into two groups, one made up of victims and the other of victimizers. The victimizers exploit the victims, who embody the various follies or vices that the author would ridicule or scourge; and, in this way, lead them to exposure or ruin. The plot then naturally resolves itself into a "network of practical jokes, some perfectly harmless, some more serious in their issues."[36]

The plot and characters of *The Sullen Lovers* will now be considered in the light of Jonsonian practice. For four acts, Lovel and Carolina play the parts of the arch-victimizers and take delight in urging the minor gullers, Ninny, Woodcock, Sir Positive, and Lady Vaine, to the easy task of making the lives of Emilia and Stanford miserable. These tricks continue in the fifth act; but, as frequently happens in the comedies of Ben, the tables are turned. Ninny and Woodcock fall victims to Emilia's trickery; and Sir Positive is deceived by Lady Vaine. By causing these characters to display their humours, Lovel and Carolina also indirectly perform the function of demonstrator.

In his portrayal of the humours, Shadwell was fairly consistent. Stanford and Emilia, described in the dramatis personae as "Morose melancholy [persons], tormented beyond Measure with the Impertinence of People, and resolved to leave the World to be quit of them," are pieces of industrious characterization. Annoyed

[35] Preface to *The Sullen Lovers.*

[36] Elizabeth Woodbridge, *Studies in Jonson's Comedy* (1898), Chapters II and III.

on every occasion, they succeed in "holding up their humours" to the end, with the exception of those moments when they are so interested in each other that they forget to rail at mankind. Ninny, who is "always troubling Men with impertinent Discourses of Poetry, and the repetition of his own Verses," is not entirely cleansed of this mania when Emilia neglects to appear at the rendezvous. But after he hears that she has married Stanford, he determines to cease writing heroic verse and henceforth to show all his "Power, and Soul, and Flame, and Mettle in Lampoon." Woodcock, who "embraces and kisses all Men" and who is so "used to his familiar endearing Expressions, that he cannot forbear them in the midst of his Anger," is silenced when he learns that Emilia has tricked him. But even then he does not neglect to use the phrase, "dear Heart." Sir Positive "pretends to understand every thing in the World, and will suffer no Man to understand any thing in his Company." When at the end of the play he learns that Lady Vaine is not the sort of person she has represented herself as being, he will not acknowledge to the company that "this is the first thing in the World that [he has] met with, which [he] did not understand."

In an attempt to be consistent in the drawing of his characters, Shadwell evidently overlooked the fact that consistency often goes hand in hand with boredom, and that "holding up a humour" does not necessarily imply holding the attention of the audience. Some of the persons who saw *The Sullen Lovers* rightly objected that there was "the same thing over and over" in that play. This repetition makes Shadwell's first comedy in places rather dull reading to-day. One passage, in my opinion, still has power to amuse—that in which Sir Positive appears as heroic dramatist.

It will be remembered that the apparent satire of Sir Robert Howard in the character of Sir Positive assured this play of success. In the preface to *The Humourists,* Shadwell disclaims any intention of representing a humour upon the stage which belongs only to one or two persons. "But I have had the Fortune, to have had a general Humour (in a Play of mine) applied to three or four Men, (whose Persons I never saw, or Humours ever heard of) till the Play was acted." Although it is uncertain whether Shadwell originally intended to ridicule this particular knight, it is likewise indisputable that he gave to Sir Positive numerous characteristics associated in the minds of theatre-goers with Sir Robert Howard.[37]

Marvell, in "The Last Instructions to a Painter about the Dutch Wars, 1667" writes:

> Of birth, state, wit, strength, courage, How'rd presumes,
> And in his breast wears many Montezumes.[38]

Likewise, Evelyn in his Diary for June 16, 1683, mentions seeing Sir Robert Howard, "that universal pretender." In his *Defence of an Essay of Dramatic Poesy*, Dryden sarcastically refers to his brother-in-law as "one, who has the reputation of understanding all things" and implies that he might make that excuse for yielding to him in the argument, "which the philosopher made to the Emperor; why should I offer to contend with him, who is master of more than twenty legions of arts and sciences?"[39]

Two years after the first production of *The Sullen Lovers*, Marvell thus mentions Howard:

> Whilst Positive walks, like Woodcock in the park,
> Contriving projects with a brewer's clerk.[40]

As late as February 16, 1684-5, Evelyn records dining at "Sr Robt Howard's, Auditor of the Exchequer, a gentleman pretending to all manner of arts and sciences, for which he had ben the subject of comedy, under the name of Sir Positive; not ill-natur'd; but insufferably boasting." According to Pepys, the Duke of York vouched for the truth of the trap-ball playing incident.[41] Dryden

[37] It seems that other persons besides Sir Robert Howard were ridiculed in *The Sullen Lovers*. Pepys heard that "my lord St. John is meant by Mr. Woodcocke." According to a contemporary annotation in the British Museum copy of the first quarto, Ninny represented Edward Howard. The latter, who was a brother of Sir Robert, was the author of some mediocre verse and a few indifferent plays. Lady Vaine may have been intended to portray Susanna Uphill, a member of the King's Company and Sir Robert's mistress.

[38] Marvell, *Works* (Fuller Worthies Library, ed. A. B. Grosart), I, 263.

[39] *Essays of John Dryden* (ed. W. P. Ker), I, 111.

[40] Marvell, *Works,* I, 324. Despite Grosart's note, I have restored the capital *W* to Woodcock. Doubtless Marvell had Woodcock of *The Sullen Lovers* in mind. In Act II, Woodcock approaches Stanford with a project of raising £20-000. Note the reference to Woodcock in Nevil Payne's *The Morning Ramble* (London, 1673) p. 70, where Townlove says to Rose: "Well, our little Projector, how go matters? I could for thy sake turn Woodcock in the Play, and alwayes be kissing."

[41] May 8, 1668.

calls one of Howard's arguments as "great a secret, as that we are all mortal."[42] Malone,[43] in this statement, rightly sees a covert allusion to the speech in which Sir Positive tells Stanford that he has thought of nothing else but mankind this month, "but betwixt you and I, let me tell you, we are all Mortal,"[44] and also thinks Shadwell may have had Howard's poem, *Against the Fear of Death*, in mind when he penned those lines.[45]

The scene in which Sir Positive appears as an heroic dramatist is introduced in the third act.[46] Here, the universal pretender, with Stanford as his second, meets the clerk who had sat in the eighteen-pence gallery and railed at his play. Sir Positive tells his friend: "if in any Dramatick Poem there has been such Breaks, such Characters, such Figures, such Images, such Heroick Patterns, such Heights, such Flights, such Intrigues, such Surprizes, such Fire, Salt and Flame, then [he is] no Judge; [he understands] nothing in this World." The clerk had offended the dramatist by saying "That shall not pass" at the point where the lady commanded her lover to hang himself. When the hero granted her request, the clerk had commented: "Fie upon't, that he should be so much overtaken."

Sir Positive considers this as good as to "call the Gentleman Fool: And 'tis the best Character in all my Play." The clerk would not be guilty of such indecorum for all the world; but he finds it strange for a man to pay eighteen-pence and not have the satisfaction of speaking a word for it. He is silenced by the retort, "Not when Gentlemen write." Sir Positive then exclaims against the invincible ignorance of the age, "now for him to hang himself at the Command of his Mistress, there's the Surprize; and I'll be content to hang my self, if ever that was shewn upon a Stage before; besides 'twas an Heroick, *Cato*-like Action; and there's great Love and Honour to be shewn in a Man's hanging himself for his Mistress, take that from me." Stanford replies that a halter is not so honorable as a poniard; but Sir Positive has seventeen arguments against this contention. "First, I'll shew you the Posture of hang-

[42] *Essays of John Dryden* (ed. W. P. Ker), I, 126.

[43] Malone, *Prose Works of John Dryden* (London, 1800), I, pt. 2, 176.

[44] Shadwell, I, 27.

[45] See J. Nichol's *Select Collection of Poems* (London, 1780), II, 330-331. In Howard's poem is the line, "We always should remember, Death is sure."

[46] Shadwell, I, 57 ff.

ing; . . . it is the Posture of a Pensive dejected Lover, with his Hands before him, and his Head aside, thus."

In order to cut short any further explanations, Stanford pretends to be convinced, and urges the fight to be concluded. But Sir Positive has a way out of this difficulty and will be satisfied if the clerk subscribes his name to a certificate. The latter then acknowledges in writing that the "Play of Sir *Positive At-All*, Knight, called *The Lady in the Lobster*, notwithstanding it was damn'd by the Malice of the Age, shall not only read, but it shall act with any of *Ben Johnson*'s, and *Beaumont*'s and *Fletcher*'s Plays." He likewise attests that the author is a "Poet, Mathematician, Divine, Statesman, Lawyer, Physician, Geographer, Musician, and indeed a *Unus in Omnibus* through all Arts and Sciences." Then upon hearing that the clerk and his second were about to play at trap-ball, Sir Positive offers to be one of the party.

The heroic drama, which is satirized in this description of Sir Positive's play, Shadwell refers to also in the preface and the prologue to *The Sullen Lovers*. In the former, he mentions slurringly the authors who have "wild Romantick Tales, wherein they strain Love and Honour to that ridiculous Height, that it becomes Burlesque." And in the prologue, he writes:

> *No kind Romantick Lovers in his Play,*
> *To sigh and whine out Passion, such as may*
> *Charm Waiting-women with Heroick Chime,*
> *And still resolve to live and dye in Rhime;*
> *Such as your Ears with Love and Honour feast,*
> *And play at* Crambo *for three Hours at least:*
> *That Fight, and Wooe, in Verse in the same Breath,*
> *And make Similitudes, and Love in Death.*

This type of play had been made popular in the Restoration theatre through the efforts of the Earl of Orrery, Sir Robert Howard, and Dryden.[47]

Shadwell's brief scene in *The Sullen Lovers* has a certain historic importance because it seems to be the first attempt in a comedy produced upon the English stage to ridicule the absurdities of the

[47] Heroic plays which had been produced before *The Sullen Lovers* were Orrery's *The General, Henry V., Mustapha,* and *The Black Prince*, Caryl's *The English Princess,* Howard's *The Vestal Virgin,* Dryden's *The Indian Emperor,* and the work written in collaboration by Dryden and Howard, *The Indian Queen.*

heroic drama, and precedes by three years and a half the presentation of the robust satire by Buckingham and his co-workers in *The Rehearsal.* The latter play, according to Briscoe's Key, printed for the first time in 1704, "had been several times *Rehears'd,* the *Players* were perfect in their Parts, and all Things in Readiness for its Acting, before the *Great Plague* [of] 1665; and that then prevented it. But what was so ready for the Stage, and so near being Acted, at the Breaking out of that *Terrible Sickness,* was very different from what you have since seen in Print. In that he call'd his poet *Bilboa;* by which Name the Town generally understood Sir *Robert Howard* to be the Person pointed at."[48] When *The Rehearsal* was actually produced in December, 1671, the satire was directed against Dryden in the person of John Bayes. Inasmuch as he was then poet-laureate and the most eminent writer of heroic plays, he was the natural choice for ridicule. But is it unreasonable to suggest that a contributory cause for the change from Howard to Dryden is to be found in the fact that the former Bilboa had become the talk of the town as Sir Positive At-all?

As a first play, *The Sullen Lovers* is decidedly above the average. It represents the attempt of a young writer, fired with enthusiasm for the work of Jonson, to present a theme suggested by *Les Fâcheux* in terms of the London of 1668. Although the humour-

[48] Malone argues (*Prose Works of John Dryden,* I, pt. 1, 97-98) that the original hero was not Howard but D'Avenant, "not only on account of the name of *Bilboa,* which alludes to his military character . . . but from the circumstance of the patch that in the course of the drama he is obliged to wear on his nose; . . . Besides, he was a much more distinguished character, not only as a Poet Laureate, but as the superintendent of the Duke of York's Company of Comedians, and the introducer of heroick plays on the English stage. The allusions to Sir Robert Howard's tragedies are so few and inconsiderable, that he never could have been the author's principal object." All this is true enough, but hardly proof that the "universal pretender" was not the victim of the burlesque. If the name Bilboa suggested military exploits, it could be used with reason for Sir Robert Howard. He joined the royalists at the outbreak of the civil wars and was knighted on the field near Newbury (June 29, 1644) for bravery in rescuing Lord Wilmot from the parliamentarians at Cropredy Bridge. Had the original draft been intended as a fling at D'Avenant, Bilboa would have worn the patch throughout the entire play. There is nothing in the later version to indicate that this was the case. On the other hand, the necessity for this ornament is visibly demonstrated. The luckless Bayes, after attempting to coach the soldiers in a difficult feat, falls with disastrous results. When he next appears, his nose is bandaged. Malone is correct in his contention that D'Avenant was a more important man in the theatrical world than Howard. Sir Robert, however, had certain personal idiosyncrasies which rendered him particularly liable to ridicule.

characters become, at times, rather monotonous,[49] they do reveal, particularly Sir Positive, the fact that their creator possesses an undeniable sense for what is effective in the theatre. This comedy also displays Shadwell in the rôle for which he was best fitted, that of satirist. Through Sir Positive At-all, considered as a caricature of the boastful Sir Robert Howard, he ridicules the heroic drama, and thus sets the pace for his later and more detailed satire of the scientific movement.

[49] A reference to three of the characters occurs in "A Satyr, In Answer to the Satyr against Man. By T. L. *of* Wadham *Colledge,* Oxon" (*Miscellanea: Or, the Second Part of Poetical Recreations. Compos'd by several Authors.* London, 1688, p. 79).

"Last night I hapned at the Tavern late,
To be where five of these great *Wits* were sate,
And was so nigh as to o'erhear their prate:
I dare to swear, that three amongst the five,
Were *Woodcock, Ninney,* and *Sir Loslitive.* [*sic*].
Had *Shadwell* heard them, he had stol'n from thence
A Second part of his Impertinence."

CHAPTER VIII

THE HUMOURISTS

THE HUMOURISTS, which was produced in 1670,[1] was received coldly by the patrons of the Duke's Theatre and saved only by the interpolation of "excellent Dancings."[2] When published in 1671 with a dedication to Margaret, Duchess of Newcastle, it was preceded by a long preface in which the author set forth his purpose of reprehending "some of the Vices and Follies of the Age" and challenged those who had accused him of reflecting upon specific persons in his writings to prove their points. This play may have been revived around 1691; for the title-page of the edition of that year described it as "Acted by Their Majesties Servants."

The plot, in some ways one of the most indecent in Restoration drama, hinges upon the loves of Crazy, a victim of the pox. In addition to receiving visits from Mrs. Striker and Mrs. Friske, who are no better than they should be and who are very jealous lest the one should replace the other in his affections, Crazy is attempting to win the hand of Theodosia. This young lady loves Raymund, who, in turn, is pursued by her aunt and guardian, Lady Loveyouth. The latter orders her niece not to think of this "Gentleman of Wit and Honour," but to consider the other suitors, among whom, in addition to Crazy, are two "Fantastick Coxcombs," Drybob and Briske.

Raymund feigns an interest in her ladyship, but makes plain to Theodosia by letter the real state of his feelings. With the assistence of the ever-ready maid, Bridget, he plans to gain admittance to his beloved's chamber in the evening. Crazy and Drybob, also desirous of a meeting with Theodosia, are directed to the wrong window by Bridget; but, when they come to the garden with ladders, they are prevented from their design by Raymund and Briske.

[1] A manuscript note by T. Holden in an old edition avouches this to have been the favorite play of a certain Anne Boothby. W. Carew Hazlitt, *Second Series of Bibliographical Collections and Notes on Early English Literature*, 1474-1700 (London, 1882), p. 554.

[2] See p. 23.

Upon their return later in the evening, they mistake Lady Loveyouth, who is awaiting Raymund, for Theodosia. Discovering the error, they take refuge in a cellar, but are caught when they flee at the cry of "Fire." During the confusion, Raymund and Theodosia elope.

Grieved by this action, Lady Loveyouth decides to settle her estate upon her cousin Richard and to marry Crazy. In the meantime, her husband, Sir Richard Loveyouth, who had left home some years before, has returned in disguise, informed her of her lord's (i.e., his own) death, and accepted the post of usher in order that he may discover grounds for divorce. Bridget arranges the marriage between Crazy and Lady Loveyouth, and informs Briske that the report of Theodosia's wedding is false. Raymund, in the guise of a scrivener, brings the deed by which Lady Loveyouth is to sign away her property, but exchanges it before the oath is sworn for a document which confers the estate upon Theodosia. Briske and Drybob marry masked women whom they believe to be Theodosia, but later find that they are Bridget and Mrs. Friske. When Crazy learns that his wife has made over her estate, he confesses the truth concerning his physical condition. But this marriage is soon annulled when Sir Richard reveals himself. He tells his wife that she must forever remain a stranger to him and declares Theodosia his heir. When Crazy attempts to transfer his affections to Striker, he is spurned.

In his preface, Shadwell avers with no small degree of pride that this play is wholly his own, "without borrowing a tittle from any Man; which . . . is too bold an Attempt for so young a Writer." This statement is substantially correct. There are no slavish borrowings in *The Humourists*, although there are frequent reminiscences of situations from earlier comedies. Like Emilia, who in Shadwell's first play is bothered by the tiresome lovers, Ninny and Woodcock, Theodosia is courted by the foolish suitors, Crazy, Drybob, and Briske.[8] There is also a slight similarity in idea between the scene in *The Wild Gallant* where Isabella and Constance happen upon Loveby, who is entertaining the so-called Lady Du Lake

[8] Mr. Miles sees in this situation a reminiscence of *Le Misanthrope*, where Célimène is wòoed by Acaste, Clitandre, and Oronte (*Influence of Molière on Restoration Comedy*, p. 231). It was not necessary for Shadwell to go to a French source for this idea: the woman courted by foolish suitors, no one of whom she intends to wed, had appeared countless time in his native dramatic literature.

and others of her kind,[4] and that passage where Briske and Crazy are caused embarrassment by the intrusion of their mistresses Friske and Striker when they are attempting to make a good impression upon Theodosia.[5] The idea of presenting as laughable the sufferings of a victim of the pox may have been suggested by the scenes of Dufoy's troubles in Etherege's *The Comical Revenge; or Love in a Tub.* The return of Sir Richard Loveyouth in disguise recalls the coming of Bonavent in *Hyde Park* (revived in 1668); and Briske, in the duel scene with Raymund, shows himself to be in the tradition of the Jonsonian and Fletcherian cowards.

Shadwell's main interest in *The Humourists,* as in *The Sullen Lovers,* lay in characterization rather than in plot. The preface states that "the Humours are new . . . and all the Words and Actions of the Persons in the Play are always suitable to the Characters . . . given . . . them." The function of Theodosia and Raymund, described as persons of wit, is, like that of Carolina and Lovel, to represent the attitude of common-sense, the norm from which the humour-characters, who are governed by their particular mental biases, depart.

Crazy, who is "in Love with most Women, and thinks most Women in Love with him," is portrayed with unswerving consistency. From the very moment that he "holds up his Humour" to Raymund by describing the bawd Mrs. Errant as a "most delicate Person" whom he loves infinitely, he remains true to his bent. He will not allow the surgeon to traduce the "person of Honour" who is responsible for his condition. When he is arrested at the suit of Pullin, he bribes the bailiff in order that he may inquire about Theodosia from Mrs. Errant, who is passing by. To repay Raymund for his assistance in overcoming the bailiffs, he offers to take him to see a "Person of Honour." During his fight with Drybob later, he promises to spare his rival's life for two minutes in order that he may speak with Mrs. Friske. He is deaf to any attempt at ending this quarrel, until Briske offers to conduct him to his mistress. After his disappointment at Theodosia's elopement with Raymund, he is quite willing to become the husband of Lady Loveyouth; upon learning that the marriage is void, he would turn to Striker.[6]

[4] Dryden, *Works* (Scott-Saintsbury ed.), II, 88 ff.

[5] Shadwell, I, 175 ff.

[6] *Ibid.*, I, 135, 141, 152, 153, 164, 166, 196, 211.

Of less importance in the action than Crazy are Drybob and Briske. The former, a "fantastick Coxcomb, that makes it his Business to speak fine Things and Wit, as he thinks; and always takes Notice, or makes others take Notice, of any thing he thinks well said," follows his bent from the time of his appearance with the little French dog which he intends as a "sacrifice to [his] Mistress," until he is tricked by marriage to Friske. An equally consistent piece of characterization is the cowardly Briske, described in the dramatis personae as a "Brisk, Airy, Fantastick, Singing, Dancing Coxcomb, that sets up for a well-bred Man, and a Man of Honour; but mistakes in every thing, and values himself only upon the Vanity and Foppery of Gentlemen."

The jealous mistresses, Striker and Friske, who are always attempting to outdo each other, are portrayed in a livelier manner than either Drybob or Briske. The spirited dialogue and animated movement of the scenes in which they appear indicate what Shadwell could do when dealing with figures from low life, types which he was to use frequently in later plays.

The Humourists differs from *The Sullen Lovers* in containing a greater amount of physical action. This appears particularly in the scenes in the garden, which soon dwindle into the wildest farce.[7] Unlike its predecessor, which had ridiculed the heroic drama, this play contains little satire of contemporary interests. There are, however, a few gibes at the French in the scene where Crazy and Raymund heap abuse upon the surgeon Pullin[8] and in Drybob's description of the parentage of his dog.[9]

In *The Humourists*, the author is successful in following his precepts. The eccentric figures "hold up their humours" to the end. As in *The Sullen Lovers*, the persons who deviate from the normal are rendered ridiculous; but Shadwell again could find no better means of effecting this end than by marrying them to the wrong persons or by not marrying them at all. The plot also is slight, and is allowed to lag whenever the opportunity for a scene of humourous exaggeration presents itself. By introducing Striker and Friske, Shadwell learned the possibilities of dealing with characters from low life. It was then but a step to the types presented in the tavern scenes of *The Miser*.

[7] *Ibid.*, I, 181 ff.
[8] *Ibid.*, I, 137 ff.
[9] *Ibid.*, I, 160.

CHAPTER IX

THE MISER

SHADWELL'S third comedy, *The Miser*, was produced at the Theatre Royal in January, 1671/2. The play on which it was based, Molière's *L'Avare*, had been acted at the Théâtre du Palais-Royal on September 9, 1668, by the troupe of the king and had been published in 1669. Shadwell's adaptation was revived at least once in the following century at Drury Lane when on June 5, 1704, Bullock, at his benefit, appeared in the part of Timothy Squeeze.[1]

Reference has been made to the English author's ill-natured statement that Molière's part in the comedy had not suffered in his hands, and that it was not *"Barrenness of Wit or Invention, . . . but Laziness"* that caused the dramatists of his country to borrow from the French.[2] This high-handed remark called forth later a well deserved rejoinder from Voltaire: "Un poëte anglais nommé Shadwell, aussi vain que mauvais poëte, la donna en anglais du vivant de Molière. . . . On peut juger qu'un homme qui n'a pas assez d'esprit pour mieux cacher sa vanité n'en a pas assez pour faire mieux que Molière. La pièce de Shadwell est généralement méprisée."[3] Tom Brown, who was also not slow to express his disapproval of Shadwell's airy self-satisfaction, writes, "Mr. *Shadwell*, in one of his last Plays, is so honest as to own, that he had stole a few Hints out of a *French* Comedy, but pretends 'twas rather out of Laziness than Want. This Confession, instead of mending Matters, would have hang'd him at the *Old Baily;* and why it should save him in *Parnassus*, I can't tell."[4]

In brief, Molière's play tells the story of the miser Harpagon,

[1] Genest, II, 300.

[2] See pp. 24-25.

[3] *Oeuvres Complètes de Voltaire* (1879), XXIII, 115. Other French writers of the eighteenth century to notice this version of *The Miser* were Béat de Muralt, in the second of his *Lettres sur les Anglais et les Francais;* and P. J. Figuet, who, in 1752, published his *Lettre sur Le Theatre Anglois* with translations of Shadwell's play and Wycherley's *Country Wife.* Figuet calls Shadwell and Wycherley "les deux Poëtes Comiques les plus célebres de ces derniers tems."

[4] *Works of Mr. Thomas Brown* (London, 1720), IV, 132.

who would marry his daughter Élise to the elderly Anselme, since the latter is willing to take her without dowry. She, on the other hand, loves Valère, a young gentleman who has saved her life and who, in order to be near her, has taken service in her father's household. Harpagon's son, Cléante, has been attracted by his fair neighbor Mariane; but, because of the efforts of the matchmaker Frosine, he finds himself and his father rivals for her hand. In desperation, he hides a casket containing the miser's treasure, which the servant La Flèche has stolen from the garden. This loss drives all other thoughts from the mind of Harpagon, who summons a magistrate and accuses Valère, at the instigation of the cook Maître Jacques, of being the thief. Finally, Anselme appears upon the scene and is revealed as the father of Valère and Mariane, the lovers are properly paired, and the casket is restored to Harpagon.

Shadwell, finding the French text to have "*too few Persons, and too little Action for an* English Theatre," added to both so much, that "[he could] *call more than half of the Play* [his] *own.*" Not only did he introduce a subplot consisting of scenes from low life, but he made a few changes and amplifications in the portion derived from Molière, and, wherever he had an opportunity, coarsened the dialogue.[5]

Shadwell's subplot is joined to Molière's main plot by the characters Theodore, Cheatly, Squeeze, and Timothy who correspond to the French Cléante, Frosine, Maître Simon, and Anselme. Theo-

[5] Shadwell's borrowings are pointed out at length in a dissertation by Franz Crull entitled *Thomas Shadwell's (John Ozell's) und Henry Fielding's Comoedien, "The Miser" in ihrem Verhältnis unter einander und zu ihr gemeinsamen Quelle* (Rostock, 1899).

The scenes borrowed from *L'Avare* appear in the following table. The text used of *L'Avare* is the "Réimpression Textuelle par les soins de Louis Lecour" (Paris, 1876).

	L'Avare	*The Miser*
Act I:	Scene 1	pp. 13-15
	Scene 2	pp. 15-16
	Scene 3	pp. 16-19
	Scene 4	pp. 19-22
	Scene 5	pp. 23-25
Act II:	Scene 1	pp. 43-44
	Scene 2	pp. 44-45
	Scene 4	pp. 31-32
	Scene 5	pp. 32-36, 48-49
Act III:	Scene 1	pp. 55-59
	Scene 2	pp. 59-60
	Scene 3	p. 60
	Scene 4	pp. 60-61
	Scene 5	p. 61
	Scene 6	p. 61
	Scene 7	pp. 61-64
	Scene 8	p. 64
Act IV:	Scene 1	pp. 65-68
	Scene 3	pp. 78-80
	Scene 6	p. 90
	Scene 7	pp. 91-92
Act V:	Scenes 1 & 2	pp. 92-94
	Scene 3	pp. 94-96
	Scene 4	pp. 96-97
	Scenes 5 & 6	pp. 97-101, with many changes and transpositions.

dore's early life has been somewhat different from that of the French original: he has passed his days and nights in the conventional pleasures of the young man of Restoration drama; he has been familiar with the daughter of Mrs. Cheatly, but has now resolved to marry the young lady Isabella who possesses the "damn'd unfashionable Qualities, call'd Virtue and Modesty." In addition to performing Frosine's labors in arranging the match between the miser and his fair young neighbor, Mrs. Cheatly appears in the rôle of "running Bawd." Although her brazen attempts to make possible a meeting between Theodora and an acquaintance of hers, "one of the handsomest and most accomplished Sparks in Town," are repulsed, she is successful in assisting her daughter to compromise Squeeze and to make away with much of his money. Instead of the elderly gentleman, Anselme, whom Harpagon has chosen for Élise, Goldingham selects for Theodora the foolish young citizen, Timothy Squeeze. This loutish creature, who "minds [his] Business as well as e'er a young Man in this City," proves an easy dupe for the cheats, Rant and Hazard, who have little difficulty in going through his purse and marrying him to Joyce. The money-lender, Squeeze, who has a more important part in the action than his prototype Maître Simon, also plays into the hands of the cheats and has to claim Lettice as his wife.

These four characters were considerably changed in the transition from the Théâtre du Palais-Royal to the King's House; otherwise, the English "Farce," in its presentation of the figures derived from the French comedy, follows the original with some closeness. Harpagon becomes Goldingham; Élise, Theodora; Valère, Bellamour; Mariane, Isabella; Maître Jacques, James; La Flèche, Robin; Dame Claude, Old Woman; Brindavoine, Roger; La Merluche, William; Le Commissaire, Justice.

In one instance, a situation in Shadwell's main plot is amplified from a suggestion by Molière. When Mariane is at her wit's end to know how she may avoid marrying Harpagon, Frosine remembers a friend who could be persuaded to impersonate a marquise and by dazzling the miser with her wealth cause him to relinquish his less affluent fiancée.[6] Nothing more is heard of this plan. In the English version, on the other hand, Cheatly offers to dress

[6] *L'Avare,* Act IV, Scene I.

Bridget, a tailor's daughter, in the clothing of a countess. She goes to the miser, gives him a glowing description of this woman who has £500 more than Isabella, and receives his assurance that he is most desirous to have an interview with her.[7] Later, when Cheatly introduces Bridget as the Countess of Puddle-Dock, Goldingham, after promising to wait upon her presently, steps into the garden to his dear gold. Returning in great rage and anguish upon discovering that his money has been stolen, he frightens Cheatly and the supposed Countess away.[8]

Shadwell also made some changes in the concluding portion of his main plot by introducing the pretended conspiracy against the government. Theodore, in order to gain mastery over his father, tells the latter about a plot which the upholders of the Good Old Cause have contrived to seize Whitehall and the exchequer. The conspirators desire to secrete arms and ammunitions in the homes of their friends and well-wishers. If Goldingham will conceal six chests of armour in his vault, he will receive forty guineas for his pains. For a moment, the miser is torn between his desire for money and fear that he may be apprehended as a conspirator. The latter motive, coupled with the fact that he now has an opportunity to take revenge for all his son's villainies, causes him to threaten to acquaint the king with this treason. Theodore then begs that the matter may be concealed and offers to return the twenty guineas which he had received as advance payment at once. When Goldingham sees the money, he immediately changes his tune: he kisses the coins and tells his son not to restore them, but to swear secrecy instead.[9]

No reference is again made to this plot until Theodore appears, after the theft of the money from the garden has been discovered, and jauntily informs his father that he will give an acquittance for the six thousand broad pieces. Goldingham, at first furious, threatens his son and then offers to spare his life if he will return the gold. Theodore replies that the money is in good hands: it is being held in mortmain; he "did but seize upon't for the King's Use." Goldingham angrily demands if his son has the impudence to accuse him of owing money to the king. Theodore retorts,

[7] Shadwell, III, 68, 76-77.
[8] *Ibid.*, III, 90-92.
[9] *Ibid.*, III, 72-76.

"Do you think, Sir, the King will let you commit Treason for nothing?" and reminds him of the ammunition in the vault. Goldingham, seeing he is caught in his own snare, can do nothing except release his son of the money before witnesses. Theodore then gives the information that the chests contain lumber and that the whole plot is a hoax. Utterly exasperated, Goldingham would gain immediate revenge by wedding Isabella; but the lady in question appears and announces her marriage to his son. Nothing is now left for the miser except to heap imprecations upon their heads and leave them with this parting malediction: "May the perpetual spirit of Contention wait on ye; may ye never in your Lives agree in one Thing; may the Name of Quiet ne'er be heard betwixt ye; and, to compleat all, may ye never be asunder: and so farewell."[10]

This final picture of the miser is very different from that presented by Molière. In the French play, Cléante agrees to return the money to his father on condition that he will be allowed to wed Mariane. Harpagon, unwilling to assent until he sees his casket, urges the objection that he has no money to bestow upon his children as wedding portions. Anselme then comes to the fore, offers to pay all the expenses of the two marriages, promises Harpagon a wedding coat, and fees the Commissaire. He then would go quickly with his children to their mother and rejoice with her at the happy conclusion of their long separation. Anselme's good-fortune does not affect Harpagon in the least; for the miser, as the play closes, can think of nothing except seeing his beloved casket once more.

The concluding picture of Harpagon illustrates well what Shadwell considered the most necessary element in a comedy of humour—unswerving consistency in character portrayal. Harpagon's humour of avarice is never forgotten; and it is accentuated with masterly touches in this final scene. After the troubles of the lovers have vanished, and when one expects that the father may for a moment show interest in his children's future, Harpagon "holds up" his humour to the concluding speech—"Et moi, voir ma chère cassette." The adapter, as we have seen, has Goldingham leave the stage, not thinking of his money, but cursing Isabella and Theodore, who have duped him by their marriage. After his exit, he

[10] *Ibid.*, III, 97-100.

is practically forgotten;[11] and the characters from the subplot again step to the foreground. The final impression is that Shadwell's play concerns itself as much with the cheats and the fools as with the miser and his household. That the English writer neglected the opportunity for humour-portraiture inherent in the character of the miser and that he was willing to give so much space to riotous scenes in taverns and stews shows how he was turning from the type of play which he had praised so highly in the preceding year[12] to a form of comedy based upon a less strict theory.

The subplot of *The Miser* echoes a device familiar to generations of English theatregoers—the gulling of a fool by a company of cheats. Middleton treats such a happening in *Michaelmas Term*, when he causes Quomodo and Shortyard for a time to get the better of Easy. Jonson, in *Bartholomew Fair*, makes Cokes an easy victim for Edgworth and his crew; Brome, in *The Sparagus Garden*, shows Tim Hoyden in the rôle of dupe to the city sharpers; and Etherege, in *Love in a Tub*, causes Sir Nicholas Cully to be made drunk and cheated by Wheedle and Palmer.

Timothy, unlike the usual prey of these rogues, is not a country squire, but the "Son of a Citizen." Happening upon Theodore and his companions at Chatolin's, he lets them understand that he is "no such contemptible Person" and that he has "Money enough" about him. Rant and Hazard, who cannot allow so likely a quarry to escape, engage him in play and ply him with drink. While intoxicated, he goes to Theodora, tells her of his recent exploits, and attempts to kiss her, but is of course repulsed. His hectoring comrades later accompany him upon a roaring expedition, during the course of which they break many windows and fight with the watch. In the morning, after this night of carousing, Timothy is shown the ring, license, and parson's certificate which prove him married to Joyce.[13]

Squeeze, the money lender, is as easy a victim for sharpers as his son. While in the apartment of Lettice, he not only pays a pretended bill for twenty pounds, but promises his mistress an addi-

[11] The Justice refers to him as having shut himself up in his closet (p. 104); and Theodore, in the closing speech, confesses to have transgressed in his duty to his father (p. 105). Nevertheless, the emphasis in the final moments of the play is upon the characters from the subplot.

[12] In his preface to *The Humourists*.

[13] Shadwell, III, 42, 70-71, 84-86, 89-90.

tional fifty pounds on the morrow, as well as a present of plate. When the roaring in the streets becomes unbearable, he retires with Lettice, leaving Mrs. Cheatly to bar the door. This precaution proves of little avail; for the house is entered and the unfortunate money lender has to make his escape from the window. The watch are not slow to arrest him and hale him before the justice. At his wit's ends, Squeeze asks advice from the ever present Mrs. Cheatly, who urges him to own Lettice for his wife. He acts according to her counsel, and thereby "saves his reputation."[14]

The other types represented in the subplot occur frequently in Shadwell's later plays. The harlots, Lettice and Joyce, are lower down in the scale than Friske and Striker of *The Humourists.* Their meeting in the concluding scene where, through marriage, one has become the mother-in-law of the other is amusingly handled.[15] Rant and Hazard, members of a long line of sharking bullies, represent Shadwell's initial attempts at drawing these types of character. The unfortunate constable and watch, who are worsted in the fight with the roarers, appear again in *The Woman-Captain, The Squire of Alsatia,* and *The Scowrers.*

The Miser is not important for the intrinsic merit of its contents. It is a transitional play in which Shadwell, for the time being, turns his back upon the kind of comedy he had written in *The Sullen Lovers* and *The Humourists* and looks ahead towards a freer type in which unswerving consistency in characterization is not the distinguishing trait.

[14] *Ibid.,* III, 80 ff., 101-102.

[15] *Ibid.,* III, 104-105.

CHAPTER X

EPSOM-WELLS

E*PSOM-WELLS*, produced in December, 1672, marks a decided advance upon Shadwell's earlier plays. Not only did it bring "great Profit to the Company" at the theatre, but it was more than once performed at court.[1] It was doubtless revived around 1693; for, in that year, a new edition of the play "As it is Acted by Their Majesties Servants" appeared. For this production, Purcell probably contributed the music for the interpolated song, "Leave these useless arts."[2]

No less a person than Steele writes of Bullock's extraordinary ability in the part of Bisket. In the seventh issue of *The Tatler*, he thus describes the benefit performance of April 25, 1709:[3]

> This evening, the comedy, called "Epsom Wells," was acted for the benefit of Mr. Bullock, who, though he is a person of much wit and ingenuity, has a peculiar talent of looking like a fool, and therefore excellently well qualified for the part of Biskett in this play. I cannot indeed sufficiently admire his way of bearing a beating, as he does in this drama, and that with such a natural air and propriety of folly, that one cannot help wishing the whip in one's own hand; so richly does he seem to deserve his chastisement. Skilful actors think it a very peculiar happiness to play in a scene with such as top their parts. Therefore I cannot but say, when the judgment of any good author directs him to write a beating for Mr. Bullock from Mr. William Pinkethman, or for Mr. William Pinkethman from Mr. Bullock, those excellent players seem to be in their most shining circumstances, and please me more, but with a different sort of delight, than that which I receive from those grave scenes of Brutus and Cassius, or Antony and Ventidius. The whole comedy is very just, and the low part of human life represented with much humour and wit.

Pinkethman, whom this writer couples with Bullock in his bestowal of praise, was the recipient of a benefit on April 2, 1715, at which

[1] See pp. 25-26.

[2] This song does not appear in the 1673, 1676, or 1693 editions. It is printed in Book II of Hudgebutt's *Thesaurus Musicus* (1694) as "A New Song in *Epsome-Wells* set by *Mr. Henry Purcell.*" See *Works of Henry Purcell,* XVI (London, 1906), xxxiii.

[3] See Genest, II, 417.

time he appeared in his old rôle of Fribble.[4] *Epsom-Wells* seems not to have been revived after July, 1726, when it was given two performances at Lincoln's Inn Fields.[5]

Shadwell had been charged with not being the real author of this play by "some impotent and envious Scriblers, and some industrious Enemies,"[6] and therefore found it necessary to insert a couplet in his own defence in the "Prologue to the King and Queen. Spoken at *White-Hall*." After boasting that this honor of a royal performance shows his life not to have been lived in vain, he refers to his play in these words:

> *If this for him had been by others done,*
> *After this Honour sure they'd claim their own.*

In *MacFlecknoe*, it will be remembered, Dryden wrote two lines which have at various times been interpreted to mean that Sedley assisted Shadwell in *Epsom-Wells:*

> But let no alien Sedley interpose,
> To lard with wit thy hungry Epsom prose.

Dryden may here have reference to the fact that the prologue for this play, no better or worse than the average Restoration prologue, was written by Sir *C. S.;* or he may have confused Shadwell's words in his dedication of *A True Widow* with those in his dedication of *Epsom-Wells.* The former Shadwell addressed to Sir Charles Sedley, whom he thanks for the "Correction and Alteration" Sedley has bestowed upon that comedy, and who he wishes had reviewed all his plays. Again, "Epsom" may have been used by Dryden without reference to any specific composition of Shadwell's. The word occurs in another line of *MacFlecknoe*, "The like was ne'er in Epsom blankets tost." This statement cannot refer to *Epsom-Wells*, since that play contains no allusion to tossing in a blanket. Because of these facts, there seems no basis for the assumption that Dryden's couplet is evidence of Sedley's assistance in the composition of *Epsom-Wells.* Furthermore, Sedley's

[4] *Ibid.*, II, 553.

[5] *Ibid.*, III, 183. Genest also lists performances at Drury Lane on July 11, 1702; December 18, 1708; December 1, 1710; February 23, October 15, 1712; June 9, December 16, 1713; December 9, 1715; March 24, May 23, 1724; at the Haymarket on October 17, 1709.

[6] Foot-note to the "Prologue Spoken at Whitehall" in the quarto.

comedy *The Mulberry Garden* (1668) is not superior in language or action to this play. A mixture of prose and heroic couplet, with plot reminiscent of Molière and Fletcher, it lacks the life and movement that *Epsom-Wells* possesses. If Sedley had "larded with wit" this comedy of Shadwell's, why do his own experiments in dramatic form appear so lame in contrast?

The plot is lively and entertaining. Carolina, a young lady of "Wit, Beauty, and Fortune," dissatisfied with Epsom society, desires to leave the Wells, but her friend Lucia wishes to remain so as to become acquainted with two gentlemen of "Wit and Pleasure," Raines and Bevil. The opportunity for this meeting presents itself when the young women, while strolling down the street in masks, are approached by Kick and Cuff. In order to escape the insults of these "sharking, cowardly Bullies," they appeal to Raines and Bevil, who are passing by, for protection. These gentlemen persuade Lucia and Carolina to unmask and procure the promise of a later meeting. In the meantime, Bevil has been pursuing an intrigue with Mrs. Woodly, whose husband professes an interest in Carolina.

When the two men later appear upon the duelling-ground to answer a summons which they believe has been sent by Kick and Cuff, the ladies are on hand to see the fun. Kick and Cuff happen along and cannot understand why Raines and Bevil accuse them of being late. Resenting the name of "cowards" by which Bevil addresses them and feeling assured that any fighting will be stopped, they draw their swords. Lucia and Carolina come to the rescue and confess sending the challenge, which is their fulfillment of the promise given at the earlier interview. This meeting has been observed by Mrs. Woodly's maid, Peg, who immediately informs her mistress.

Filled with jealousy, Mrs. Woodly sends Bevil a note signed "Carolina," appointing a place and time of meeting. He naturally mistakes Mrs. Woodly, who comes to the rendezvous masked, for his new love, and addresses her by the name of that lady. She soon makes herself known, however, and upbraids him for his lack of constancy. Angered by discovering herself no longer foremost in his affections, she determines to estrange Lucia and Carolina from their new friends, and therefore informs them that Bevil and

Raines have boasted of their acquaintance throughout the entire town. Although the young ladies turn from their lovers, Bevil insists upon explaining the matter to Carolina. In the conversation which follows, he announces that he is pursued by Mrs. Woodly; and Carolina confesses that she has been perpetually importuned by Mr. Woodly. At this, husband and wife, who unknown to each other have been spying upon the lovers, step forward in great anger. Mrs. Woodly accuses Bevil of lying. Bevil, in turn, demands satisfaction of Woodly for traducing him to Carolina.

Mrs. Woodly, determined to be rid of either Bevil or her husband, then sends to the former a challenge which he thinks is from Woodly, and confesses to the latter that Bevil, after again soliciting her virtue, awaits her in the field behind their lodgings. Woodly hastens to the supposed place of meeting and, after being disarmed in the ensuing duel, asks Bevil if he did not come to meet another person. Upon seeing the challenge, he is greatly angered at what he knows to be the work of his wife. Thereupon, he hastens to his lodgings where, in the presence of friends, the Woodlys sign articles of separation, kiss, and part. Lucia and Carolina, not at present willing to marry Raines and Bevil, admit them to their company as "servants."

Joined to the main intrigue are two subplots: that of Clodpate and that of the citizens and their wives. The country justice Clodpate, who bears an inveterate hatred towards London, woos Lucia; but, when he learns of her predilections for that city, he quickly turns to Carolina. Mrs. Woodly's maid, Peg, hearing of his humour, urges her sister Mrs. Jilt, with whom Bevil has been familiar, to feign a love for the country. This she does; and Clodpate, after he has been gagged, dressed like a ghost, and frightened while awaiting a supposed meeting with Carolina, eagerly marries her. Immediately after the ceremony, Mrs. Jilt appears in her true character of a Londoner and makes all sorts of demands upon her disappointed spouse. Peg offers to release him from his marriage for a reward, which he willingly pays. She then produces the parson, who proves to be Mr. Woodly's man in disguise.

The other subplot has for its theme the cuckolding of Bisket and Fribble. The former, a hen-pecked comfit maker, and the latter, a surly and domineering haberdasher, spend their days in bowling and their nights in drinking. Mrs. Bisket, observing the humble attitude Mrs. Fribble takes towards her husband, urges her to pluck up spirit. Acting upon this advice, Mrs. Fribble asks her husband if he has the confidence to leave her when he suggests to Bisket that they make merry in the evening. This unexpected display of energy on the part of his wife causes Fribble to think her distracted. When, however, she "gives him a Dash on the Chaps," he is no longer able to restrain his anger, but beats her until she cries for pardon. Bisket, impressed with what he has seen, determines to treat his wife in a similar manner. Mrs. Bisket does not accept the epithet of "Sow" with calmness. After striking her husband, who returns the blow, she renders him helpless by snatching away his stick and beating him unmercifully. When Fribble comes to the assistance of his friend, she turns upon him and gives him a taste of the same treatment. Both men are then forced to leave her sole victor on the field of battle. In the evening, the wives take Kick and Cuff to their lodgings, where the husbands discover them later in a compromising situation.[7] Bisket and Fribble go for the constable and watch, who arrest the wives and lovers and hale them before the justice. Recognizing in Kick and Cuff the persons who had won his money earlier in the day, Clodpate sends them to jail. The wives fall upon their knees and beg for forgiveness, which the husbands quickly grant. Bisket is overjoyed to receive his wife's promise that he may command her from that day.

In plot-details, there are but few reminiscences of the work of Jonson. The marriage of Clodpate to Mrs. Jilt, who proves very different from the person he had supposed her to be, may have been suggested by the experience of Morose with Epicoene in *The Silent Woman.* In both plays, the unlucky husband is released from what proves to be a "trick-wedding" by agreeing to pay a sum of money to the instigator of the match.[8] The treatment of Bisket, who is

[7] This situation is referred to in prologue to Duffett's *Psyche Debauched* (1675). Fribble, Cuff, and Kick are mentioned in "Tunbridge-Wells, A Satyr," printed in *Works of . . . the Earls of Rochester and Roscommon,* 3d ed. (London, 1709), pp. 66-67.

[8] After Morose signs a paper allowing his nephew £500 yearly for the rest of his life and the remainder of his estate after death, Dauphine removes Epicoene's peruke and other disguises (*The Silent Woman,* Act V). Clodpate signs a warrant provided by Peg, who thereupon pulls the disguise from the so-called parson (Shadwell, II, 285).

beaten by his wife,[9] may owe something to the behavior towards Captain Otter of his termagant spouse.[10] Somewhat similar to the passage in which Littlewit displays his wife's beauties to Winwife,[11] is the episode in which Bisket and Fribble vie with each other in calling the attention of Kick and Cuff to the attractive qualities of their wives.[12] The foolish husband in *Bartholomew Fair* praises his love's "strawberry breath, cherry lips, apricot cheeks, and soft velvet head" and urges his friend to kiss her; likewise, the citizens in *Epsom-Wells* exhibit their wives' "delicious" eyebrows, "pretty, plump, red lips," "sweet breaths," "stately" foreheads, "fine, round, small white" hands, and tell them to kiss their newly made acquaintances.

The main plot, in general outline, bears a closer resemblance to *She Would If She Could* than to any other play.[13] Etherege's second venture, which Shadwell in his preface to *The Humourists* called "the best Comedy that has been written since the Restauration of the Stage," was first produced in 1668, on which occasion Mrs. Shadwell appeared as Lady Cockwood. In this comedy, Sir Oliver and Lady Cockwood go to the city for practically the same reasons that Mr. and Mrs. Woodly betake themselves to the Wells. As Lady Cockwood pursues Courtal,[14] so Mrs. Woodly makes advances to Bevil.[15] The two young men, Courtal and Freeman, are anxious to become acquainted with Ariana and Gatty who flirt with them while masked[16] in a manner similar to that pursued by Lucia and Carolina during their first encounter with Raines and Bevil.[17] In each play, the men exact promises for a later meeting from the women. Both Lady Cockwood and Mrs. Woodly, in order to discover the state of their gallants' affections, counterfeit letters to the men in the girls' names.[18] Lady Cockwood is angered when she hears from Sentry that Courtal because of an important engagement

[9] Shadwell, II, 264.

[10] Mrs. Otter (*The Silent Woman,* Act IV, scene I), after overhearing her husband's uncomplimentary description, "falls upon him, and beats him."

[11] *Bartholomew Fair,* Act I.

[12] Shadwell, II, 240-241.

[13] This general resemblance was first noticed by James Wright in *Country Conversations: Being an Account of some Discourses That Happen'd in a Visit to the Country last Summer, on divers Subjects; Chiefly Of the Modern Comedies, Of Drinking, Of Translated Verse, Of Painting and Painters, Of Poets and Poetry* (London, 1694), pp. 5-6.

[14] Etherege, *Works* (ed. Verity), pp. 123, 131-133.

[15] Shadwell, II, 197.

[16] Etherege, pp. 140-145.

[17] Shadwell, II, 199-202.

[18] Etherege, p. 189; Shadwell, II, 234.

—the anticipated interview with Gatty—cannot meet her in Gray's Inn Walks. Mrs. Woodly, after sending the letter to Bevil, goes to the rendezvous and becomes enraged upon discovering his love for Carolina. Because of the rebuff, Lady Cockwood tells her husband that Courtal "misconstruing [her] civility, in most unseemly language made a foul attempt upon [her] honour."[19] Impelled by jealousy, Mrs. Woodly also confides to her husband that "*Bevil* . . . again had the Impudence to sollicite [her] Virtue."[20] Lady Cockwood resorts to this device in order that Sir Oliver shall hate Courtal and justify her banishing him from the house; Mrs. Woodly, on the other hand, desires a duel, hoping that either her husband or former lover will be killed. At the close of Etherege's comedy, Ariana and Gatty agree to admit Courtal and Freeman in the quality of servants, but finally seem willing to comply with Sir Joslin's suggestion that they hasten the wedding ceremony.[21] In *Epsom-Wells*, Lucia and Carolina, after seeing what failures Bisket, Fribble, and Woodly have made of matrimony, receive Raines and Bevil for a couple of servants "upon . . . good Behaviour." Bevil, however, feels assured that "one Fortnight's conversing" with him and his friend "will lay such a Scandal upon 'em, they'll be glad to repair to Marriage."[22]

Mr. Miles sees in Cuff, Kick, and Clodpate reminiscences of Acaste, Clitandre, and Alceste in *Le Misanthrope*,[23] but he neglects to cite specific references. Cuff and Kick are cheating bullies who succeed in cuckolding Bisket and Fribble; the marquises Acaste and Clitandre are suitors to Célimène. I am unable to discern the slightest resemblance between these characters or the actions in which they appear. Clodpate, like Alceste, is a fault-finder; but he is abusive only when talking of the city. On the other hand, he speaks of the country in terms of superlative praise. Alceste, it will be remembered, is disgusted with all human society because of the manifestations of insincerity which he sees displayed on every side.

Mr. Miles may be more correct when he calls attention to the resemblance between the final episode of Act IV and the first three scenes of *Le Médicin malgré lui*. In the former of these passages,

[19] Etherege, p. 193.
[20] Shadwell, II, 277.
[21] Etherege, p. 234.
[22] Shadwell, II, 287.
[23] Miles, *Influence of Molière on Restoration Comedy*, p. 230.

Fribble, after a vituperative combat with his wife during which she gives him a "Dash on the Chaps," beats her and forces her upon her knees to beg his pardon. When Bisket asks his neighbor to hold, Fribble threatens to "mischief" him. In the scenes from Molière, Sganarelle, after quarreling with his wife, Martine, seizes a stick and belabors her. Attracted by her cries, M. Robert comes to the rescue; but he is forced to draw back when Martine, after giving him a blow, vows she likes to have her husband beat her. Sganarelle then gives a taste of the stick to his zealous neighbor, who is forced to concede that his help is not wanted. Husband and wife agree to make up; but she determines under her breath that he will pay for his treatment. Shadwell must have been familiar with this episode from Lacy's adaptation, *The Dumb Lady; or The Farrier made Physician* (printed in 1672).[24] But he need not have had this particular passage from Molière in mind; for scenes of quarreling husbands and wives were in the tradition of English comedy from the days of Noah's Wife to those of Mrs. Snore.[25]

Despite the fact that *Epsom-Wells*, in some instances, resembles earlier plays, it would be quite incorrect to think of the comedy as anything but an original piece of work. To the watering-place of Epsom, situated fourteen miles from the metropolis, Shadwell transplants a group of Londoners from the drawing-rooms, Mulberry Garden, and Hyde Park. Hither he also brings from Cheapside, Bisket, Fribble and their wives, and, from Sussex, the Justice Clodpate. That the Wells was the gathering place of such a company as Shadwell depicts is attested by Pepys. On July 26, 1663, the diarist notes, "Up and to the Wells, where great store of citizens, which was the greatest part of the company, though there were some others of the better quality." While riding through the town, he was pleased to see so many citizens "that I could not have thought to have seen there or that they ever had it in their heads or purses to go down thither." On July 27, "it being much a warmer day than yesterday there was a great store of gallant com-

[24] *Dramatic Works of John Lacy* (Maidment-Logan ed.), p. 17 ff.

[25] When D'Avenant "corrected and enlarged" *The Wits* (originally presented in 1636) for performance in 1667, he considerably expanded the scenes in which Constable Snore, his wife, and neighbor Mrs. Queasy appear. These additions were first published in the folio edition of 1673.

pany, more than then to my greater pleasure." He also mentions the Bowling-Green "where I have seen so much mirth in my time," and observes that "under one of the trees on the common, a company got together that sung." Settle in his prologue to *The Empress of Morocco* alludes to the popularity of the Wells among another class of persons:

> *The* Wells *have stoln the* Vizar Masks *away.*
> *Now punk in penitential Drink begins,*
> *To purge the surfeit of her* London *Sins.*[26]

St. Évremonde correctly couples *Epsom-Wells* with *Bartholomew Fair* as plays in which the unity is preserved by representing "various things that happen to several persons in publick places."[27] There is, however, a difference between the methods employed by Shadwell and Jonson in dealing with these "publick-places." Shadwell makes Epsom merely the scene for his action, and introduces no characters primarily of the Wells. Jonson, on the other hand, used the Fair not only as the setting for his plot, but also as the natural environment for Ursula, the pig-woman, Leatherhead, the toyman, and Nightingale, the ballad-singer. These persons, essentially of the Fair, play important parts in the action.

But in addition to the unity noticed by St. Évremonde, there is a deeper unity in Shadwell's play—that of subject-matter. Marriage is the theme which unites the various threads of the plot of *Epsom-Wells.* The four groups of characters—Mr. and Mrs. Woodly; Bisket, Fribble, and their wives; Clodpate and Mrs. Jilt; Carolina, Lucia, Raines, and Bevil—combine to present an unfavorable picture of the wedded state.

Woodly, although describing wedlock to Raines and Bevil as "the happiest Condition of Life," expresses his real opinion to Carolina when he depicts the marital relationship as "the least Engagement of all; for that only points out where Man cannot love." Mrs. Woodly, who "values herself . . . much upon her Virtue" and thus convinces her husband she is true to him, is known

[26] See also epilogue to Ravenscroft's *The Wrangling Lovers* (London, 1677) and prologue and epilogue to Tate's *A Duke and No Duke* (London, 1685).

[27] *Works of Monsieur de St. Evremond, Made English from the French Original: with Life of the Author: by Mr. des Maizeaux* (2d Edition, London, 1728), II, 171.

by Bevil to be "a damn'd Wife, but a very good Mistress." When this ill-mated pair at length find out the truth about each other, they gladly sign articles of separation.

Mrs. Bisket and Mrs. Fribble also play the game of deceit. While the husbands are drinking and making merry, the wives are entertaining stray gallants. Mrs. Fribble has discovered that her husband can be kept away if she begs him to remain at home. Mrs. Bisket has her helpmate even better trained: he goes so far as to invite gentlemen of her choosing to visit her. When the wives are revealed in their true characters, Bisket and Fribble do not follow the example of the Woodlys. After they bring Kick and Cuff before the justice, their anger subsides as they think of the damages that can be secured when these bullies are tried before a "good substantial Jury of all married Men."

The outcome of these matrimonial experiments, as well as the short-lived marriage of Jilt and Clodpate, has been observed by Carolina and Lucia. "See what Matrimony comes to," is Lucia's comment. Their lovers, Raines and Bevil, who have run riot among the women of the Wells, but who are now tamed to a condition of wedlock, cannot prevail upon these "Ladies of Wit, Beauty, and Fortune" to marry them. Lucia and Carolina are not willing to venture their future upon such an uncertain bark. Instead, they tell the men that they will not accept them as husbands, but that they will receive them as "servants" upon good behavior.

This solution seems the logical result of the preceding action; and the play closes with the men acceding to these terms, while Woodly is treading on air for joy of being rid of his wife. Then comes the epilogue in which the dramatist tags a moral to his play. In this, Shadwell scolds the audience for the condition in which matrimony is held and begs the gallants to take wives:

> *Repent, for Shame, your* Covent-Garden *Lives.*
> *Fear not the Fate of us, whom in the Play*
> *Our bawdy Poet Cuckolded to-Day;*
> *For ours are* Epsom *Water-drinking Wives,*
> *And few in that lewd Town lead stricter Lives:*
> *But for the rest he'd have it understood,*
> *By representing few ill Wives, he wou'd*
> *Advance the Value of the many Good.*

The dialogue in *Epsom-Wells* is more spirited than that in Shadwell's three earlier comedies. The scenes between the lovers move with animation. A passage near the end of the second act may serve as an example. While Bevil and Raines are awaiting the persons who had challenged them to a duel, Carolina and Lucia appear masked. Not recognizing their acquaintances of the morning, the men begin a flirtation; whereupon the women reveal their identity.

CAROLINA: Who says they are not a couple of Constant Men?
BEVIL: What, I warrant, you think we did not know you?
LUCIA: O! yes, as *Falstaff* did the true Prince, by Instinct. You are brisk Men, I see; you run at all.
RAINES: The wilder we are, the more Honour you'll have in reclaiming us.
BEV: 'Tis in your Power to make us a couple of as constant dull Fellows as ye could wish.
CARO: Ye have Constancy enough of all Conscience, for the Use we shall have of it.
LUCIA: And for Dulness, for our own Sakes, we do not wish it you; since I find ye are resolv'd to be acquainted with us, whether we will or no.
CARO: Is it not pity that witty Men should be so scandalous, that if we converse with them, we must do it with the same Privacy that Statesmen debauch?
BEV: If Wit be a scandalous Thing, you are the most scandalous Women I have met with; but, methinks, Fools should rather be scandalous, since they can have but one way of passing their Time with you.
LUCIA: You rally well, but your Wit is never without Extravagancy; you drink *Burgundy* perpetually, and Scower, as you call it.
BEV: We hate debauching, but love Complaisance, Madam. And can no more deny a Friend that calls for another Bottle, than you can deny to turn up a Card at *Ombre*.
RAINES: We use Wine, Madam, to elevate our Thoughts; but Love has done it for me a pleasanter Way.
BEV: And, Madam, your Beauty has already reclaim'd me.
LUCIA: If you're as soon Drunk, as you're in love, you're the weakest Drinkers in Christendom.
RAINES: You see, Madam, the Strength and Spirit of your Beauty.
LUCIA: For Love, I bar you; can't we converse, without remembring we are of different Sexes?
CARO: If you will accept of such Conditions, we may sometimes admit you into our Privy-Council.
RAINES: Would you have us spend our Time like some visiting Fools,

that never aspire at more, than playing at *Langtriloo* with Women, all Days of their Lives?

BEV: Our Communication would then be as dull and insipid, as the Mirth of Statesmen.

In many respects, *Epsom-Wells* is the best of Shadwell's first four comedies. The action is rapid and lively, and is not clogged with scenes in which humour-characters tediously parade their eccentricities. Although Clodpate,[28] with his hatred for London, is as consistently drawn as Crazy or Sir Positive, he does not obtrude himself so tiresomely as do those characters from the earlier comedies. The dialogue is sprightly; nevertheless, as usual in Shadwell's plays, it is frequently coarse. The setting must have impressed the theatregoers who, in 1672, were accustomed to having the scenes of their realistic comedies laid in London, as being very original. It seems reasonable to place *Epsom-Wells* with *An Evening's Love*, *She Would If She Could*, and *Love In A Wood* as the four best comedies produced on the English stage in the years 1668-1672.

[28] The Epistle Dedicatory to Settle's *The Female Prelate: Being the History of the Life and Death of Pope Joan. A Tragedy* (London, 1680), contains a reference to *Epsom-Wells*. The writer, in speaking of himself, says "nor am I like *Clodpate's* Fidler, that sings against his Conscience." The passage alluded to is found in Shadwell, II, 232-234. Clodpate is referred to also in "The Stage Vindicated: A Satyr. By I. H. Esq.," printed in *The Muses Mercury, for the Month of July, 1707*, p. 159. "*Hugh Clodpate* of Merry Memory" is mentioned by John Dennis in *Original Letters, Familiar, Moral, and Critical* (London, 1721), I, 164. Thomas Rymer (*Short View of Tragedy*, p. 113), in discussing the passage where Othello stops the fight between Cassio and Montano, remarks: "Consider also throughout this whole Scene, how the Moorish General proceeds in examining into this *Rout;* No Justice *Clod-pate* could go on with more Phlegm and deliberation." The Reverend Richard Davies confused the names of Shadwell's justice and Shakespeare's Shallow when he wrote, some time between 1688 and 1708, in the earliest extant account of Shakespeare as a poacher: "his [Shakespeare's] revenge was so great that he [i.e., Sir Thomas Lucy] is his Justice Clodpate."

CHAPTER XI

THE VIRTUOSO

THE VIRTUOSO, the comedy in which Shadwell returned to that form of dramatic writing abandoned upon the comparative failure of *The Humourists*, was acted in May, 1676.[1] It evidently was well liked; for Gildon, in 1699, vouches that this "Play . . . has always found Success."[2] It may have been revived after Shadwell's elevation to the laureateship; for, in 1691, an edition "As it is Acted By Their Majesties Servants" was published. In 1704, the comedy was again reprinted. The final production occurred upon March 31, 1705, at which time the play was performed at a benefit for Cave Underhill at the theatre in Lincoln's Inn Fields, "it being the last time of acting in this house."[3]

The Virtuoso tells of the love of Bruce and Longvil for Clarinda and Miranda, the nieces and wards of Sir Nicholas Gimcrack. In order to obtain admittance to his house, they inform his friend, Sir Formal Trifle, that they are interested in scientific experiments; and, in consequence, they are invited to be present at the dissection of a lobster. But Lady Gimcrack determines to have these "Gentlemen of Wit and Sense" for herself. Upon finding Bruce alone, she attempts with many protests of honor to lure him into a grotto. She is prevented by Longvil, to whom she also conveys the broadest hints. The fruition of her design, however, is thwarted by Sir Formal, who escorts the gentlemen to Sir Nicholas. The virtuoso, who had previously displayed the "speculative part of swimming," now describes his numerous curious discoveries. This discourse is of slight interest to Bruce and Longvil, who, wishing to be alone with the nieces, arrange for Hazard to summon Lady Gimcrack and for Flirt to send for Sir Nicholas.

Living with the virtuoso is his uncle Snarl. Although a professed hater of the vices of the age, he has a mistress, Figgup, whom he meets in the room later visited by Lady Gimcrack and

[1] See pp. 30-31.
[2] P. 178.
[3] Genest, II, 329. Underhill probably acted the part of Snarl.

Hazard. The two are forced to hide at the approach of the new-comers, who, in turn, are interrupted by Sir Nicholas and Flirt. Lady Gimcrack is soon frightened from the woodhole in which she has taken refuge and confronts her husband, who charges her with being false. The two bandy accusations and explanations back and forth until the virtuoso is persuaded of his wife's innocence. Then Snarl is discovered, and straightway becomes the laughing-stock of all. In order to be revenged, he incites a band of weavers against his nephew, whom he accuses of inventing the engine-loom. The rabble are about to break open the door when they are frightened away by the pistol-shots of Bruce and Longvil.

By promising to wear a certain ring and bracelet, Clarinda persuades Sir Formal to conduct her and her sister to Sir Samuel's masquerade. At this entertainment, Lady Gimcrack takes her nieces' lovers on different occasions to the retiring-room and gives each a note. When these letters are opened later, Bruce's is signed "Miranda" and Longvil's "Clarinda." At this disclosure, the men accuse each other of treachery and commence fighting. The girls, who have watched the whole affair, reveal themselves and inform their lovers that the notes are in Lady Gimcrack's handwriting. Bruce then discovers that he has been loving Clarinda with a passion which is not returned. Longvil, on his part, learns that he has been wasting his sighs upon Miranda, who really loves Bruce. Such a predicament offers but slight difficulty to these "Gentlemen of Wit and Sense," who quite readily turn to the women who love them.

Sir Nicholas threatens to put aside his wife because she, mistaking him for Hazard at the masquerade, had expressed pleasure in fooling him earlier in the day. Lady Gimcrack then announces that she will publish the letters he has received from his mistresses and send them to Gresham College. After the steward informs him that engineers and glass-makers have seized upon his property for debt, the virtuoso is willing to forgive his wife; but Lady Gimcrack thinks that to preserve her estate without encumbrance is better than to return to her erratic husband. Sir Formal arrives with the announcement that he has married Clarinda; he discovers, however, after the wearer of the bracelet and ring has unmasked, that his wife is the maid Betty. Snarl further thwarts his nephew by becoming the husband of Figgup. Sir Nicholas tells his nieces that their money, which he has in trust, will redeem his estate; but they inform him that they have transferred their guardianship to Bruce and Longvil. Deserted by all to whom he might turn for assistance, the virtuoso bemoans the fact that he has studied spiders instead of mankind.

Like *The Sullen Lovers* and *The Humourists*, *The Virtuoso* is built around a love story. The two pairs of lovers are bothered by a group of eccentric humours whom they present to the audience by means of asides and characterizing speeches.[4] The four humours designated by the author as "entirely new" are Sir Nicholas Gimcrack, Sir Formal Trifle, Sir Samuel Hearty, and Snarl.

Sir Nicholas Gimcrack "does not," says Pope, "maintain his character with equal strength to the end."[5] While in his study explaining the wonders of his discoveries to Bruce and Longvil, he is every inch the virtuoso. When, however, he forsakes his laboratory in order to keep an appointment with Flirt, he sloughs off this character of the preoccupied scientist and appears as the conventional man of the Restoration world engaged in the usual intrigue. Upon returning to his scientific apparatus, he again becomes the virtuoso. He "holds up his humour" admirably in his final speech: "Well, now 'tis time to study for Use: I will presently find out the Philosopher's Stone; I had like to have gotten it last Year, but that I wanted *May-Dew*, it being a dry Season."[6]

Sir Formal is a much more consistent bit of character portrayal than Sir Nicholas.[7] Priding himself upon the floridity of his ora-

[4] Shadwell, I, 316, 317, 324, 325, etc.

[5] Joseph Spence, *Anecdotes, Observations and Characters, of Books and Men* (London, 1820), p. 13. In his discussion of Aristophanes, Thomas Rymer writes: "The *Vertuoso*'s Character, and *Ben Johnson*'s *Alchymist* give some shadow of his *Clouds*." *A Short View of Tragedy* (London, 1693), p. 24.

[6] Shadwell, I, 416. The author of *The Tatler*, Nos. 216 and 221, gives his virtuoso the name of Sir Nicholas Gimcrack.

[7] Sir Formal is twice mentioned in other plays by Shadwell. In *A True Widow*, Lump says to Lady Cheatly, "I walk to *Hampstead*, dine at the *Queen's-Head*, come back in my Coach, visit Sir *Formal Trifle*" (*Works*, III, 129). In *The Woman-Captain*, Mrs. Gripe thus addresses Phillis, "Dear Fair One, if you had not resolv'd to see me, your Letter had been in vain; if I could tell you my Transport at the Reading of it, I should be more eloquent than Sir *Formal* himself" (*Works*, III, 416).

Tate, in his preface to *Brutus of Alba* (London, 1678), after referring to the "*Capital crime of inserting* Learning *into his Play*," writes: "*Sir* Formal *got rid of the* Silk-weavers *with* much Confusion." Otway, in the preface to *Don Carlos*, speaks of a "certain writer" as a "fine facetious witty person, as my friend Sir Formal has it."

tory, he never forgets his bent. His "Speeches are all so subtilly design'd, that whatever [he speaks] in Praise of any Thing, with very little Alteration, will serve in praise of the contrary." On two occasions he is rendered ridiculous by this belief in the efficacy of oratory. When the lovers desire to be rid of him, they draw him to the trap-door leading to Sir Nicholas' vault and urge him to compose an oration upon a mouse caught in a trap. Unable to resist the temptation of displaying his gift, he commences a foolish polysyllabic harangue with disastrous result: the trap is sprung, and his fate becomes that of the animal he has been describing. In the last act, when the weavers are storming Sir Nicholas' house with the angry demands that the inventor of the engine-loom show himself, Sir Formal is ready to meet them with eloquence, a weapon more potent than gunpowder. He tells the mob that they "will be soundly punish'd upon a *Quare fremuerunt Gentes*" if they destroy his friend's property. After he has continued speaking of "Passion . . . which with its sudden, and, alas! too violent Circumgyrations does too often shipwreck those that are agitated by it; while it turns them into such giddy Confusion, that they can no longer trim the Sails of Reason, or steer by the Compass of Judgment," one of the weavers vows that his tongue is well hung, "but I know not what he means by all this Stuff." Refusing to listen longer, they beat and kick him, a treatment described by the unfortunate Sir Formal as a "Barbarity, which *Scythians* would blush at." Because of being tricked into marriage with Betty, the orator is cleansed of his mania for florid speeches: "I am amaz'd! I am struck dumb! I ne'er shall speak again!"[8]

Snarl is described in the dramatis personae as an "old pettish Fellow, a great Admirer of the last Age, and a Declaimer against the Vices of this; and privately very vicious himself." He decries the women of the day: "they have so many Tricks to disguise themselves, washing, painting, patching, and their damn'd ugly new-fashion'd Dresses, that a Man knows not what to make on 'em." He cannot "endure to see Plays, since Women came on the Stage." What the theatres now offer are "either damn'd insipid dull Farces, confounded toothless Satyrs, or plaguy rhiming Plays." He continues his fault-finding to the end. Even after his intrigue with

[8] Shadwell, I, 366, 367, 398, 413.

Figgup has been discovered, he rails at the people who are attending Sir Samuel's masquerade: "The Men are all Rogues and Fools, and the Women all Strumpets, by the Mass, or which are ten times worse, scandalous honest Women. In sadness, it is a shame such Bawdy doings should be suffer'd in a civil Nation. . . . It was not so in the last Age."[9]

Sir Samuel Hearty, "a brisk, amorous, adventurous, unfortunate Coxcomb," "that thinks that all Mirth consists in Noise, Tumult, and violent Laughter," is a tiresome bit of characterization. He is forever appearing before Miranda in disguise. In his continued use of such expressions as "Tace is Latin for a candle" and "Whip-stitch," he does not square with Shadwell's definition of a "humour." In the epistle dedicatory to this play, the author says "Nor do I count those Humours, which a great many do; that is to say, such as consist in using one or two By-words."

The Virtuoso contains echoes of Shadwell's earlier comedies. Sir Formal's comments upon the floridity of his style recall similar remarks by Drybob. Sir Formal marries Betty masked, thinking her Clarinda, as Drybob and Briske marry Friske and Bridget masked, believing their brides to be Theodosia.[10] Longvil is as willing to retire with Lady Gimcrack[11] as Bevil is with Mrs. Woodly.[12] In *The Virtuoso*, one may also note a resemblance to *She Would If She Could*, a comedy which is undoubtedly echoed in *Epsom-Wells*. As Lady Cockwood in Etherege's play pursues the lover of Gatty, so Lady Gimcrack attempts to win the gallants of her husband's nieces.[13]

Mr. Miles sees in Sir Formal, Sir Samuel, and Snarl reminiscences of Acaste, Clitandre, and Alceste, which he had also found in *Epsom-Wells*.[14] In my opinion, there is nothing in the Marquis Acaste to suggest the florid orator Sir Formal, nor is there any trait in the character of Clitandre that might have given hints for Sir Samuel, the fop who delights in disguises and nonsensical by-words.

[9] *Ibid.*, I, 326, 328, 407.

[10] *Ibid.*, I, 209.

[11] *Ibid.*, I, 355.

[12] *Ibid.*, II, 219.

[13] James Wright in *Country Conversations* (London, 1694), pp. 4-6, has something to say about the dependence of this play on *She Would If She Could*. He also mentions the "Men of Wit and Sense," who "admire the Name of *Lucretius*, and seem to have a Judgment above the Common Doctrines of Religion," an obvious reference to Bruce and Longvil. See Shadwell, I, 313-314.

[14] Miles, *Influence of Molière on Restoration Comedy*, p. 240.

The only point held in common by the fools of Shadwell and Molière is that they are in love with women who do not return their affection, a situation belonging to the stock equipment of English comedy. Alceste and Snarl resemble each other only in professing displeasure with contemporary life and manners; otherwise, they are very different persons. "The treatment of Clarinda and Miranda shows influence from *L'Ecole des Maris*," says Mr. Miles. Clarinda and Miranda are kept within the precincts of the house of their uncle, Sir Nicholas; Isabelle is carefully guarded by Sganarelle. The methods pursued by these women in the duping of their guardians are not the same.

In this comedy, Shadwell directs his satire against the experimental scientist or "virtuoso," a type associated with the newly-formed Royal Society.[15] This organization, which received a royal charter in 1662, had for its aim the purpose of improving "the knowledge of naturall things, and all useful Arts, Manufactures, Mechanick practises, Engynes and Inventions by Experiments," of attempting the recovery of "such allowable arts and inventions as are lost," and of examining "all systems, theories, principles, hypotheses, elements, histories, and experiments of things naturall, mathematicall, and mechanicall, invented, recorded, or practised by any considerable author ancient or modern."[16] It is needless to recall how the high ideals of this learned body were amply justified by the numerous important discoveries of its members. But some of the experiments described by the contributors to the *Philosophical Transactions* could easily impress a person of non-scientific mind, particularly if he was on the hunt for subjects inviting satire, as puerile or useless. It was to experiments of this nature that Shadwell chiefly turned when collecting material for the humour of Sir Nicholas Gimcrack.

Although Shadwell was the first playwright to present a full-length portrait of a virtuoso, he was not the first to make such a person the subject of dramatic satire. St. Serfe, in his episodic third act of *Tarugo's Wiles: or The Coffee House*,[17] writes some

[15] A good discussion of the satires upon seventeenth century science is contained in Carson S. Duncan's *The New Science and English Literature in the Classical Period* (University of Chicago dissertation, 1913).

[16] C. R. Weld, *History of the Royal Society* (London, 1848), I, 146-147.

[17] Tho. St. Serfe, *Tarugo's Wiles: or The Coffee House* (London, 1668), pp. 16 ff. Not mentioned by Duncan.

rather ponderous humor in ridicule of the virtuosi. Tarugo, in order to escape arrest, steps inside a coffee-house and exchanges clothes with a servant. At one of the tables, a group of customers is disputing over "the new invention of the *Vertuosi* of Transfusion of the blood." A member of the company maintains that he is able to perpetuate himself to eternity by this process of transfusion. "When once his own blood decays through Age, that by letting it out, and filling its place with the blood of a young Hog, then immediately he returns into the Age of Fifteen." A hog is chosen for this experiment, he concludes, because "it resembles most a Man." At another table, two customers are debating the merits of a painting. A third customer, commenting upon their remarks, observes, "I perceive these blades would fain be reckon'd among the *Vertuosi* of the time, for all their knowledge in Painting consists in the naming of famous Artists basely apply'd." In the meanwhile, two scholars indulge in learned gibberish while one instructs the other in the celestial-globe. A barber and a baker, who desire to be among this erudite gathering, come to the coffee-house. The baker is followed by his wife who complains of the way he has neglected her and their four children since he has become a "*Vertuoso*-Hunter." Among the items read from the Gazette is one to the effect that in Amsterdam "the States have taken the Allowance from the *Vertuosi* that were to find out the longitude, and bestow'd it upon their Gazeteers, for finding out dextrous lies to conceal the defeats they had from the English." After the master of the house has asked the company to leave because of a dispute which arose among a group of reformadoes, he designates the virtuosi as "a company of empty fellows."

This depicting of a conversation of virtuosi is the first considerable dramatic treatment of the subject before Shadwell's. With this rather heavy passage in mind, one is better able to appreciate the humor of the scene in which Sir Nicholas is introduced.[18] Bruce, Longvil, and Lady Gimcrack step into the virtuoso's study and discover that gentleman lying prone upon a table and learning to swim by imitating the motions of a frog.

BRUCE: Let's not interrupt them, Madam, yet, but observe a little this great Curiosity.

[18] Shadwell, I, 340 ff.

LONG: 'Tis a noble Invention.

L. GIM: 'Tis a thing the College [i.e., Gresham College] never thought of.

SIR NICH: Let me rest a little to respire. So; it is wonderful, my noble Friend, to observe the Agility of this pretty Animal, which, notwithstanding I impede its Motion, by the Detention of this Filum, or Thread, within my Teeth, which makes a Ligature about its Loins, and though by many sudden Stops I cause the Animal sometimes to sink or immerge, yet with indefatigable Activity it rises, and keeps almost its whole Body upon the Superficies, or Surface, of this humid Element.

SIR FORM: True, noble Sir; nor do I doubt but your Genius will make Art equal, if not exceed Nature: nor will this or any other Frog upon the Face of the Earth out-swim you. . . .

SIR NICH: . . . But having sufficiently refrigerated my Lungs by way of Respiration, I will return to my swimming—

SWIM MAST: Admirably well struck! rarely swum! he shall swim with any Man in *Europe*.

SIR FORM: Hold, Sir *Nicholas*; here are those Noble Gentlemen and Philosophers, whom I invited to kiss your Hands; and I am not a little proud of the Honour of being the grateful and happy Instrument of the Necessitude and familiar Communication, which is like to intervene between such excellent Virtuoso's.

BRUCE: We are *Sir Nicholas*'s and your most humble Servants.

LONG: We shall think our selves much honoured with the Knowledge of so celebrated a Virtuoso.

SIR NICH: You are right welcome into my poor Laboratory; and if in ought I can serve you in the way of Science, my Nature is diffusive, and I shall be glad of communicating with such eminent Virtuoso's, as I am let to know you are.

LONG: We pretend to nothing more than to be your humble Admirers.

SIR FORM: All the ingenious World are proud of Sir *Nicholas*, for his Physico-Mechanical Excellencies.

SIR NICH: I confess I have some Felicity that way; but were I as praecelling in Physico-mechanical Investigations, as you in Tropical Rhetorical Flourishes, I would yield to none.

LONG: How the Asses claw one another! (*Aside*.

BRUCE: We are both your Admirers. But of all quaint Inventions, none ever came near this of swimming.

SIR FORM: Truly, I opine it to be a most compendious Method, that in a Fortnight's Prosecution has advanced him to be the best Swimmer of *Europe*. Nay, it were possible to swim with any Fish of his Inches.

LONG: Have you ever try'd in the Water, Sir?

SIR NICH: No, Sir; but I swim most exquisitely on Land.

BRUCE: Do you intend to practise in the Water, Sir?

SIR NICH: Never, Sir; I hate the Water, I never come upon the Water, Sir.

LONG: Then there will be no use of Swimming.

SIR NICH: I content my self with the speculative Part of swimming, I care not for the Practick. I seldom bring any thing to Use; 'tis not my way. Knowledge is my ultimate End.

The interest of the virtuoso in matters having but remote, if any, relationship to the practical affairs of life is continually emphasized in Shadwell's satire. "To study for Use," says Sir Formal, "is base and mercenary, below the serene and quiet Temper of a sedate Philosopher." When Sir Nicholas avers that he has travelled all over Italy, Bruce naturally queries, "Did you not observe the Wisdom, Policies, and Customs of that ingenious People?" The virtuoso replies, "O, by no means! Tis below a Virtuoso to trouble himself with Men and Manners. I study Insects." At another time Longvil, who has asked Sir Nicholas why he weighs air, receives the answer, "To what end should I? to know what it weighs. O, Knowledge is a fine thing; why, I can tell to a grain what a Gallon of any Air in *England* weighs." Snarl calls his nephew a "Coxcomb, [who] has study'd these twenty Years about the nature of Lice, Spiders and Insects." Miranda designates the virtuoso as "One, who has broken his Brains about the nature of Maggots, who has studied these twenty Years to find out the several sorts of Spiders, and never cares for understanding Mankind." After Bruce, who is amazed at the ridiculous assertions made by Sir Nicholas, turns to his friend and exclaims, "No Phanatick, that has lost his Wits in Revelation, is so mad as this Fool," Longvil replies, "You are mistaken; this is but a faint Copy to some Originals among the Tribe."[19]

The objects of Sir Nicholas' curiosity are manifold. He has built a vault which is filled with bottled air collected for him by his factors throughout England. These men "bottle up Air, and weigh it in all Places, sealing the Bottles Hermetically." He has found that the air from Teneriff is the lightest, while the heaviest is from Sheerness and the Isle of Dogs.[20] He intends to publish a book on the geography of the moon, a subject on which he is amply

[19] *Ibid.*, I, 343, 362, 393, 331, 324, 395.

[20] *Ibid.*, I, 387. The virtuoso's bottled air is referred to in *Heraclitus Ridens*, No. 6, p. 2 (March 8, 1681) and in the *Letter to Sir John Sands* (*Works of Tho. Brown*, IV, 248). The other references in this paragraph are found in Shadwell, I, 394, 389, 341, 389, 360, 362.

able to write, having seen "Several Battles fought there." In addition to skill in the "*Rosacrucian* Learning," he has so "much advanced in the Art of flying, that [he] can already out-fly that ponderous Animal call'd a *Bustard;* nor should any Grey-Hound in *England* catch [him] in the calmest Day, before [he] got upon Wing." He has "Bills ready written for [the cure of] all Diseases"; he has perceived that the ant is "the most politick of all Insects" and that the government of these insects is a "Republick, resembling that of the States-General"; he is "in constant Correspondence with all the Virtuoso's in the North and North-East Parts" and is "beholden to *Finland, Lapland* and *Russia* for a great Part of [his] Philosophy." In short, Sir Nicholas Gimcrack is a burlesque *unus in omnibus* of all branches of scientific endeavor in the early years of the Restoration period.

Many of Shadwell's hits are mere exaggerations of passages in the *Philosophical Transactions of the Royal Society.*[21] Sir Nicholas' remark, "I my self have read a *Geneva* Bible by a Leg of Pork"[22] is but an absurd extension of Boyle's statement in the course of his discussion of the luminosity of a piece of veal, "having by me the curious *Transactions* of this month, I was able so to apply that flexible paper to some of the more resplendent spots, that I could plainly read divers consecutive letters of the Title."[23] Again, the reviewer of Sengwerdius's work on the tarantula affirms that all who are bitten by this insect "delight in Musick, and are thereby moved either to dance, or to gesticulate. . . . The cure of the poisonous effect, he [Sengwerdius] with others assigneth to be Musick, and the dancing, consequent thereto; which the Patients do perform as if taught: . . . the *Tune,* which is suitable to the person bitten, is also suitable to the *Tarantula* it self . . . as also, that not only men, but other Animals, as Cocks, Wasps, *&c* bitten

[21] See Duncan, *op. cit.,* p. 101, for list of articles in *Philosophical Transactions* used by Shadwell in his satire. Duncan errs twice. The letter from Leeuwenhoek, dated Delft, April 21, 1676, was printed in No. 127 of the *Transactions* (July 18, 1676), which was published at least a month and a half after the production of *The Virtuoso,* and so could not be the source for the "Eels in Vinegar." The description of the spider and the fly was also not derived from I. Wray's discussion in the *Transactions* for 1668. Both came from Hooke's *Micrographia,* a work not mentioned by Duncan as a source of Shadwell's satire.

[22] Shadwell, I, 393.

[23] "*Some Observations about Shining Flesh, made by the Honourable* Robert Boyle, Febr. 15, 1671/72" in *Philosophical Transactions,* VII, 5108 ff.

by the Spiders, do dance; and that the effects of the wound depend not on the life of the wounding Spider."[24] Sir Nicholas, who is interested in the effect of the music upon the tarantula, has observed that there are three sorts of this kind of spider, "Black, Grey and Red, that delight in three several Sorts and Modes of Musick." To Bruce's question concerning how he made this curious discovery, the virtuoso replies, "Why, I put them upon three several Chips in Water; then caus'd a Musician to play, first, a grave Pavin, or Almain, at which the black *Tarantula* only mov'd; it danc'd to it with a kind of grave Motion, much like the Benchers at the Revels."[25]

The Stentrophonical Tube, through which its inventor hopes "a General may speak himself to his whole Army; an Herald may make a proclamation, to be distinctly heard by many thousands; an Overseer of Works, give orders to many hundreds of Workmen, without changing his station,"[26] Sir Nicholas desires to perfect with the result that "there needs but one Parson to preach to a whole County; the King may then take all the Church-Lands into his Hands, and serve all *England* with his Chaplains in Ordinary." At the present experimental stage, Sir Nicholas has found that "of all Languages, none is heard so far as *Greek;* your *Ionick* Dialect of *Oio* does so roll in the Sound."[27] The actual experiment of transfusing the blood from a mangy into a sound dog resulted in "no alteration at all, any way, to be observed in the Sound Dog. But for the Mangy Dog, he was in about 10 dayes or a fortnights space perfectly cured."[28] Not so with Sir Nicholas—not only did the "*Mangy Spaniel* [become] sound, and the *Sound Bull-Dog* Mangy," but "the *Spaniel* became a *Bull-dog,* and the *Bull-dog* a *Spaniel.*"[29] Longvil mentions the results of transfusing the blood of a sheep into a mad-man, an undoubted allusion to an experiment performed upon Arthur Coga on November 23, 1667, with no ill effects.[30] This experiment, however,

[24] Account of Book, "I. W. Sengwerdius P. D. *de* Tarantula" in *Philosophical Transactions,* II, 660 ff.

[25] Shadwell, I, 362.

[26] "*An Account of the* Speaking Trumpet, *as it hath been contrived and published by Sir* Sam. Moreland *Knight and Baronet; together with its Uses both at Sea and Land,*" in *Philosophical Transactions,* VI, 3056-3058.

[27] Shadwell, I, 393-394.

[28] "An *Account Of another Experiment of* Transfusion, *viz. of Bleeding a* Mangy *into a* Sound *Dog,*" in *Philosophical Transactions,* II, 451-452.

[29] Shadwell, I, 343-344.

[30] "An Account Of the Experiment of *Transfusion,* practised upon a *Man* in *London,*" in *Philosophical Transactions,* II, 557-559.

is short of many performed by Sir Nicholas, whose patient became wholly ovine or sheepish, bleated perpetually, and chewed the cud.[31]

Frequently Shadwell's wording is almost identical with that of the *Transactions:*

Philosophical Transactions	*The Virtuoso*
He makes *Respiration* to be a Motion of the Thorax and Lungs, whereby the Air is sometimes impelled by the Nose, Mouth, and Wind-pipe into the Lungs; and thence again expelled; farther to elaborate the Bloud, by *Refrigerating it*, and by Separating its *fuliginous steams*.[32]	Why, I have found out the use of Respiration, or Breathing, which is a motion of the Thorax and the Lungs, whereby the Air is impell'd by the Nose, Mouth and Wind-pipe into the Lungs, and thence expell'd farther to elaborate the Blood, by refrigerating it, and separating its fuliginous Steams.[34]
. . . the *Black* ones will seize on the *Red*, never leaving to pinch them on the head with their *Forceps* or Claws, till they have killed them upon the place.[33] Etc.	The Black will pinch the Dark-Brown with his Forceps, till it kills it upon the Place.[35] Etc.

In addition to the *Philosophical Transactions*, Shadwell found material for his satire in Hooke's *Micrographia*, a work which describes what the author had been able to observe through the microscope. Sir Nicholas' description of the eels in vinegar, which "resemble other Eels, save in their Motion; which in others is sideways, but in them upwards and downwards"[36] follows Observation LVII[37] almost verbatim, except that Sir Nicholas transfers the sharpness from the nose to the tail. Likewise, the idea of the "Blue upon Plums [being] nothing but many living Creatures"[38] was suggested by Observation XX, "*Of* blue Mould, *and of the first Principles of Vegetation arising from* Putrefaction." The discussion of the nature of this mould leads Hooke to venture the possibility of tracing from "fluidity, or body without any form" the evolution "of a brute Animal's Soul, making the steps or

[31] Shadwell, I, 346-347.
[32] *Philosophical Transactions*, II, 535.
[33] *Ibid.*, II, 425.
[34] Shadwell, I, 343.
[35] *Ibid.*, I, 360.
[36] *Ibid.*, I, 385-386.
[37] Robert Hooke, *Micrographia: or some Physiological Descriptions of Minute Bodies made by Magnifying Glasses with Observations and Inquiries thereupon* (London, 1665), p. 216.
[38] Shadwell, I, 386.

foundations of [the] Enquiry, *Fluidity*, *Orbiculation*, *Fixation*, *Angulization*, or *Crystallization Germination* or *Ebullition*, *Vegetation*, *Plantanimation*, *Animation*, *Sensation*, *Imagination*."[39] This list of steps just cited is used by Sir Nicholas to explain how the plum becomes blue. But the most interesting of the borrowings from Hooke is Evelyn's communication on the spider, printed as Observation XLVIII. A comparison of the two passages will show how closely Shadwell followed the original:

Such [a spider] I did frequently observe at *Rome*, which espying a Fly at three or four yards distance, upon the Balcony (where I stood) would not make directly to her, but craul under the Rail, till being arriv'd to the *Antipodes*, it would steal up, seldom missing its aim; but if it chanced to want any thing of being perfectly opposite, would at first peep, immediately slide down again, till taking better notice, it would come the next time exactly upon the Fly's back . . .	SIR FORM: As soon as it [the spider] has spy'd its Prey, as suppose upon a Table, it will crawl underneath, till it arrive to the Antipodes of the Fly, which it discovers by sometimes peeping up;
But, if the capricious Fly took wing, and pitch'd upon another place behind our Huntress, then would the Spider whirle its body so nimbly about, as nothing could be imagin'd more swift; by which means, she always kept the head towards her prey, though to appearance, as immovable, as if it had been a Nail driven into the Wood, 'till by that indiscernable progress (being arriv'd within the	and if the capricious Fly happens not to remove it self by crural Motion, or the Vibration of its Wings,
sphere of her reach) she made a fatal leap (swift as Lightning) upon the Fly, catching him in the pole, where she never quitted hold till her belly was full, and then carried the remainder home. I have beheld them instructing their young ones, how to hunt, which they	it makes a fatal Leap upon the heedless Prey; of which, when it has satisfied its Appetite, it carries the remainder to its Cell, or Hermitage.

[39] Hooke, *Micrographia*, p. 127.

would sometimes discipline for not well observing; but, when any of the old ones did (as sometimes) miss a leap, they would run out of the field, and hide them in their crannies, as asham'd and haply not be seen abroad for four or five hours after.[40]

SIR NICH: It will teach its young Ones to hunt, and discipline 'em severely, when they commit Faults; and when an Old one misses its Prey, it will retire, and keep its Chamber for Grief, Shame and Anguish, ten Hours together.[41]

In *The Virtuoso*, then, Shadwell returned to the kind of comedy he had discontinued writing five years earlier because of the public's coldness towards *The Humourists.* He followed his bent towards satire by ridiculing the contemporary scientific movement in the person of Sir Nicholas Gimcrack. By documenting himself in publications by members of the Royal Society and by exaggerating those communications and articles which to him seemed most to invite exaggeration, he was able to produce an effective satire. The weakness of his play lies in the fact that he aimed at too many spots in the armor of the scientific movement; and, as a result, the scenes in the virtuoso's laboratory, by reason of being crammed with a superabundance of material, are cumbersome. In its own day, *The Virtuoso* was by no means a failure. Its success proved to the author that he could satisfy the public with a satirical play of humour. Because of this fact, his next venture in comedy, *A True Widow*, was also of that kind.

[40] *Ibid.*, pp. 200-201.

[41] Shadwell, I, 361.

CHAPTER XII

A TRUE WIDOW

A *TRUE WIDOW*, despite Sir Charles Sedley's "Correction and Alteration" and despite Dryden's prologue (which was later to be transferred to Mrs. Behn's posthumously acted *The Widow Ranter*), was not so well liked as its predecessors.[1] It may have been revived in 1688 or 1689; for, in the latter year, an edition of the play as "acted by His Majesty's Servants" was published. There is no indication that the comedy was produced after 1689.

The main plot contains the most Jonsonian situation in all the plays of Shadwell. Lady Cheatly causes the false report of her wealth to be spread throughout London by her Steward, her brother Lump, the credulous Maggot, and Lady Busy. Because of her reputation as a woman of business, the scriveners and citizens fairly force their money upon her. But the Steward threatens to divulge the true state of affairs if she does not marry him. She consents, and then persuades one of her admirers, Prig, to act the part of chaplain. After the mock-marriage, Lady Cheatly sends the Steward with a hundred pounds to a kinsman, the master of a ship bound for the Indies. Expecting that he will be clapt under hatches and sold into slavery, she is unprepared for his escape and return. When he learns that the marriage is void, he hastens away to inform the customers of how they have been cheated by the use of disappearing ink upon their bonds. They come to her and demand their money. The Steward then commits the blunder of whispering to his mistress and promising to deny everything if she will agree to marry him. She informs the assembled creditors of this proposal and, by persuading Prig to deny the Steward's assertions, she turns the tables upon her accomplice. Those who have been duped clamor for his arrest and will not listen to his denunciation of Lady Cheatly. More angry creditors arrive; but they are driven away by those who were present at the exposure of the Steward's infamy. Lady

[1] See pp. 32-33.

Cheatly escapes all blame and marries Maggot. When he finds her to be poor, he is much disturbed; but, upon learning that she may yet have a good estate although it belongs of right to other people, he is willing to assist her with his knowledge of law.

In general, this plot resembles that of *The Alchemist.* Jonson's comedy presents with great vividness the attempts of Face, Subtle, and Dol Common to dupe the credulous Londoners who come to the house of Lovewit during his absence in the belief that they are visiting the home of an alchemist. For a time, the cheats are entirely successful; then, for a moment, it looks as if the tables would be turned by the sceptical Surly, but his efforts are fruitless. The ending of *A True Widow,* in which the worst of the cheats, after duping everyone, escapes scot free, while the accomplice is made to suffer, recalls the conclusion of Jonson's play where the worst rogue of all, Face, turns against his comrades, Subtle and Dol, who are thereby forced to flee, leaving him to continue in the good graces of his master and actually to receive commendation for his wit.

The humour-characters, of which there are more in *A True Widow* than in *The Sullen Lovers, The Humourists,* or *The Virtuoso,* are among the persons who visit the house of Lady Cheatly. Lady Busy, Selfish, and Prig are designated by Shadwell in his dedication as "wholly new, not so much as touch'd upon before." The first of these, described in the dramatis personae as a "Woman of Intrigue, very busie in Love-Matters of all kinds, too old for Love of her own, always charitably helping forward that of others, very fond of young Women, very wise and discreet, half Bawd, half Match-maker," attempts in vain to persuade Isabella to become the mistress of a young lord in a scene which the author thinks "will live, when the Stuff of such Scribblers [i.e., those who condemn his plays] . . . shall be consum'd in Grocery-ware, Tobacco, Band-boxes, and Hat-Cases, and be rased out of the Memory of Men." The subject-matter of the vulgar scene upon which Shadwell thus prides himself had been used by Beaumont and Fletcher in *A Wife for a Month*[2] and by Rowley in *All's Lost by Lust.*[3] In the former play, the waiting-woman, Cassandra, tries to convince Evanthe of the desirability of becoming the mistress

[2] Act. IV.

[3] Act II, scene I.

of Frederick; in the latter, Malena urges Jacinta to sacrifice her virginity to King Roderigo. Lady Busy, however, is more subtle than either Cassandra or Malena. She does not state her purpose baldly, but attempts to smooth the way by anticipating the arguments of the person she would convince, and ends her plea with the statement that since custom has so run down wedlock, they should "make use of the next thing to it."

Of the two other characters which the author says have not been "touch'd upon before," Selfish, "a Coxcomb conceited of his Beauty, Wit and Breeding, thinking all Women in Love with him; always admiring and talking of himself," has some traits found in earlier Shadwellian humours. Like Crazy, he thinks all women in love with him; like Drybob and Sir Formal, he is well pleased with himself. But a more original figure than Selfish is Prig, the "universal Gamester, an admirable Horse and Dog Herald," who "knows all the remarkable Ones, their Families and Alliances," and who expresses his creed in the question, "What a Pox should a Gentleman think of, but Dogs, Horses, Dice, Tennis, Bowls, Races, or Cock-Fighting?" He talks of nothing but sports, even urging Lady Cheatly to marry him a day earlier than was intended in order that he may go to Newmarket where he has laid some money upon a cock fight.

Among the characters which Shadwell calls "new in the greatest Part" are Lump and Young Maggot. Lump, the "methodical Blockhead, as regular as a Clock, and . . . as true as a *Pendulum*," is at times suggestive of characters in Jonson's comedies. Like Sir Politick Would-Be,[4] he keeps a journal with meticulous care, but his entries deal with future happenings rather than with past events.[5] He is also a Puritan. In this character, he visits the theatre, which he denounces as a "Sink of Sin,"[6] and thus shows himself to be in the tradition of Zeal-of-the-Land Busy, who breaks into the puppet-play and announces his purpose of removing that heathenish idol Dagon.[7] Since Lump is a "mortal Enemy to Wit," he is in direct contrast to Young Maggot, "an Inns-of-Court Man, who neglects his Law, and runs mad after Wit, pretending much to Love, and both in spight of Nature; since his

[4] *Volpone,* Act IV, scene I.
[5] Shadwell, III, 129.
[6] *Ibid.,* III, 184.
[7] *Bartholomew Fair,* Act V, scene III.

Face makes him unfit for one, and his Brains for the other." This young man, by means of poetic activities, is able to keep his weight down. On one occasion, when he is about to entertain the company with a set of verses which he "purged, and bled, and enter'd into a Diet about," his uncle, a professed enemy to wit and a firm believer in the solid virtues displayed by men of business, creeps in unseen, and before the luckless nephew is aware of his presence, snatches the composition from him and tears it to pieces. Then, compelling the unfortunate poet to stand still, he searches his pockets and draws out bundles of papers, which he refuses to return despite the pleadings of all present.[8] This scene, in which worthless verse is destroyed, may have its origin in that episode in *Every Man In His Humour* in which Justice Clement orders Matthew's pockets to be searched. After finding a "commonwealth of paper" in the hose of the foolish poet, the good justice, who is heartily opposed to "paper-pedlars," sets the entire bundle on fire.[9]

The persons who play the parts of the lovers are Isabella and Bellamour, Theodosia and Carlos. Isabella, the antithesis of her foolish sister Gartrude, seems out of place in the household of her mother, Lady Cheatly. Because of her "Virtue and other inestimable Perfections," Bellamour, after vainly hoping that she may become his mistress, proposes marriage. Theodosia, the vivacious young woman who keeps her lover at arm's length, is of the school of Lucia and Carolina. Like her sisters in *Epsom-Wells*, she refuses to marry Carlos until he has served a certain period of probation. Bellamour and Carlos conform to the type of Shadwell's men of "Wit and Sense." Both are represented as having returned to the town after an absence, one in the country, the other on the continent. With the assistance of the livelier Stanmore, they perform the function of "demonstrators" for the humours.

Certain episodes in the plot of *A True Widow* are reminiscent of earlier plays. Mr. Saintsbury[10] has called attention to the resemblance between the motive of the disappearing ink used by Lady Cheatly[11] and the incident of the vanishing wax and writing which Overreach in *A New Way to Pay Old Debts* discovers have been put upon the deed to Welborne's estate.[12] Mr. Lawrence[13] has

[8] Shadwell, III, 170.
[9] Act V, scene I.
[10] In Mermaid edition of Shadwell, p. 121.
[11] Shadwell, III, 202.
[12] Act V, scene I.
[13] W. J. Lawrence, "Plays within Plays" (*Englische Studien*, XXXIII, 401).

noted the likeness between the hasty exit of Lump—who, upon becoming obstreperous at the Play-House, is spirited away by "*two Mock-Devils*" at a whistled signal from Lady Cheatly[14]—and the hurried departure of Squire Softhead in *The Dumb Lady*. In the latter play, "*Elysium opens; many women's voices sing, 'John, come kiss me now'; after that a dance; they draw up* SQUIRE SOFTHEAD *with a devil, and he cries out.*"[15] Also the situation in which Prig and Young Maggot are carried up in their chairs and left hanging in the air[16] may owe something to the passage in *Sir Martin Mar-all* where Moody and Sir John Swallow are hoisted up in their chairs and abandoned by their friends while in this lofty position.[17]

Just as *The Sullen Lovers* made fun of the heroic drama and *The Virtuoso* satirized the new scientific movement, so *A True Widow* attempts to "expose" the type of play associated in Shadwell's mind with the word "Farce." From the dedicatory epistle to this comedy, we may gather that the main elements in this detested dramatic form are the chief ingredients used by the "little Poetasters of the fourth rate" who "hold that Wit signifies nothing in a Comedy; but the putting out of Candles, kicking down of Tables, falling over Joynt-stools, impossible Accidents, and unnatural Mistakes (which they most absurdly call Plot)." This kind of play Shadwell ridicules in his fourth act, where he represents the interior of a theatre during the performance of a farce. Many difficulties were encountered in staging this scene: "In the Action, many doubted which belong'd to the Farce in the Play, and which to the Play it self, by reason of promiscuous speaking; and I found by venturing upon that new Thing, I ran a great Risque: For some, I believe, wish'd all the Play like that part of a Farce in it; others knew not my intention in it, which was to expose the Style and Plot of Farce-Writers, to the utter confusion of damnable Farce, and all its wicked and foolish Adherents."[18]

That portion of the "Farce" which is performed before the quarrel in the audience is of the most absurd nature. Two characters designated as a Lover and a Wife, after a short dialogue of

[14] Shadwell, III, 185.
[15] Act IV, scene I.
[16] Shadwell, III, 185.
[17] Dryden, *Works* (Scott-Saintsbury ed.), III, 92.
[18] Note in 1679 edition of *A True Widow*.

long speeches larded with polysyllabic words, retire. The Husband comes unexpectedly, knocks at the door, and turns his back, a signal for the Lover to give him several sound kicks. Believing the Devil to be at hand acting as pander for the rogue who is with his wife, the Husband determines to surprise them and leaves. A second Lover, seeing the Wife return with her paramour, hides under the table. The Husband then enters, falls over a form, and puts out the candle he is carrying. The latter mishap is immediately remedied when he "blows it in again." He then threatens to kill his Wife, who vows she is alone. If he sees anyone, it must be the Devil. *"If thou strik'st it, it will tear thee in Pieces,"* she adds. This statement so terrifies the Husband that, imagining he sees the cloven foot and glaring eyes, he calls upon Heaven for help and begs his wife to forgive him. In the meantime, the Lover seeks refuge under the table where he encounters his rival. In jealous anger, the two men "scuffle under the Table, rise with it on their Backs; the Table falls down; they draw their Swords and fight." These happenings convince the Husband of his wife's faithlessness. How he intends to deal with her is left untold; for, at this moment, the play is interrupted by the fighting in the audience occasioned by Prig's striking the bully.[19]

I have been unable to find any particular episode in the printed drama of the years immediately preceding the production of *A True Widow* which Shadwell might have been imitating in this scene.[20] The stilted language of the Wife and the Lover also has no counterpart, except for humorous effect, in any Restoration play

[19] Shadwell, III, 175 ff.

[20] The nearest approach to a resemblance is found in the fourth act (pp. 42-47) of D'Urfey's *A Fond Husband: or, The Plotting Sisters,* published in 1677. Ranger, upon discovering his love Emilia with his rival Rashley, hides from them. When their conversation is interrupted by the knocking of the husband Bubble upon the door, Rashley secretes himself under the table. Stepping from his place of hiding, Ranger confronts Emilia with the declaration that the dice are his. She, however, immediately throws suspicion upon him by dropping the doorkey into his pocket, laying hold of him, and shouting "A rape!" When Bubble and Maria burst into the room, Emilia accuses Ranger of having forced himself into her presence. As Bubble rushes at him in jealous rage, he knocks over the table and discovers Rashley. In reply to Bubble's angry demands, Rashley answers that he had watched two hours to frustrate Ranger's design and that Emilia told him not to discover himself for fear of arousing her husband's jealousy. Bubble finally begs his wife to forgive him. In both the "Farce", and D'Urfey's play, one lover hides in order to spy upon the wife and his rival, the rival hides under the table in order to avoid meeting the husband, and the husband finds the wife in the room with two lovers.

known to me. No comic dramatist of the sixteen-seventies seriously wrote lines approaching these in heaviness: "*But since Fortune (by so many frequent Signalizations) has demonstrated how much she is a Friend to us, in assisting us with so many Subterfuges, when most we have needed them, it will be a heinous Tergiversation from her, to abandon that Trust we formerly have reposed in her; and she may justly take a Picque at our Infidelity, and, in that Caprice, may continue a Revenge suitable to our Delinquency.*" Shadwell could not have been ridiculing actual dramatic practice in this passage; instead, he was again satirizing that kind of "florid" style which he had previously burlesqued in the speech of Sir Formal Trifle.

Scenes laid inside theatres had been shown at least three times by Restoration dramatists before the production of *A True Widow.* D'Avenant, in *A Play-House to be Let,*[21] represents a Tire-Woman, a Char-Woman, a House-keeper, a Player, a Musician, a Dancing-Master, and a Poet discussing conditions within the theatre. In *The Humorous Lovers,* the characters go to the playhouse in order to see the masque provided by Sir Anthony Altalk for the purpose of causing Boldman to fall in love with the Widow.[22] Buckingham and his co-workers show Johnson, Smith, and Bayes at the rehearsal of an heroic play. In the first of these comedies, the only persons represented are employees of the theatre; in the second, the audience is composed solely of characters who have appeared in the preceding acts; in the third, the spectators are merely Bayes and the gentlemen who are criticizing his play.

Shadwell, however, in the fourth act of *A True Widow,* attempts something new in Restoration drama—a picturing of the typical theatrical audience. In addition to the characters from the earlier acts, he brings into his scene persons representing types to be found in the audiences of his day. After the guests of Carlos have seated themselves, a great knocking is heard at the door of the play-house. The door-keeper announces that several ladies and gentlemen are clamoring to get in. Carlos permits the ladies to be admitted free, but orders the door-keeper to collect a fee from the men.

[21] Act I.

[22] Newcastle, *The Humorous Lovers,* (London, 1677), pp. 27 ff.

Several more come in, Women mask'd, and Men of several sorts. Several young Coxcombs fool with the Orange-Women.

ORANGE WOM: Oranges! will you have any Oranges?

1 BULLY: What Play do they play? some confounded Play or other.

PRIG: A Pox on't, Madam! what should we do at this damn'd Play-house? Let's send for some Cards, and play at Lang-trilloo in the Box. Pox on 'em! I ne'er saw a Play had any thing in't; some of 'em have Wit now and then, but what care I for Wit?

SELFISH: Does my Cravat sit well? I take all the Care I can it should; I love to appear well. What Ladies are here in the Boxes? really I never come to a Play, but upon account of seeing the Ladies.

CARLOS: Door-keeper, are they ready to begin?

DOOR-KEEP: Yes, immediately.

. . .

YOUNG MAGGOT: You'll find it an admirable Plot; there's great Force and Fire in the Writing; so full of Business and Trick, and very fashionable; it pass'd through my Hands; some of us help'd him in it.

1 BULLY: Dam' me! when will these Fellows begin? Plague on't! here's a staying.

2 MAN: Whose Play is this?

3 MAN: One *Prickett*'s, Poet *Prickett.*

1 MAN: O hang him! Pox on him! he cannot write; pr'ythee let's to *White-Hall.*

Y. MAG: Not write, Sir! I am one of his Patrons; I know the Wits don't like him; but he shall write with any of 'em all, for an Hundred Pound.

PRIG: Ay, that he shall. They say he puts no Wit in his Plays; but 'tis all one for that, they do the Business; he is my Poet too; I hate Wit.

Enter several Ladies, and several Men.

DOOR-KEEP: Pray, Sir, pay me; my Masters will make me pay it.

3 MAN: Impudent Rascal! do you ask me for Money? Take that, Sirrah.

2 DOOR-KEEP: Will you pay me, Sir?

4 MAN: No: I don't intend to stay.

2 DOOR-KEEP: So you say every Day, and see two or three Acts for nothing.

4 MAN: I'll break your Head, you Rascal.

1 DOOR-KEEP: Pray, Sir, pay me.

3 MAN: Set it down; I have no Silver about me; or bid my Man pay you.

THEODOSIA: What, do Gentlemen run on Tick for Plays?

CARLOS: As familiarly as with their Taylors.

2 MAN: Pox on you, Sirrah! go, and bid 'em begin quickly.

After the play begins, the audience comment upon the action.

One man exclaims, "Dam' me! I don't like it." Another prefers "Drums, and Trumpets, and much ranting, roaring, huffing, and fretting, and good store of Noise in a Play." Losing interest in what is happening on the stage, one of the spectators *"sits down, and lolls in the Orange-Wench's Lap"*; others commence flirting with the vizard-masks. Prig amuses himself by rapping people on the back, twirling their hats, and then appearing demure as if he had done nothing. By attempting this trick once too often, he precipitates the quarrel which frightens the actors from the stage and drives the audience from the play-house. The bustle, life, and movement of this scene in the theatre make it unique in Restoration drama and not unworthy of being mentioned in the same breath with the opening passages of the first act of *Cyrano de Bergerac*.

A True Widow shares with *Epsom-Wells* and *The Virtuoso* the right to be called one of the three best comedies written by Shadwell before *The Squire of Alsatia.* The "humours" are more numerous than in any of his earlier comedies. The main plot representing Lady Cheatly's successful duping of all the persons who place confidence in her and her escape without punishment in the end is Jonsonian. The representation of the audience within the playhouse was a novelty in Restoration drama. With all these seeming advantages, *A True Widow* was not successful. Seeing a play of this type again meet with disapproval, Shadwell once more did as he had done several years earlier: he stopped writing comedies of humour and turned to forms of dramatic composition more certain of success.

CHAPTER XIII

THE WOMAN-CAPTAIN

THE *WOMAN-CAPTAIN* with its "*Plenty of Noise, and Scarcity of Wit*"[1] was able to please the theatre-going public for a longer period than *A True Widow.* It was performed the second time "for sixteen years" at the theatre in Lincoln's Inn Fields on October 25, 1703.[2] On March 21, 1710, Norris and Mrs. Bradshaw appeared in the rôles of Gripe and his wife at Drury Lane.[3] The summer company acted this play at Lincoln's Inn Fields, the first time in seven years on June 29, 1716, when J. Leigh was Sir Humphrey; Griffin, Gripe; Bullock, Sir Christopher Swash; and Mrs. Thurmond, Mrs. Gripe.[4] After this production, theatrical records are silent concerning *The Woman-Captain.* On October 10, 1744, at the Haymarket, however, *The Prodigal: or, Recruits for the Queen of Hungary,* an alteration of Shadwell's play by Thomas Odell, was presented.[5]

[1] See pp. 33-34.

[2] Genest, II, 303.

[3] *Ibid.,* II, 437.

[4] *Ibid.,* II, 589.

[5] In his dedication to Charles, Earl of Middlesex, Odell flatters himself that his alterations have improved Shadwell's play. The prologue ends as follows:

"*Our Bard to-night, but with a trembling Heart,*
One Play has ventur'd to reduce to Art;
New plant the Fable, and the Plot refin'd,
Whence strikes the instructive Moral to the Mind.
Sirs, as the Woman-Captain *heretofore,*
Has, with Applause, been acted o'er and oer,
For this, our Prodigal thence ta'en, we pray
Your kind Indulgence, as old Shadwell's *Play;*
His Wit still stands in Force, his Humour free,
And thence our Bard most humbly begs, by me,
That you'll not damn him now for Regularity."

The names of the characters are changed: Sir Humphrey becomes Sir Anthony Wildwit; Bellamy, Gayly; Wildman, Freeman; Gripe, Scrape; Richard, Timothy; Sir Christopher, Sir Toby Riot; Heildebrand, Bounce; Blunderbuss, Bluster; Sir Nicholas Peakgoose, Sir Nicholas Spottey; Mrs. Gripe, Mrs. Scrape; Phillis, Harriot; Cloris, Isabella; Celia, Charlotte.

There are many omissions (practically all of Shadwell's songs are left out) and some transpositions (the scene between the miser and his wife in Act I is shifted to Act II after the departure of the drunken Timothy). Moral rime tags close each act. The only important alteration in the plot is in the character of Harriot (Phillis in *The Woman-Captain*). When Sir Anthony is about to leave, after saying that his misfortunes have freed him of his riotous companions and have cleared his understanding, Harriot expresses joy to learn that he has condescended to make a sober use of his senses. She returns his settlement and bids him farewell for ever, saying that she will

The Woman-Captain begins with a representation of the prodigality of Sir Humphrey Scattergood, who, upon coming into his estate at the age of twenty-four, determines to devote his life to the object of pleasing all his senses. In this resolution, he is aided by Bellamy and Wildman; but his steward, who knows that the property will soon be consumed, begs him to be less extravagant. This old servant is sent to negotiate a loan from Gripe, a usurer, who starves his servant Richard and keeps his wife under lock and key for fear of being cuckolded. In order to obtain his signature, Gripe goes to the house of the wastrel, who is loath to be disturbed during his birthday celebration. Sir Christopher Swash with his "roaring" companions, Blunderbuss and Heildebrand, also calls upon Sir Humphrey, who persuades them all to go with fiddles and collation to the home of the money-lender. Just before these visitors appear, Mrs. Gripe has informed her husband that her twin brother will take revenge for the indignities she has been forced to suffer. Later, with the aid of Sir Humphrey, she escapes from the house.

Sir Christopher and his bullies, after breaking windows and terrifying passers-by, return to Sir Humphrey's, well pleased with their adventures. Here they enjoy much mirth while forcing drink upon Sir Nicholas Peakgoose, a married man browbeaten by his mistress Celia. This carousing is interrupted by the constable and watch, who have come to search for the usurer's wife. But they are soon forced to beat a retreat; and Gripe and Richard, who have accompanied them, are taken prisoners by the revellers.

In the meantime, Mrs. Gripe has dressed herself in the uniform of an army captain and gone to Sir Humphrey's residence. Representing herself as her twin brother, she interviews her husband whom she forces to take the shilling, the emblem of enlistment.

pass the rest of her life in solitude in the country. He begs her to remain as "my dearest Wife, my truest Friend, and everlasting Love."

Odell's moral is driven home in the concluding verses:

"The Lessons, Sirs, our labour'd Scenes disclose,
Shew first, that Trencher-Friends are real Foes;
That Whores, when pamper'd, are so prone to change,
Their Cully-Keepers, scarce, can think it strange:
That woful Want had follow'd wanton Waste,
Had not this Girl I kept, because the Taste,
This Phoenix! gen'rous prov'd, and sav'd me at the last.
But hence, let Prodigals ne'er hope that they,
Shall by some Miracle be sav'd, as in our Play."

She also forces the shilling upon Sir Christopher and his companions, who are willing to don the uniform in order to escape arrest by the bailiffs. Once enlisted, all are compelled to submit to the strictest discipline.

In time, Sir Humphrey's land, the richest in the country, is seized. The spendthrift then turns to his companions for help. Bellamy refuses to be of aid because Sir Humphrey has no land to offer as a counter-security; Wildman withholds assistance on account of an oath he has taken. Phillis, upon whom Sir Humphrey has settled his estate, now assures him that she will no longer allow "lewd Companions, Sotting and Drinking" within the walls of *her* house.

Mrs. Gripe, again in woman's clothes, goes to her husband, feigns discontent because of the treatment he has received at the hands of her supposed brother, and advises him to agree to the captain's demand that he pay her £3000 outright or £400 a year separate maintenance. Gripe dislikes the idea but, when she offers to return the deed to him after he has signed it, is willing to consider the matter further. While in the disguise of captain, Mrs. Gripe had won the interest of Phillis, Cloris, and Celia, to all of whom she promised appointments for eight o'clock in the evening. But when the hour arrives and the officer does not appear, these women lose no time in finding other lovers. Cloris and Celia become the mistresses of Wildman and Bellamy. Sir Humphrey, in order to obtain the remnants of his estate, marries Phillis. Mrs. Gripe, once more in military uniform, accepts the deed by which she is granted freedom, reveals herself, and then brings the play to a close with a warning to husbands.

The Woman-Captain is a play of plot rather than a play of character, and recalls, instead of Shadwell's earlier comedies of humour, Mrs. Behn's comedies of intrigue, which were very popular during the sixteen-seventies. The two threads of the story, that dealing with the prodigality of Sir Humphrey and that relating to the display by Mrs. Gripe of the "liberty of a She-Subject of *England*," are joined by the character of Gripe to whom Sir Humphrey sends for money. The plot in which Sir Humphrey figures is composed of elements suggested by three plays of the early part of the century—*Timon of Athens*, *The Scornful Lady*, and *The Alchemist*.

The idea of transferring a portion of the story of Timon to an English setting doubtless occurred to the writer while he was engaged in adapting Shakespeare's play. Sir Humphrey, however, is a very different person from Timon; his prodigality is caused by the desire to please every sense, while Timon's lavishness is due to generosity. In each play, the spendthrift has a steward who is much grieved at the wastefulness of his lord and who attempts to halt his expenditures. As Flavius is compelled to inform Timon that his land which at one time reached to Lacedaemon is forfeited,[6] so the steward brings the news that Sir Humphrey's "Land in *Essex* is extended by [his] Creditors; and [his] Furniture, the richest in the County, all seiz'd upon."[7] When he hears this disheartening information, Timon dispatches his servants to his supposed friends. Lucullus tells Flaminius, after listening to his errand, "that this is no time to lend money, especially upon bare friendship, without security."[8] Similarly, Bellamy and Wildman, when approached by Sir Humphrey, express a readiness to venture their lives for him, but are unwilling to supply the necessary money without counter-security.[9] From this point, resemblances cease. Timon invites his friends to a feast, rebukes them for their selfishness, and leaves the city to lead the life of a misanthrope. Sir Humphrey, on the other hand, after thanking the gentlemen for clearing his understanding and exclaiming "This is the World I find," takes the desperate means of marrying his mistress, Phillis, to regain his property.

Shadwell's treatment of Sir Humphrey and his extravagant companions may also owe something to *The Scornful Lady*, a play mentioned in *The Sullen Lovers*.[10] In Beaumont and Fletcher's comedy, the Elder Loveless, who has been repulsed by his beloved, leaves his estate in charge of his younger brother, and orders the steward Savil to keep a sharp eye upon the latter's extravagance. In his absence, the Younger Loveless entertains a Captain, a Traveller, a Poet, and a Tobacco-Man. With the assistance of these wasteful companions and against the protest of Savil, he decides to spend his money on wine and women. The task of furnishing the latter is given to Savil.[11] In a like manner, Sir Humphrey and

[6] *Timon of Athens*, Act II, scene II.
[7] Shadwell, III, 413.
[8] *Timon of Athens*, Act III, scene I.
[9] Shadwell, III, 413-414.
[10] *Ibid.*, I, 19.
[11] Act I, scene II.

his friends, after naming the meats, fishes and drinks they intend to consume, order the steward to "provide a World of Strumpets."[12] Later, in the course of a drinking-bout with his comrades and mistresses, Young Loveless orders Savil to "kiss [his] *Helen*, And court her in a dance." The steward, greatly dismayed by this command, pleads for consideration and begs to be killed.[13] Likewise, the steward in *The Woman-Captain*, after Sir Humphrey has given the order that in his house "Chastity shall be Fellony, and Sobriety High-Treason," begs to be whipped or hanged rather than indulge in his master's vices.[14] After the death of the Elder Loveless has been announced, Savil goes to the usurer Morecraft, who is willing to accommodate the prodigal with a thousand pounds on condition that "his land lie for the payment."[15] Similarly, Sir Humphrey's steward visits Gripe to "borrow Money on a Mortgage."[16] Young Loveless and his companions follow Savil to Morecraft, who desires to purchase the estate outright. Despite the steward's pleadings against such an action, the spendthrift assents to the money-lender's demands.[17] Instead of having Sir Humphrey go to the house of the usurer in order to negotiate the loan, Shadwell has Gripe accompany the steward to the home of the prodigal and there obtain his seal and signature.[18] From this point, a similarity in the development of the actions of the two plays ceases.

In addition to these reminiscences of Shakespeare and Beaumont and Fletcher, there is also an element from Jonson in this play. The author of an article on "Shadwell's Dramatic Works" in *The Retrospective Review* thinks that Sir Humphrey Scattergood is a modification of Sir Epicure Mammon, and that some of the ideas and speeches of this character have been adopted by Shadwell with slight variation.[19] With the first statement, I am in hearty agreement. Sir Humphrey's anticipations of the delights in store for the man who will please all his senses are of a kind with Sir Epicure's air-castles of what he shall do when presented with the philosopher's stone. There is, however, slight resemblance between the beauty of the lines in which Sir Epicure indulges his imagina-

[12] Shadwell, III, 352.
[13] Act II, scene II.
[14] Shadwell, III, 390.
[15] Act II, scene III.
[16] Shadwell, III, 360.
[17] Act II, scene III.
[18] Shadwell, III, 362.
[19] *The Retrospective Review, and Historical and Antiquarian Magazine: Second Series* (London, 1828), II, 56.

tion and the antiphonal reciting of the menu-card by Sir Humphrey and his hedonistic companions.

Sir Epicure speaks of his feasts in this manner:

> My meat shall all come in, in Indian shells,
> Dishes of agat set in gold, and studded
> With emeralds, sapphires, hyacinths, and rubies.
> The tongues of carps, dormice, and camels' heels,
> Boil'd in the spirit of sol, and dissolv'd pearl,
> Apicius' diet, 'gainst the epilepsy:
> And I will eat these broths with spoons of amber,
> Headed with diamond and carbuncle.[20]
> Etc.

Shadwell uses no selection in his list of foods, but names everything on the bill of fare:

> SIR HUMPH: And then for Fish, what the vast Seas afford, Ponds, immense Lakes and Rivers too; Brett, Mullet, Turbet, Smelt, Plaice, Scate, Cod-Whiting, and the old Organ-Ling with Gold Flakes, with heightning Sturgeon to stir up my Blood; provoking Oisters, and the lusty Lobster; Crabs, Shrimps, Crafish-Pottage, Muscles and Cockles, and dissolved Pearl and Amber in my Sauce.
>
> WILD: The Luscio, Eel, the Trout, Char Tench, Perch, calver'd Salmon: And from the Ponds, over-grown Pikes, Carps, Breams, Torecells; The *German* Fish as fat as Bucks in *August*.[21]
> Etc.

Sir Humphrey's idea of wantoning in the baths undoubtedly also came from *The Alchemist;* the beauty of the original, however, is lost in the transcript.

> MAM: . . . My mists
> I'll have of perfume, vapour'd 'bout the room,
> To lose ourselves in; and my baths, like pits
> To fall into; from whence we will come forth,
> And roll us dry in gossamer and roses.[22]

> I'll have my Baths prepared full of most fragrant Scents; . . . there we'll lye soaking till we be refreshed. Then we'll come out, be rub'd, and be anointed with precious Oyls and Essences; and then we'll roll our selves in Beds of Orange-Flowers.[23]

[20] *The Alchemist,* Act II, scene I.
[21] Shadwell, III, 351-352.
[22] *The Alchemist,* Act II, scene I.
[23] Shadwell, III, 355.

I have been unable to find a direct source for the other plot—that dealing with the revenge of Mrs. Gripe upon her miserly husband. Dr. Marti has shown that Ward, who ventures the opinion that *The Woman-Captain* "is indebted to Fletcher and Shirley's *The Night Walker*,"[24] is mistaken in this instance.[25] He suggests Moll in *The Roaring Girl* as a probable hint for Mrs. Gripe after she dons male attire. It would not, however, have been necessary for Shadwell to turn to a play by Middleton for the idea of his heroine since women who dressed as men were familiar figures in the drama of the 1670's. *The Woman turn'd Bully* has the character of Betty Goodfeild, who goes to London in order to avoid marriage with Sir Alexander Simple. In the clothing of a man, she swaggers up to her brother and his friend Truman, who are conversing with Lucia and her maid in Temple Garden, huffs, and arranges to meet each man at a duel on the morrow. When the men arrive at the duelling place, she discloses her identity.[26] In *The Morning Ramble*, Honour and Rose, who wish to see the inside of a tavern, dress themselves as men and proceed to the Rose.[27] Mrs. Gripe's desire, "I cannot Drink: yet I have a great Curiosity to see what it is, that charms Men to sit up whole Nights at Eating-Houses and Taverns,"[28] recalls the purposes of these women. Similarly, Hillaria in *The Careless Lovers* dresses as a man and goes to a tavern in order to discover how her lover comports himself. Here she finds Lovell and Careless in company with the wenches, Clappam and Breedwel. The latter, who are immediately attracted by the supposed young man, become jealous of each other and send the drawer to whisper to Hillaria. When Careless draws his sword to fight for the woman he loves, Hillaria makes herself known and leaves.[29] The old situation of the wenches' falling in love with a woman in disguise and consequently becoming jealous of each other is echoed in the scenes in which Phillis, Cloris, and Celia attempt to arrange a meeting with the

[24] A. W. Ward, *English Dramatic Literature* (London, 1899), III, 457 n.

[25] Paul Marti, *Fletcher's Play, The Night Walker and Shadwell's Comedy, The Woman Captain* (Berne, 1910).

[26] *The Woman turn'd Bully. A Comedy, Acted at the Duke's Theatre* (London, 1675).

[27] [Nevil Payne], *The Morning Ramble, or, The Town-Humours: a Comedy. Acted at the Duke's Theatre* (London, 1673), pp. 30-36.

[28] Shadwell, III, 405.

[29] *The Careless Lovers: A Comedy. Acted at the Duke's Theatre. Written by Edward Ravenscrofts* [sic], *Gent.* (London, 1673), pp. 49-55.

so-called captain.[30] Mrs. Gripe then ought to be considered as a composite of recollections of many characters.

The miser Gripe in his hatred of anyone who comes between him and his money, follows in the footsteps of Goldingham, Shadwell's rendering of Harpagon. His treatment of his half-starved servant Richard may owe something, as Mr. Miles suggests, to that scene in *L'Avare* where Harpagon orders his servants to be particularly careful in their method of serving food at his contemplated dinner.[31] There are, however, no likenesses in specific details between the methods of careful housekeeping practised by Harpagon and Gripe. Mr. Miles also avers that the "conduct of Mrs. Gripe is a reflection of the *L'École des Maris motif.*" In each play, a woman outwits the man who will not allow her to leave his house; but the methods employed are different.

Sir Christopher Swash and his bullying comrades are in the tradition of English comedy. Sir Christopher is an exponent of lip-valour; as soon as he is faced down by the woman-captain, he has as little to say as Bobadill. Heildebrand and Blunderbuss, ferocious in words but powerless in deeds, are reminiscent of Pistol. The cheating of Sir Nicholas Peakgoose while drunk reminds one of the treatment given Timothy Squeeze by Rant and Hazard.[32] In the conflict between the roisterers and the watch, Shadwell also revives a subject which he had not treated since *The Miser;* but the scene in *The Woman-Captain* is much livelier than its predecessor.

One should consider this play, then, as a comedy of intrigue filled with reminiscences of the writings of numerous Elizabethan and Restoration dramatists. Containing much action and many boisterous scenes of horseplay, it must have amused an audience that demanded *"Plenty of Noise and Scarcity of Wit."* Although a mere pot-boiler, it has a real interest for the student of Shadwell. Sir Christopher, Heildebrand, and Blunderbuss whose conversation contains an occasional touch of Alsatian cant are preliminary studies of the denizens of Whitefriars—figures that were later to give *The Squire of Alsatia* a success known to few plays of its generation.

[30] Shadwell, III, 401-405, 414-416.

[31] Miles, p. 241. Passage referred to is in *L'Avare,* Act III, scene I.

[32] Shadwell, III, 50 ff.

CHAPTER XIV

THE LANCASHIRE WITCHES

THE LANCASHIRE WITCHES, and Tegue O'Divelly, The Irish Priest met with opposition when first presented, but was able to weather the storm.[1] Records of performances in the first quarter of the eighteenth century are plentiful. On August 10, 1704, Pinkethman acted Young Hartfort at Drury Lane;[2] on July 1, 1707, at the Haymarket, Bullock appeared as Tegue, Norris as Sir Timothy, and Johnson as Tom Shacklehead.[3] The revival of August 3, 1711, with Mills, Booth, Johnson, the two Bullocks, Norris, Pack, Mrs. Powell, Mrs. Mills, and Mrs. Bradshaw in the cast,[4] occasioned the letter which was printed in No. 141 of *The Spectator* on August 11. The play was performed on June 4, 1723,[5] at the benefit for Widow Bowen and Widow Leigh, and on May 13, 1724,[6] at the benefit for the prompter Chetwood. The last recorded production of *The Lancashire Witches* was that of October 30, 1727.[7]

The play, which was published with the passages expunged by the Master of the Revels printed in italics, is a hodge-podge. No one realized this fact better than the author who, in his preface, wrote that, since the town has now run entirely into politics, a person cannot "touch upon any Humour of this Time" without offending one of the parties. For this reason, he saw "there was no Scope for the writing of an entire Comedy," and therefore "resolved to make as good an Entertainment as [he] could, without tying [him]self up to the strict Rules of a Comedy; which was the Reason of [his] introducing of Witches." To Downes,

[1] See pp. 52-54.
[2] Genest, II, 301.
[3] *Ibid.*, II, 373.
[4] *Ibid.*, II, 482.
[5] At Drury Lane. Genest, III, 106.
[6] At Drury Lane. Genest, III, 134.
[7] At Drury Lane. Genest, III, 199. Genest also records performances at Drury Lane on December 22, 1702; June 22, September 4, 1708; March 11, 1710; October 12, 1711; June 12, 1713; March 31, November 16, 1714; July 8, November 11, 1715; July 4, October 29, 1717; November 7, 1718; June 8, 1720; August 18, October 30, 1721; October 29, 1724; April 3, 1727; at Dorset Garden or Drury Lane on October 29, 1705; at the Haymarket on July 25, October 29, 1707. Mr. J. L. Hotson informs me that it was acted on May 27, 1697, by the Theatre Royal Company.

this play appeared as a "kind of Opera, having several *Machines* of Flyings for the Witches, and other Diverting Contrivances in't."[8]

The scene is laid in and around the dwelling of Sir Edward Hartfort in Lancashire. This worthy gentleman intends to marry his son and his daughter Isabella respectively to Theodosia and Sir Timothy, the children of his neighbor, Sir Jeffery Shacklehead. The young ladies care nothing for their awkward suitors, but instead love Bellfort and Doubty, Yorkshire gentlemen whom they had met the previous summer at the Spa. Hoping to prevent their impending weddings, they tease their destined husbands at every opportunity. While journeying to Whalley, Bellfort and Doubty lose their way during a storm, but are fortunately directed by Clod, a country fellow, to the home of Sir Edward Hartfort, who begs them to accept of his hospitality.

The countryside is troubled with witches, beings in whom Sir Edward and his visitors place little credence, but who are very real to Sir Jeffery and Lady Shacklehead. Tegue O'Divelly, an Irish priest, comes with holy water and relics to rid the neighborhood of these creatures. When Sir Edward's chaplain, Smerk, complains of pain as the result of eating the "charmed" substance which the chambermaid Susan has mingled with his food in order to make him love her, Tegue sprinkles him with holy water. But the bottle flies from the hand of the priest, who is belabored by the witch, Mother Demdike.

The young men plan to wed their loves during the night. In the meantime, Doubty has been pursued by the amorous Lady Shacklehead, to whom he promises a meeting. She goes to the rendezvous, but is forced to beat a hurried retreat after she mistakes Tegue for her gallant. The priest does not notice at first that the witch, Mother Dickenson, has taken the lady's place. When he discovers the identity of his companion, he shrieks with fright, arouses the household, and thus prevents the lovers from consummating their design. After the house again becomes quiet, Doubty is once more bothered by Lady Shacklehead. This time, however, he is rescued by Sir Jeffery, who happens along with a light. In order to avert suspicion, his lady pretends to be walking in her sleep.

[8] P. 38.

Mother Dickenson again visits Tegue, lays hold upon him, and accuses him of promising marriage. When he cries for help, Tom and Clod hurry to his assistance and apprehend the witch. Young Hartfort, who would go hunting on his wedding morning before the ceremony, and Sir Timothy are likewise attacked by the witches, who are shortly afterwards taken prisoner and sent to Lancaster by Sir Jeffery.

After the tenants have arrived to make merry with their landlords at the weddings that are to bind the two families, Bellfort, Doubty, Isabella, and Theodosia appear, kneel before the parents, and announce their marriages. Sir Jeffery and his lady depart in anger, meditating revenge. Sir Edward, after recovering from his surprise, wishes his daughter and son-in-law happiness. Smerk, upon whom Susan's charm has worked, then begs Sir Edward's pardon for marrying his chambermaid. Because the chaplain had made love to his daughter and corrupted his son by teaching that the Plot was Presbyterian rather than Popish, Sir Edward refuses to continue him in his service. On the other hand, he bestows a farm of forty pounds a year upon Susan. Finally, a messenger comes with a warrant for Kelly, alias Tegue O'Divelly, who is accused of being implicated in the Popish Plot. The priest, before leaving, consoles himself with the thought that hanging will make him a saint.

The suggestion of writing a play upon witchcraft very likely came from a reading of *The Late Lancashire Witches* by Heywood and Brome.[9] From this work, Shadwell derived his setting, the idea of witches engaged in playing tricks upon the country people, and a few of the incidents.[10] These may be summarized as follows:

[9] This play, which was occasioned by the Lancashire witch-prosecutions of 1633, was evidently produced at the Globe Theatre at the time when four of the accused women—Margaret Johnson, Frances Dickonson, Mary Spenser, and Hargrave's wife—were in London awaiting trial. See Wallace Notestein, *History of Witchcraft in England* (Washington, 1911), pp. 146-158, and Montague Summers, *History of Witchcraft and Demonology* (New York, 1926), p. 295. Chapter VII of the latter work contains an excellent account of the witch in dramatic literature.

[10] Ernest Ammann in his *Analysis of Thomas Shadwell's Lancashire Witches and Tegue O'Divelly the Irish Priest* (Bern, 1905), says, "Though some resemblance may be traced between Shadwell's Lancashire Witches and the plays of his predecessors we shall be entirely wrong in thinking that he imitated these writers. The chief material for his witch-scenes and magic art which we cannot discover in Middleton, Shakespeare nor

1. In the earlier play, Master Arthur, Mr. Shakstone, and Mr. Bantam return from hunting, disappointed because their sport was "crost in th' height." Arthur thinks the hare, which vanished the instant his "Dog had pincht her," must have been a witch or devil. Shakstone is certain that "these are accidents all game is subject to" and will accept no explanation based upon superstition.[11] In the later play, Sir Jeffery and Sir Edward, with retainers, hunt a hare which disappears in the course of the chase. Sir Jeffery is positive that the animal must have been a witch; Sir Edward avers that a person shows "Incorrigible Ignorance" in holding such a thought.[12]

2. Sir Edward, like Generous, breathes the soul of hospitality. Arthur describes his host as "the sole surviving sonne Of long since banisht Hospitality."[13] Sir Edward endeavors to "imitate the Life of [the] *English* Gentry, before [they] were corrupted with the base Manners of the *French.*"[14]

3. The Lancashire dialect of Clod, Thomas ô Georges, and Tom Shacklehead is similar to that spoken by Lawrence and Parnell.[15]

4. When Robin refuses to get the gray gelding for Mrs. Generous, she immediately bridles him and drives him to the meeting of the witches.[16] Similarly, Mall Spencer bridles Clod and flies away with him to Madge's initiation.[17] The words of charm spoken in both plays are nearly the same:

Heywood	*Shadwell*
Horse, horse, see thou be,	*A Horse, a Horse, be thou to me,*
And where I point thee carry me.	*And carry me where I shall flee.*

5. At the wedding of Lawrence and Parnell, the musicians are bewitched and play "*every one a severall tune.*" Later, they are unable to make a sound.[18] At Sir Edward's, the musicians "*gape and strain, but cannot sing, but make an ugly Noise.*"[19]

Heywood he collected from ancient or modern witch-mongers" (p. 35). He makes no mention of Shadwell's indebtedness to the *Masque of Queens,* and he notes merely two resemblances, numbered 1 and 9 in my list, between the plays by Shadwell and Heywood.

[11] *Dramatic Works of Thomas Heywood* (London, 1874), IV, 171-172.

[12] Shadwell, III, 233-234.

[13] Heywood, IV, 177.

[14] Shadwell, III, 252.

[15] Cf. Heywood, IV, 183, with Shadwell, III, 240.

[16] Heywood, IV, 211.

[17] Shadwell, III, 275.

[18] Heywood, IV, 215-216.

[19] Shadwell, III, 294.

6. A portion of the scene in Heywood's play[20] where the four witches call their attendant spirits seems in diction to have suggested a part of the scene where Madge is to be initiated into the ranks of witchhood.[21]

Heywood	*Shadwell*
GIL: Therefore sing *Mawd*, and call each spright.	DEMD: . . .
Come away, and take thy duggy.	Where's my *Mamillion?* Come, my Rogue,
(*Enter foure spirits*)	And take thy Dinner.
MEG: Come my Mamilion like a Puggy.	DICKEN: Where's my *Puggy?* Come to me, and take thy Duggy.

7. The soldier who sleeps in the mill belonging to Generous is awakened by Mrs. Generous, Mall, the witches, and their spirits whom he beats off with a sword.[22] In a similar manner, Tom Shacklehead cuts at Mother Hargrave, Madge, and the other witches, who spit like cats and scratch him.[23] In each encounter, the hand of one of the witches is cut off.

8. In both plays, the witches are taken prisoners and ordered to the court for trial.[24]

9. The names of some of the witches are the same in both plays. "Mal Spencer" is used by Shadwell and Heywood; so is "Goody Dickison," who is called "Mother Dickenson" by Shadwell. "Mother Hargrave," who appears in Shadwell's comedy, is mentioned in the earlier play. Shadwell's "Mother Demdike" was suggested by the blind beggar of Pendle forest, Elizabeth Southerns or "Old Demdike," who, in 1612, died in prison while awaiting trial as a witch.

To the material suggested by the play of Heywood and Brome, Shadwell, in the scenes portraying the rites and ceremonies of the witches, added an element derived from Ben Jonson. In his preface, the author writes: "For the Magical Part, I had no Hopes of equalling *Shakespear* in Fancy, who created his Witchcraft for the most part out of his own Imagination; (in which Faculty no Man ever excell'd him) and therefore I resolv'd to take mine from Authority. And to that End, there is not one Action in the Play,

[20] Heywood, IV, 187.
[21] Shadwell, III, 275.
[22] Heywood, IV, 244-245.
[23] Shadwell, III, 310.
[24] Heywood, IV, 256-259; Shadwell, 317.

nay, scarce a Word concerning it, but is borrow'd from some Ancient or Modern Witchmonger which you will find in the Notes, wherein I have presented you a great part of the Doctrine of Witchcraft, believe it who will." Langbaine knows "nothing that we have in this Nature, in Dramatick Poetry, except *Ben Johnson's Masque of Queens,* which is likewise explained by Annotations."[25] But Langbaine did not notice that the subject-matter of Shadwell's scenes in which the witches appear was found in part in the *Masque of Queens,* and that the learned comments to which the author refers are in twenty-seven cases based upon Jonson's notes.[26]

As a matter of fact, the first paragraph of Shadwell's note *d* in the first act is drawn from note *m* in *Masque of Queens* with some omissions. Also, note *a* in Shadwell's second act is an enlarged version of note *n* in Jonson's masque.[27] In this case, a comparison of the language used by the two authors seems to admit of the interpretation that Shadwell wrote this note to *The Lancashire Witches* with an open copy of the *Masque of Queens* before him.

Jonson	*Shadwell*
Their little Martin is he that calls them to their conventicles, which is done in a human voice, but coming forth, they find him in the shape of a great buck goat, upon whom they ride to their meetings, *Delr. Disq. Mag.* quaest. 16, lib.	They call the Devil, that calls them to their Sabbaths or Feasts, little *Martin*, or little Master. *Delrio Disquis. Mag. quaest.* 16. *lib.* 2. and *Bodin Demonoman. lib.* 2. *cap.* 4. have the same Relation out of *Paulus Grillandus.* He is

[25] P. 448.

[26] A list of Shadwell's notes which are derived in whole or in part from *The Masque of Queens:*

	Lancashire Witches (Vol. III, 1720 ed.)	*Masque of Queens* (Vol. VII, Gifford Cunningham ed.)
Act I.	b	1 (p. 111)
	d	m (p. 111)
	e	m (p. 111)
	f	m (p. 111)
	g	m (p. 111)
	h	e (p. 108)
	k	e (p. 124)
	l	f (p. 125)
	m	6 (p. 125)
Act II.	a	n (p. 112)
	e	t (p. 116)
	f	5 (p. 118)
	g	5 (p. 119)
	h	4 (p. 118), 7 (p. 119)
	i	g (p. 109), 4 (p. 118)
	k	2 (p. 117)
	m	u (p. 117), 10 (p. 120)
	q	2 (p. 117)
	u	1 (p. 127)
Act III.	e	f (p. 109)
	g	o (p. 112), c (p. 123)
	i	9 (p. 120)
	k	12 (p. 121)
	l	3 (p. 117)
	m	8 (p. 120)
	n	11 (p. 121)
	c	m (p. 128), n (p. 130)

[27] Jonson, VII, 112; Shadwell, III, 328.

ii. And *Bod. Daemon.* lib. ii. cap. 4, have both the same relation from Paulus Grillandus, of a witch.

said to call them with a human Voice, but to appear in the Shape of a Buck-Goat.

The Restoration writer, however, did not borrow the quotations for all his notes from the *Masque of Queens.* In fact, about seventy per cent of the material contained in them is probably derived directly from classic poets or authorities on witchcraft.[28]

Certain portions of Shadwell's text show the undoubted influence of specific passages from Jonson:

Jonson	*Shadwell*
The ditch is made, and our nails the spade, *With pictures full, of wax and of wool;* *Their lives I stick, with needles quick;* *There lacks but the blood, to make up the flood.*	I' th' Hole, i' th' Ditch (our Nails have made) Now all our Images are laid, Of Wax and Wool, which we must prick, With Needles urging to the Quick. Into the Hole, I'll pour a Flood.
The sticks are across, there can be no loss, *The sage is rotten, the sulphur is gotten* *Up to the sky,' that was in the ground.*	HARG: Here's Sage, that under Ground was rotten, Which thus a-round me I bestow. SPENC: Sticks on the Bank a-cross are laid.
A murderer, yonder, was hung in chains, The sun and the wind had shrunk his veins; I bit off a sinew.	From a Murderer, that hung in Chains, I bit dry'd Sinews, and shrunk Veins.

[28] The works cited by Jonson in his notes to the *Masque of Queens* are listed in *Ben Jonson,* ed. Herford and Simpson, I, 252-253; those referred to by Shadwell are given in Summers, *History of Witchcraft and Demonology,* 296-297. Shadwell quotes passages which are not used by Jonson from Ovid, Propertius, Lucan, Tacitus, Horace, Virgil, Lucian, Juvenal, Pliny, Aristotle, Tibullus, Seneca, Petronius, Theocritus, and Theophrastus; also from Jean Bodin's *De Magorum daemonomania,* Martin Delrio's *Disquisitionum Magicarum,* Nicholas Remy's *Daemonolatria,* Philip Ludwig Elich's *Daemonomagia,* Bartolommeo Spina's *Quaestio de Strigibus seu Maleficis,* John Nider's *Formicarius,* and the *Malleus Maleficarum* by James Sprenger and Henry Institor. Shadwell adds the following to Jonson's authorities: Johann Wier, *De Praestigiis Daemonum;* Olaus Magnus, *Historia de Gentibus Septentrionalibus;* Reginald Scot, *Discoverie of Witchcraft;* Burchard, *Decretum;* Girolamo Cardano, *De Subtilitate;* Francesco Maria

I have been gathering wolves hairs, The mad dog's foam, and the adder's ears.	A mad Dog's Foam, and a Wolf's Hairs; A Serpent's Bowels, Adder's Ears.
The screech-owl's eggs, and the feathers black, The blood of the frog, and the bone in his back.[29] Etc.	The Bones of Frogs I got, and th' Blood, With Screetch-Owl's Eggs, and Feathers too.[30] Etc.

For one phrase, Shadwell acknowledges indebtedness to Jonson's *The Sad Shepherd.*

Jonson	*Shadwell*
. . . and where the sea Casts up his slimy ooze, search for a weed To open locks with . . .[31]	DICKEN: From the Sea's slimy Ouse a Weed I fetch'd, to open Locks at need.[32]

The Sad Shepherd may also have suggested the name "Puck-Hairy" given by Madge to the imp she suckles.[33] The similarity between Alken's description of the witch's abode and the words of Mother Demdike[34] seems more than a mere coincidence.

Jonson	*Shadwell*
ALKEN: Within a gloomy dimble she doth dwell, Down in a pit, o'ergrown with brakes and briars, Close by the ruins of a shaken abbey.	DEMD: Within this shatter'd Abby Walls, This Pit o'er-grown with Brakes and Briers, Is fit for our dark Works.

So much for Shadwell's borrowings from Ben! There is also a large amount of material in the witch-scenes found in neither Jonson nor Heywood. The sacrifice of the black lamb, the banquet with the devil, and the initiation of Madge are drawn in

Guazzo, *Compendium Maleficarum;* Sylvester Mazzolini, *De Strigimagarum, Daemonumque Mirandis;* Gabriel Naudé, *Apologie pour tous les grands Personnages qui ont esté faussement soupconnez de Magie;* and Pierre le Loyer, *IV Livres de Spectres* in English translation of Z. Jones.

[29] Jonson, VII, 111-112, 125, 119, 117, 120.

[30] Shadwell, III, 236, 237, 255, 256, 276.

[31] Jonson, VI, 276.

[32] Shadwell, III, 276.

[33] Jonson, VI, 279; Shadwell, III, 275.

[34] Jonson, VI, 276; Shadwell, III, 275.

large part from books on witchcraft.[35] Shadwell also introduces in these passages numerous songs, dances, and machines—operatic features of a kind with those he had devised for *Psyche* and *The Tempest*. The fusion of these diversified elements is accomplished but clumsily, with the result that the scenes in which the witches appear are among the least successful in the play.

The author is happier in his portrayal of the "non-magical" characters. Sir Edward Hartfort, Bellfort, and Doubty are used as mouthpieces for what Shadwell intends as common-sense. Sir Edward, who may have been suggested by Generous in *The Late Lancashire Witches*, is an embodiment of the self-satisfied country gentleman, a John Bull who thinks the English gentry are the noblest works of God. He upbraids his chaplain Smerk for meddling in family affairs and emphatically denies the existence of witches. To Bellfort, he represents "the Golden Days of Queen *Elizabeth*." He holds that there were "never good Days, but when great Tables were kept in large Halls, the Buttery-Hatch always open; Black Jacks and a good Smell of Meat and *March* Beer." He expresses his creed in a passage which the censor saw fit to delete: *"I am a true* English-*Man; I love the Prince's Rights and People's Liberties, and will defend them both with the last Penny in my Purse, and the last Drop in my Veins, and dare defie the witless Plots of Papists."* He is sure that the English "Constitution is the noblest in the World," and hopes to see the day when the "Prince and People [will] flourish . . . in spite of Jesuits." The younger men are in agreement with Sir Edward, Bellfort going so far as to think "there's Virtue in an *English* Sir-loin."[36]

Sir Jeffery Shacklehead presents a decided contrast to Sir Edward. Credulous in the extreme, he believes all the local supersitions concerning the efficacy of charms and prides himself upon his ability as a witch-finder. The scene in which he and his wife, after listening to the reports of the Constable and Thomas ô Georges against Mother Hargrave and Mall Spencer, name the remedies to be applied is a compendium of countryside superstition.[37] His son, who, despite his Oxford and Inns-of-Court breeding, is very much of a fool, and the equally loutish son of

[35] Shadwell, III, 236, 254, 275.
[36] *Ibid.*, III, 257 ff.
[37] *Ibid.*, III, 270 ff.

Sir Edward, who thinks of nothing but his sports, are the sources of much of the comic action.

Of the women, the vivacious Isabella and Theodosia profess a willingness to rebel against marrying the husbands selected by their fathers. In the manner of Mrs. Gripe, who in *The Woman-Captain* determines to have the "liberty of a She-Subject of *England*,"[38] Isabella tells Theodosia that she is a "a free *English* Woman, and will stand up for [her] Liberty, and Property of Choice."[39] Lady Shacklehead, in addition to assisting her husband in the examination of witches, plays the part of the amorous older woman, the Lady Gimcrack or the Lady Loveyouth of the countryside.

The characters which caused the censor greatest concern, Tegue and Smerk, now claim our attention. In his preface, Shadwell denies intending a reflection upon the Church of England in the person of Smerk. This character, whose name Ward[40] thinks is taken from that of the parson in Etherege's *The Man of Mode*, is represented as an "infamous Fellow, not of the Church, but crept into it for a Livelyhood." He is treated with the utmost contempt by Sir Edward, who makes him understand that his office is that of a "*Mechanick Divine, to read Church Prayers Twice every Day, and once a Week to teach* [*the*] *Servants Honesty and Obedience*." He is not "*to govern Men of Sense and Knowledge*." When Smerk attempts to argue that he has a "*Power Legantine*" from Heaven, Sir Edward demands to see his credentials and orders him to pack up his books and marry "*some cast Chamber-Maid . . . Charm'd with a Vicaridge of Forty Pound a Year*." Smerk, who immediately repents of his rashness, begs to be forgiven. Sir Edward then receives him with the understanding that he must omit controversial sermons, not meddle with government, not inquire into the business of the family, and devote his care to the other world.

Despite the orders given him by Sir Edward, Smerk, in another expurgated scene, makes love to Isabella and receives a box on the ears for his pains. She turns upon him with these words: "*Thou most insolent of Pedants! thou silly formal Thing, with a stiff*

[38] *Ibid.*, III, 360.
[39] *Ibid.*, III, 231.
[40] Ward, *English Dramatic Literature*, III, 458.

plain Band, a little Parsonical Grogram, and a Girdle thou art so proud of, in which thou would'st do well to hang thy self; some have vouchsafed to use it for that Purpose: Thou that never wert but a Curate,—a Journey-man Divine, as thy Father was a Journey-Man Taylor, before he could set up for himself, to have the Impudence to pretend Love to me!" In a contemptuous tirade, she then pictures the life of a country clergyman. Since he thinks it atheistical not to believe in witches, Smerk proves good timber for the Roman Catholic propaganda of Tegue. After acknowledging, in the presence of Bellfort and Doubty, that the Plot is not Papist, but Presbyterian, he utters sentiments in opposition to Parliament. *"With my Bible in my Hand, I'll dispute with the whole House of Commons. Sir, I hate Parliaments; none but Fanaticks, Hobbists, and Atheists, believe the Plot."* These statements lead the young men to think Smerk a rascal *"conceal'd in the Church, and . . . none of it."* When Sir Edward finally learns the true character of his chaplain, he refuses to retain him in his household: "I'll not have a Divine with so flexible a Conscience; there shall be no such Vipers in my Family."[41]

Shadwell gives to the Irish priest through whom he ridicules the Church of Rome the assumed name of Tegue. He intends this as a disguise for Dominick Kelly, one of the supposed murderers of Sir Edmund Berry Godfrey, for whose attachment the House of Lords passed an order on December 27, 1678.[42] "Tegue" (also spelled "Teg" or "Teague") was familiar to Restoration theatre-goers as the name of the Irish servant in *The Committee*. The lines written for the latter character by Sir Robert Howard are not in dialect. Shadwell's priest, however, speaks a sort of stage-Irish, a language very like that used by Captain Whit in *Bartholomew Fair* and the Irishmen in Jonson's *Irish Masque*.

Tegue attempts to avert the powers of the witches by means of "St. *Caaterine* de Virgin's Wedding Ring," "shome of de Sweat of St. *Francis*," and a "Piece of St. *Lawrence*'s Grid-Iron." When these relics prove of no avail, he sprinkles everyone with holy water. He is ambitious of becoming an "Eerish *Cardinal*"; he is willing to pray souls out of purgatory, if he is paid money

[41] Shadwell, III, 243, 268, 322.

[42] *Journals of the House of Lords*, XIII, 441.

enough; he holds that "*a Cooncel is infallible; . . . de Cardinals are infallible too, upon Occasion, and dey are damn'd Hereticks Dogs . . . dat do not believe every oord dey vill speak indeed.*" In his interview with Sir Jeffery, he answers questions with mental reservation: "I did never taake Holy Orders since I was bore,—(*Aside*) In *Jamaica*"; "I did never shee *Rome*, in all my Life,—(*Aside*) Vid de Eyes of a Lyon." When he is arrested on the charge of being implicated in the Popish Plot, he manifests pleasure: "if dey vill hang me, I vill be a shaint indeed. *My hanging Speech was made for me long ago by de Jesuits, and I have it ready, and I will live and dy by it, by my shoul.*"[43]

The Lancashire Witches, because the various diversified elements which make up the plot are not well blended, is as a whole inferior to many of Shadwell's plays. The characters of Smerk and Tegue, mere excrescences upon the story of the lovers and the witchridden countryside, might have been omitted with little harm to the rest of the comedy. They give the impression of being dragged in by the heels in order that the author may have an opportunity to take part in the political war in the theatre. Although professing to be "somewhat costive of Belief," Shadwell introduces his witches as real in order to prevent his opponents from clamoring against his play as atheistical. After presenting them as substantial creatures, he causes Sir Edward, Bellfort, and Doubty, characters with whom he evidently intends the audience to sympathize as representatives of common-sense, to profess continually a disbelief in their existence. *The Lancashire Witches* is, nevertheless, almost unique among plays of the time. It brought to the theatre-goers of the Restoration a touch of the English countryside; it introduced the rural gentry and their households, types that must have been a welcome relief from the never-ending fops and rakes of Hyde Park and the drawing-rooms.

[43] Shadwell, III, 287-290, 317, 322.

CHAPTER XV

THE SQUIRE OF ALSATIA

THE SQUIRE OF ALSATIA, the comedy with which Shadwell after an absence of seven years returned to the theatre, was a triumph when first produced in May, 1688. It was printed at least five times before 1700.[1] Robert Gould, although linking it with farces, vouches for its popularity in "The *Play-house* A Satyr":

> The Emp'rour of the Moon, *'twill never tire;*
> *The same Fate has the fam'd* Alsatian Squire.[2]

That it was also well liked in Dublin appears in a letter of John Dunton, dated April 20, 1699: "For the Play . . . I need say nothing, it is so well known; it was pretty to see the Squire choused out of so fair an estate with so little ready rhino. . . . In a word, no Church I was in while at Dublin could I discern to be half so crowded as this place [i.e., the play-house]."[3]

I have elsewhere noted the actors and actresses who made up the superlative original cast.[4] The revivals during the eighteenth century likewise called forth the efforts of the best players of that time. Among those who appeared as Sir William Belfond were Pinkethman,[5] Estcourt, Spiller, Harper, Miller, Macklin, Yates, and Shuter; the Belfond Seniors were Bullock, Miller, Chapman, the younger Cibber, and Woodward; the younger Belfond afforded Wilks, Bridgewater, Walker, Milward, Hale, Havard, and Smith an opportunity to display their abilities; Sir Edward was performed by Keen, Quin, Thurmond, Lacy, Bridgewater, and Gibson. Of the women, Mrs. Knight, Mrs. Thurmond, Mrs. Egleton, Mrs.

[1] 1688 (two), 1692, 1693, 1699.

[2] *Works of Mr. Robert Gould* (London, 1709), II, 238.

[3] *Life and Errors of John Dunton* (London, 1818), II, 563-564. An edition of *The Squire of Alsatia* was published in Dublin in 1738.

[4] See pp. 76-77. It was acted in the hall of the Inner Temple on November 1, 1689. *Calendar of Inner Temple Records* (London, 1901), III, 271.

[5] Cibber says he has "seen Leigh extremely well imitated" in the part of Sir William by Pinkethman, "who, tho' far short of what was inimitable in the original, yet as to the general resemblance was a very valuable copy of him."

Pritchard, Mrs. Kilby, and Mrs. Vincent acted Mrs. Termagant; Mrs. Oldfield, Mrs. Younger, Mrs. Mills, and Miss Hallam performed the part of Teresia; while Mrs. Rogers, Mrs. Horton, and Mrs. Clive appeared as Isabella.

The last important revival of *The Squire of Alsatia* was by Woodward at Covent Garden on November 18, 1763.[6] At this time, the play received about seven performances. Dibdin accounts for its withdrawal on the ground that it contained "too much of the low and vulgar."[7] It did not entirely disappear from the boards after this production, however, since sporadic performances are recorded for December 12, 1765, and October 23, 1766.[8] Shadwell's play was later to be remembered by those critics who accused Cumberland of borrowing the plot of *The Choleric Man* (produced December 19, 1774) from the earlier comedy.[9]

The Squire of Alsatia tells the story of the two sons of Sir William Belfond. The elder has been bred in the country with great severity by his father; the younger has been brought up in the city with kindness and liberality by his uncle. While the father is attending to business on the continent, the elder son with his servant Lolpoop goes to London. Here he falls in with a company of rascals, Cheatly, Shamwell, and Captain Hackum, who dare not stir out of the district known as Alsatia, the sanctuary of rogues. Sir William, upon returning to London, overhears bullies speaking of the scouring exploits of Belfond. Thinking this to be his younger son, he goes to his brother, Sir Edward, and ex-

[6] Genest, V, 53.

[7] *Complete History of the Stage,* IV, 245.

[8] Genest, V, 105, 129. Genest also records performances at Drury Lane on December 29, 1703; September 13, November 14, 1704; June 4, 1707; April 26, October 25, 1708; May 22, November 23, 1711; October 20, 1712; November 16, 1713; November 29, 1714; October 20, 1720; January 23, November 8, 1723; January 20, November 3, 1725; September 23, October 23, 1736; March 13, May 17, 1738; December 10, 1739; December 28, 1748; December 18, 1749; May 2, 1758; at Drury Lane or Dorset Garden on October 25, 1705; November 6, 1707; at Lincoln's Inn Fields on December 15, 1715; October 21, 1717; November 24, 1719; April 3, December 21, 1722; November 25, 1723; October 27, 1724; November 29, 1725; January 8, 1728; May 11, 1730; at Covent Garden on April 6, 15, May 3, 1734; May 16, 1735; May 7, 1739; February 28, October 11, 1744; December 26, 1746.

[9] For discussion of this play and the criticisms against it, see S. T. Williams, *Richard Cumberland. His Life and Dramatic Works,* (New Haven, 1917), pp. 111-113. Paul P. Kies (*Modern Philology,* XXIV, 65-90) thinks that Lessing derived the outline of the plot of *Miss Sara Sampson,* the principal characters, and many details from *The Squire of Alsatia.*

claims against the latter's method of education. Sir Edward, however, feeling certain that there must be a mistake, takes Sir William to the lodgings of Belfond Junior. But here the father's misgivings are strengthened when he finds Termagant, a woman by whom his younger son has had a child, and Lucia, a girl recently seduced by him, secreted in his apartments.

Meanwhile, the elder Belfond makes merry at Alsatia. When Sir William intrudes upon his son's companions, he is forced by the rabble to take to his heels. After hearing of this experience, Belfond Junior determines instantly to learn who is using his name. In amazement to find his elder brother, whom he had thought to be in the country, at the George, he attempts in vain to draw him away from his riotous comrades. Later, Sir William, upon discovering his elder son in Alsatia and upon being addressed by him in the canting language of the place, becomes furious and summons a constable to arrest him. The rabble of the district, who are aroused by this action, take Sir William prisoner and threaten to place him under the pump. Belfond Junior with several gentlemen from the adjoining Temple comes to the rescue in the nick of time and orders that Cheatly, Hackum, and Shamwell receive the punishment they would have given his father.

The younger Belfond and his friend Truman love the niece Isabella and daughter Teresia of the hypocritical Puritan Scrapeall. In order to obtain admittance to their company, Truman dresses in sober attire and ingratiates himself with their governess Ruth. The jealous Termagant, pretending that her brother intends to kill her because of the dishonor she has brought upon her family, takes refuge in the house of Scrapeall and tells of her desertion by Belfond Junior for an attorney's daughter. Isabella, moved by this story, then spurns her lover. But after Belfond has sworn that he has never been contracted to any woman and that he has abandoned all thoughts of vice and folly, she and her cousin leave their prison and accompany their lovers to the dwelling of Sir Edward.

Termagant, ceaseless in her attempts at revenge, is later introduced as a fortune to the elder Belfond by the denizens of Whitefriars. He is about to marry her when his younger brother appears and saves him from ruin. She has also informed the attorney of the relationship between Lucia and her former lover. Belfond Junior, in what he considers a lawful lie, assures the attorney of his daughter's innocence. Termagant, now dressed in male attire, again tries revenge by having two affidavit men swear that Isabella has for months been contracted to "him." Belfond Junior, who refuses to believe this charge, pulls off the accuser's wig and discovers his former mistress. Sir Edward then settles an annuity upon Termagant on condition that she will no longer torment his nephew and also makes a gift to Lucia. Belfond Senior, after repenting of his actions, is forgiven by his father, who for the first time in his life treats him with kindness. Sir Edward plans to prosecute the rogues who had cheated his nephew. Sir William has to confess that his brother's method of education is superior to his own. Truman and Teresia marry, and Belfond Junior, pleased at having such a wife as Isabella, bids farewell to vice.

Langbaine, never slow to notice dramatic borrowings, holds that the "Ground of this Play, is from *Terence* his *Adelphi;* especially the two Characters of *Mitio* and *Demea,* which . . . are improv'd."[10] The plot of the Latin play has been summarized thus:

> Demea having two sons, Æschinus and Ctesipho, allowed the one to be adopted by his brother Micio, but kept the other. Demea was a grim and harsh father, and Ctesipho being captivated by the charms of a cithern-player was sheltered by his brother Æschinus, who allowed rumour to ascribe the intrigue to himself. Further he carried off the girl from the slave-dealer who owned her. Æschinus had himself seduced an Athenian lady of scanty means and pledged himself to marry her. Demea angrily protested against the affair, but on the truth becoming known Æschinus married the lady and Ctesipho was left in possession of the fiddle-girl.[11]

In *The Squire of Alsatia,* Shadwell has produced a free adaptation of the *Adelphoe.* The part of the harsh father Demea is taken by Sir William; that of his more complacent brother by Sir Edward. Micio, whose methods of education differ radically from

[10] *Account of the English Dramatic Poets,* p. 450. Referred to as adaptation from *Adelphoe* in Charles Gildon's "A Letter to Mr. D'Urfey" prefixed to his *The Marriage-Hater Match'd: A Comedy* (London, 1692) and in Preface to *Fortune in her Wits: A Comedy* (London, 1705) by Charles Johnson. The situations common to Terence and Shadwell are noted by Heinemann in his *Shadwell-Studien* (Kiel, 1907), pp. 12 ff.

[11] Terence, With an English Translation (ed. Sargeaunt in Loeb Classical Library), II, 217.

those of Demea, believes that the spirit of a true father is to accustom his son to do right by inclination rather than by fear. When Demea brings to his brother information concerning the latest escapade of Æschinus, Micio is willing to be indulgent. If Demea were flesh and blood, he answers, he would allow his son to enjoy his youth, instead of causing him to look forward to the day of his father's death.[12] In the English play, Sir Edward, after Sir William angrily relates what he has heard about the person he thinks to be his younger son, grants that the adopted boy is subject to the extravagancies of youth, but excuses him on the ground that he is no sot and that he is private in his debauches. To Sir William, such faults as these loom large; he thinks a son will later bless his father if he has been treated with severity and not allowed too much liberty or money when young.[13]

Shadwell has added to Terence by making the believer in the sterner method of training argue for schooling in the practical things of life and by causing his better-humoured brother to believe in the type of education which develops "a compleat Gentleman, fit to serve his Country in any Capacity." The instruction of the elder Belfond has been of such a nature that "he knows a Sample of any Grain as well as e'er a Fellow in the North: Can handle a Sheep or Bullock as well as any one: Knows his Seasons of Plowing, Sowing, Harrowing, laying Fallow: Understands all sorts of Manure: And ne'er a one that Wears a Head can wrong him in a Bargain." Sir Edward thinks him a "very pretty Fellow for a Gentleman's Baily." He, on the other hand, sent his adopted son to Westminster School "till he was Master of the *Greek* and *Latin* Tongues," then to the university for three years where he read "the Noble *Greek* and *Roman* Authors," Natural Philosophy, History, and Mathematics, then to the Temple to be instructed in "some old Common-Law Books, the Statutes, and the best Pleas of the Crown, and the Constitution of the old true *English* Government," and finally to the continent where he "saw two Campaigns; studied History, Civil Laws and Laws of Commerce. . . . He made the Tour of *Italy*, and saw *Germany*, and the *Low-Countries*, and return'd well-skill'd in Foreign Affairs."[14]

In the last act of the *Adelphoe*, Demea compares his life which

[12] Act I, scenes I, II.

[13] Shadwell, IV, 26-30.

[14] *Ibid.*, IV, 43-45.

has been spent in misery with that of his brother, who has lived for himself and won the esteem of everybody. His sons love Micio, but await his own death. After determining to emulate his brother, Demea acts in a friendly manner to Syrus, Geta, and Æschinus. Aided by the latter, he wheedles Micio into agreeing to marry Sostrata, into giving a farm to Hegio, and into not only granting Syrus his freedom, but also advancing him money by which to live. When the generous brother asks the cause of this sudden change in his ways, Demea replies that his purpose was to demonstrate that what his sons found to be good-nature in Micio did not spring from justice and goodness, but from indulgence. If they wish someone to reprove them when their inexperience would lead them to excesses, he will gladly supply that office.[15]

Like Demea, Sir William, after seeing his "carefully nurtured" son repudiate his former training and praise the life of the Alsatians, compares his position with that of his brother, who, in addition to enjoying all pleasures, has won the respect of the world and the love of his adopted son. All this goes to prove, says Sir Edward, that severity will do nothing; Sir William must win his son back by love.[16] The moral which the author would point in this play, and that he intends to point a moral is indicated in the prologue where he speaks of desiring to conform to the rules of Master Ben, who "to correct, and to inform, did write," is well summed up in the concluding speech of Sir Edward:

> You, that would breed your Children well, by Kindness and Liberality endear 'em to you: And teach 'em by Example,
>
> Severity spoils ten for one it mends:
> If you'd not have your Sons desire your Ends,
> By Gentleness and Bounty make those Sons your Friends.

From the *Adelphoe*, then, Shadwell takes two contrasting points of view in the training of youth—that based upon unmitigated severity, and that founded upon kindness tempered with indulgence. In the original, the follies resulting from the soft method are stressed; in the adaptation, the benefits growing out of the soft method are accentuated. Shadwell's shift in emphasis may have

[15] Act V, scenes IV-IX.

[16] Shadwell, IV, 97.

been due to the influence of *L'École des Maris,* Molière's comedy based upon the *Adelphoe.* In this play, two brothers, Sganarelle and Ariste, act as guardians for the sisters, Isabelle and Léonor. Sganarelle's severe treatment causes Isabelle to deceive him by wedding Valère; whereas Ariste's kindness leads to his own marriage with Léonor.

The influence of Molière is again evident, as Mr. Miles has indicated,[17] in that scene in which Sir Edward urges the reasons why the match between the elder Belfond and Scrapeall's niece would not be happy. Every argument of his is met by Sir William's reply, "Fifteen Thousand Pounds."[18] Likewise, in *L'Avare,* Harpagon, when discussing with Valère the marriage of his daughter to Anselme, replies "sans dot" to all objections.[19]

In adapting his material to contemporary London, Shadwell had to change considerably the characters and escapades of the sons of Sir William. Belfond Junior, who corresponds to Æschinus in the *Adelphoe,* is the typical young man of Restoration comedy. Described in the dramatis personae as an "ingenious, well-accomplished Gentleman: A Man of Honour, and of excellent Disposition and Temper," he is presented at the conclusion of a career of youthful extravagancies. Having fallen in love with Isabella, he is now "content to abandon all other Pleasures, and live alone for her; she has subdu'd [him] even to Marriage." The troubles resulting from his follies are also instrumental in causing him to leave the "foolish, restless, anxious Life" he has been leading. After Sir Edward has made the proper settlements upon the former mistresses of his adopted son, Belfond Junior kneels before Isabella with this promise: "A long farewell to all the Vanity and Lewdness of Youth: I offer my self at your Feet as a Sacrifice without a Blemish now." When his future wife expresses the fear that he may return to his old practices, he replies: "I look on Marriage as the most solemn Vow a Man can make; and tis, by consequence, the basest Perjury to break it." By the end of the play, he has become quite virtuous:

> Farewell for ever all the Vices of the Age:
> There is no Peace but in a virtuous Life,
> Nor lasting Joy but in a tender Wife.[20]

[17] *Influence of Molière on Restoration Comedy,* p. 238.
[18] Shadwell, IV, 73.
[19] *L'Avare,* Act I, scene VII.
[20] Shadwell, IV, 35, 94, 107 ff.

The presentation of this character is rather confusing. Shadwell intended to show that Sir Edward's method of managing youth is superior to Sir William's, yet the illustration, the Younger Belfond, is not always a convincing example. His "reformation" at the close results as much from the difficulties in which he finds himself because of his previous actions as from the training he has been given by Sir Edward. His protest that he is now a "Sacrifice without a Blemish" seems woefully inept.[21]

In his portrayal of the women whose fates are more or less bound up with Belfond's, Shadwell is most successful in his drawing of Lucia. Possibly he is too successful for he presents this "beautiful Girl, of a mild and tender Disposition," who has been seduced by the young rake, in such a manner as to draw one's interest towards her and away from Isabella, who later becomes Belfond's wife. The jealous and revengeful Mrs. Termagant reminds one of Maria in *The Libertine*, who dresses in male attire and pursues her seducer with the purpose of vengeance.[22] In Termagant, there may also be a slight trace of Angelica Bianca, the courtezan in *The Rover*, who is jealous of any person to whom her lover Willmore shows affection. On one occasion, she goes to him in masking habit, draws a pistol which she holds to his breast, and upbraids him for his lack of constancy.[23] This passage may have suggested, although there is no similarity in the details of the two scenes, the episode in which Termagant attempts to shoot Belfond.[24]

[21] See E. Bernbaum, *The Drama of Sensibility* (Boston, 1915), pp. 67-69. Chapter III of the "Considerations on the Stage, and on the Advantages which arise to a Nation from the Encouragement of Arts," printed with *The Triumphs of Love and Honour, A Play . . . By Mr. Cooke* (London, 1731), contains "A Criticism on The Squire of Alsatia." The author commends the teaching in this play: "An Audience, which is convinced of the good Effects of Sir *Edward Belfond*'s prudent Management of his Son, will not go contrary to it when they have Occasion to follow the Example; nor is the Consequence of Sir *William*'s Manner of Behaviour any encouragement to follow it. The Lenity of Sir *Edward*, and his taking proper Opportunitys to instill such Maxims into his Son as these, *young Fellows will never get Knowledge but at their own Cost, there's Nothing but Anxiety in Vice, and every drunken Fit is a short Madness, that cuts off a good Part of Life*, made his Son reflect on his Actions, and profit from every Reflection; but the Severity of Sir *William* made his Son eager in Pursuit of what he had been tyrannically restrained from, and had so blunted his Understanding that he was scarcely capable of enjoying the benefit of Reflection, till Destruction, the Product of Vice and Folly, stared him in the Face" (p. 61 f.).

[22] Shadwell, II, 121 ff.

[23] *Works of Aphra Behn* (ed. Summers), I, 93 ff.

[24] Shadwell, IV, 105.

Belfond Senior, whose part in the comedy corresponds to that played by Ctesipho in the Terentian play, is an elder son upon whom his father's estate is entailed. He goes to the city and there repeats the adventures of a long line of unsophisticated country fellows, who, after falling into the clutches of clever rascals, emerge from their experiences poorer, but wiser, men. The actions of Belfond Senior are not dissimilar to those in *The Sparagus Garden* of Tim Hoyden, who journeys to London with his man Coulter. Here he meets Monylacks, Springe, and Brittleware, who soon relieve him of his four hundred pounds and give him lessons in how to behave as a gentleman.[25]

The attempt on the part of a rustic to improve his vocabulary was a device occasionally used in the earlier drama. In *A Fair Quarrel* of Middleton and Rowley, the Cornishman Chough and his servant Trimtram repair to the Roaring School. After studying such expressions as "Briarean brousted," "bronstrops," and "minotaur," they sally forth, meet Captain Albo, address him with these high-sounding terms, and cause him to resolve also to take lessons in roaring.[26] This learning of expressions, which are later handled with surprising effect, is practised by Belfond Senior, who at first merely repeats with growing interest the words employed by his companions. After becoming proficient in their use, he throws them in the teeth of his father when the latter confronts him in Alsatia.[27]

Genest thinks that Lolpoop, the servant of the elder Belfond, is from the *Truculentus* of Plautus.[28] The character he has in mind is the crusty servant of Strabax. At first, Stratilax is very surly towards Astaphium, the maid of the courtesan Phronesium. When he is next seen, he has changed his behavior and willingly accompanies her to her residence.[29] Lolpoop, who attempts to make Belfond Senior believe that the persons into whose hands he has fallen are "Rogues, Cheats, and Pickpockets" and who forever urges his master to return home, is finally ensnared by the prostitute Betty.[30]

A touch of novelty was injected into Shadwell's play by laying

[25] Act II, scene III; Act III, scenes VII, XI; Act IV, scenes IX, X, XI.

[26] Act IV, scenes I, IV.

[27] Shadwell, IV, 85 ff.

[28] Genest, I, 459.

[29] Act II, scene II; Act III, scene II.

[30] Shadwell, IV, 19-21, 46, 56 ff.

the scene of Belfond's undoing in Whitefriars. This section of London, at one time the seat of the Carmelites, was in 1688 notorious as a sanctuary for rogues. Edward I had given the order of Carmelites or White Friars a plot of land in Fleet Street upon which to build their house. Here the establishment flourished for more than two centuries, until, in the reign of Henry VIII, the brethren were compelled to surrender their property. At the time when Stow was writing his *Survey*, the Church had disappeared, but within the district there had been many "fayre houses builded, lodgings for Noble men and others."[31]

In 1608, the immunities which had been granted to the inhabitants of Whitefriars were confirmed in a charter of James I. Those living within the precincts were to be "quit and exonerated of and from all taxes, fifteenths, and other burdens of scot, and of watch and ward, through or within the city of London, to be paid, made, sustained or contributed" except certain charges for defence and for pavements. All non-freemen residing within the city were to be taxed equally with the citizens, except those who dwelt in Blackfriars and Whitefriars.[32] This district naturally became the rendezvous of a gang of nondescript rascals, glad of a place of refuge from bailiffs and creditors.

The term "Alsatia" as a name for this locality was familiar to the theatre-goers of the seventies and eighties. In the prologue to *Pastor Fido*, Settle writes:

> *And when poor Duns, quite weary, will not stay,*
> *The hopeless Squire's into* Alsatia *driven.*[33]

In *Tunbridge-Wells, or a Dayes Courtship*, Owmuch tells Fairlove that he is "as foul mouth'd as a decayed sinner in the lower *Alsatia*."[34] Otway, in *The Cheats of Scapin*, has his hero ask Shift if he cannot "counterfeit a roaring bully of Alsatia."[35] In *The Soldier's Fortune*, this same dramatist makes Courtine, who has been railing against his fate, express himself in this manner:

[31] Stow, *Survey of London* (ed. C. L. Kingsford, Oxford, 1908), II, 46-47.

[32] *Historical Charters and Constitutional Documents of the City of London* (London, 1884), pp. 144-145.

[33] [Settle], *Pastor Fido: or, The Faithful Shepherd* (London, 1677).

[34] [Rawlins], *Tunbridge Wells, or a Day's Courtship* (London, 1678), p. 4.

[35] *Works of Thomas Otway* (London, 1812), I, 215.

"Tis a fine equipage I am like to be reduced to; I shall be ere long as greasy as an Alsatian bully; this flopping hat, pinned up on one side, with a sandy weather-beaten peruke, dirty linen, and, to complete the figure, a long scandalous iron sword jarring at my heels."[36] Likewise, Mrs. Behn in *The Lucky Chance* causes Bredwel to describe the lodging of Mr. Wasteall as situated in a "nasty Place called *Alsatia*, at a Black-Smith's."[37] In *The Woman-Captain*, Sir Christopher Swash, after military discipline proves too severe, suggests going "to the *Temple* or *Alsatia* for Refuge."[38]

Although references to this district and its inhabitants were not unusual, Shadwell was the first to make dramatic capital of Alsatia. He sketches three dwellers in the place—Cheatly, "who by reason of Debts dares not stir out of *White-fryers*"; Shamwell, "who being ruin'd by *Cheatly*, is made a Decoy-Duck for others; not daring to stir out of *Alsatia*, where he lives"; and Captain Hackum, "a Blockheaded Bully of *Alsatia;* a cowardly, impudent, blustering Fellow; formerly a Serjeant in *Flanders*, run from his Colours, retreated into *White-Fryers* for a very small Debt; where by the *Alsatians*, he is dubb'd a Captain." William Oldys reports that the latter according to "old John Bowman the player" was drawn to expose Bully Dawson, the notorious sharper.[39] Hackum is presented as a person with "Terror in [his] Countenance and Whiskers." He and his comrades, who, like the brave-mouthed Swash, Blunderbuss, and Heildebrand in *The Woman-Captain*, are cowards at heart, display their true characters when they submit without protest to the insults of the younger Belfond.[40] The

[36] *Ibid.*, I, 371-372.

[37] *Works of Aphra Behn* (ed. Summers), III, 201.

In D'Urfey's *Love for Money: or, The Boarding School* (London, 1691), p. 59, occurs this conversation:

"*Jilt*(all). What means the Fellow: Who is this Rascal, *Oyley?*

Oyley. Some pitiful Shaggrag or other, Madam, of *Alsatia*, that wants to be kicked by your Ladyships Footman."

In Robert Gould's *The Corruption of the Times by Money. A Satyr* (London, 1693), p. 20, is a reference to Alsatia as a retreat. *The Post-boy rob'd of his Mail: Or, the Pacquet Broke Open* (London, 1692), p. 29, mentions "a Title of Honour for an *Alsatian* spunger." E. Lewis, writing to Robert Harley on September 27, 1707, refers to "Mr. Cornwallis, an ancient inhabitant of Alsatia" (*MSS. of Duke of Portland*, IV, 453 in *App. Hist. MSS. Comm. Report XV, Pt. IV*).

[38] Shadwell, III, 419.

[39] *Notes and Queries*, 2d Series, XI, 182. It will be remembered that Sir Roger de Coverley "kicked Bully Dawson in a public coffee-house for calling him youngster." See *Spectator*, No. 2.

[40] Shadwell, IV, 63-64.

George Tavern, in which Shadwell lays some of his Alsatian scenes, was, according to Joseph Moser, an actual place, "not only the temple of dissipation and debauchery; but also [a house containing] under its ample roof the recesses of *contrivance* and *fraud*, the nests of *perjury*, and the apartments of *prostitution*."[41]

The scenes in the Friars are alive with action. Especially is this true of that passage in which Sir William Belfond, after being bantered by his son, summons "*a Tip-staff, with the Constable and his Watch-Men*." At the cry of "An Arrest," the denizens of the place are aroused, and, armed with all sorts of weapons, they flock to the fight with the representatives of the law. In the combat which follows, the rabble fall upon the constable, beat him, and cause the tipstaff to take to his heels. Then they seize Sir William and are about to put him under the pump when the younger Belfond and his company come from the adjoining Temple, fall upon the Alsatians, and worst them in the struggle.[42]

Shadwell inserted a touch of realism in these scenes in Whitefriars by giving to the inhabitants a "particular Language which such Rogues have made to themselves, call'd Canting, as Beggars, Gipsies, Thieves, and Jail-Birds do." This use of slang was thought by Peregrine Bertie to be the reason for the success of the play.[43] In the initial episode of the comedy, the elder Belfond hears a goodly number of Alsatian words—"ready," "cole" and "rhino" for "money"; "putt" for "one who is easily cheated"; "clear" for "very drunk"; "meggs" for "guineas"; "smelts" for "half-guineas"; "tatts" and "the doctor" for "false dice"—expressions which cause him to consider it a blessing that he has met such persons as Shamwell, Cheatly, and Hackum.[44]

When the squire is later confronted by his father,[45] he has become proficient in the language of Whitefriars and answers Sir William's question, "Were you not educated like a Gentleman?" in this manner:

[41] John Nichols, *Literary Anecdotes of the Eighteenth Century*, VIII (London, 1814), 353. According to Nichols, I, 4, 5, William Bowyer the elder in 1699 "removed his printing-office into *White Fryars*, to a house which had formerly been the George Tavern." A foot-note adds the further information: "In which some of the scenes of Shadwell's 'Squire of Alsatia' are painted."

[42] Shadwell, IV, 90-91.

[43] See p. 75.

[44] Shadwell, IV, 15 ff.

[45] *Ibid.*, IV, 85 ff.

No; like a *Grasier*, or a *Butcher*. If I had staid in the Country, I had never seen such a *Nab*, a rum Nab, such a modish *Porker*, such spruce and neat Accoutrements; here is a *Tattle*, here's a *Famble*, and here's the *Cole*, the *Ready*, the *Rhino*, the *Darby:* I have a lusty *Cod*, Old *Prig*, I'd have thee know, and am very *Rhinocerical;* here are *Meggs* and *Smelts* good store, *Decusses* and *Georges;* the Land is entail'd, and I will have my *Snack* of it while I am young, adad, I will. Hah!

Such a reply stumps the irascible Sir William, who calls his son a "most confirm'd *Alsatian* Rogue."

The Squire of Alsatia, although the first play to use this particular canting language extensively, was not the first play to represent it on the stage. Etherege's *The Man of Mode* contains an earlier attempt to insert in drama the slang of Whitefriars. In an episode in the third scene of the third act,[46] three ill-fashioned fellows enter singing and have this brief conversation:

1 MAN: Dorimant's convenient, Madam Loveit.
2 MAN: I like the oily buttock with her.
3 MAN: What spruce prig is that?
1 MAN: A caravan lately come from Paris.
2 MAN: Peace, they smoke.

In *The Woman-Captain,* Shadwell adds to the four expressions used by Etherege:

BLUND: Ounds! what Prigg is yon talking with your Natural?—
HEILD: Shall I pluck out Porker and lay him on thick?

. . . .

HEILD: Are you sure the Doctors are in, *Blunderbuss?*[47]

Finally, the glossary prefixed to *The Squire of Alsatia* contains no less than forty-seven canting terms.

Shadwell, during his residence in the parish of St. Bride's, had had ample opportunity to hear this Alsatian slang as well as to observe the disorder and license of the district. Through the mouth of Sir Edward, he forcefully expresses disapprobation:

I'll rout this Knot of most pernicious Knaves, for all the Privilege of your Place. Was ever such Impudence suffer'd in a Government? *Ire-*

[46] *Works of Sir George Etheredge* (ed. Verity), p. 309.

[47] Shadwell, III, 367, 394.

land's conquer'd; *Wales* subdu'd; *Scotland* united: But there are some few Spots of Ground in *London*, just in the Face of the Government, unconquer'd yet, that hold in Rebellion still. Methinks 'tis strange, that Places so near the King's Palace should be no Parts of his Dominions. 'Tis a Shame to the Societies of the Law, to countenance such Practices: Should any Place be shut against the King's Writ, or *Posse Comitatus?*[48]

Whether Dennis was correct or not in holding that Shadwell's play "was a good deal instrumental in causing that nest of villains to be regulated by public authority,"[49] the fact remains that "An Act for the more effectual Relief of Creditors in Cases of Escapes & for pventing Abuses in Prisons and pretended priveleged Places" was passed in 1696-7. Article Fifteen states that "after the said First Day of May it shall and may be lawfull for any Person or Persons who have or hath any Debt or Debts Sum or Sums of Money due or oweing to him from any person or psons who now is or hereafter shall be and reside within the White Fryars Savoy Salisbury Court Ram-Alley Mitre Court Fullers Rents Baldwyns Gardens Mountague Close or the Minories Mint Clink or Deadmans Place upon legal Processe taken out against such Person or Persons to demand and require the Sheriffs of London," to take Posse Comitatus and arrest within these privileged places. The Act also provides a severe penalty for the rescue of a prisoner.[50]

After the right of sanctuary was lost to Whitefriars, the place became almost deserted. Ned Ward, in *The London-Spy Compleat*, describes the main street of "these Infernal Territories where Vice and Infamy were so long Protected, and Flourish'd without Reproof, to the great Shame and Scandal of a Christian Nation" as "so very thin of People, the Windows broke, and the Houses untenanted, as if the Plague, or some such like Judgment from Heaven, as well as Executions on Earth, had made a great Slaughter amongst the poor Inhabitants."[51] The ruined condition of Alsatia is also mentioned by Steele in *The Tatler*, No. 66.

The Squire of Alsatia, as we have seen, is a free adaptation to conditions in contemporary London of the central theme of the

[48] *Ibid.*, IV, 109.

[49] Joseph Spence, *Anecdotes, Observations, and Characters of Books and Men* (London, 1820), p. 43. Dennis is also quoted as saying, "The story it was built on was a true fact."

[50] *Statutes of the Realm . . . From Original Records and Authentic Documents* (1820), VII, 273 ff.

[51] [Ward], *The London Spy Compleat* (London, 1703), p. 153.

Adelphoe. The author, who, in his prologue, sets forth his aim of correcting and informing in this comedy, emphasizes the superiority of Sir Edward Belfond's method of training youth and exposes the evils of Whitefriars. The situation in which a country fellow, desirous to be made a city gentleman, is cheated by a band of cowardly bullies had been pleasing to Middleton and Brome. Shadwell added novelty to this old dramatic trick by placing the scene of Belfond's undoing in Alsatia and by giving the dwellers in that place their characteristic slang.[52] The action of this realistic comedy of manners is continuous; for not one moment does the author halt his story, as he frequently did in earlier plays, in order to emphasize the eccentricities of a humour-character. The triumphant success of *The Squire of Alsatia* proved to Shadwell that he had not lost any of his dramatic sense during his period of silence.

[52] Sir Walter Scott in the introduction to *The Fortunes of Nigel* writes that "from the *Squire of Alsatia* [he] derived some few hints, and learned the footing on which the bullies and thieves of the Sanctuary stood with their neighbours, the fiery young students of the Temple, of which some intimation is given in the dramatic piece." The time of this novel is in the reign of James I. Because he commits a Star-Chamber offense by drawing his sword upon Dalgarno within the precincts of the Court, Glenvarloch is forced to take refuge in Whitefriars. Here Duke Hildebrod with ceremony allows him the privilege of sanctuary. Colepepper is a coward somewhat like Captain Hackum. The only cant terms in Shadwell's list used by Scott's Alsatians are "decuses," "smelts," and "doctors."

CHAPTER XVI

BURY-FAIR

B*URY-FAIR*, acted in 1689, at first met "with a kind Reception from all, but some of the late Loyal Poets."[1] It was, however, unable to hold for long the audiences of the eighteenth century. On April 10, 1708, after remaining unacted for five years, it was produced at Drury Lane with Mills, Johnson, Bullock, Cibber, Bowen, Mrs. Porter, Mrs. Bradshaw, and Mrs. Powell in the cast.[2] It was also performed on December 31 of that year.[3] The last revival noted by Genest, a production in which Mrs. Thurmond was Gertrude, occurred on October 10, 1716, at the theatre in Lincoln's Inn Fields.[4]

The scene of the play is laid in Bury St. Edmunds, a town situated about seventy miles from London. Here dwells Mr. Oldwit, a believer in the wit of the days before the Commonwealth and an admirer of Sir Humphrey Noddy, a great lover of puns and practical jokes. But Mr. Oldwit is by no means pleased with the way his third wife, Lady Fantast, and his step-daughter ape the breeding of the French. Neither Gertrude, his daughter by a former marriage, nor her suitor, Wildish, can abide the affectations of Lady Fantast. In order to render the affected women ridiculous, Wildish persuades a French peruke-maker to masquerade as a count and make addresses to the daughter.

In his disguise as the Count de Cheveux, La Roch has slight difficulty in winning the interest of Mrs. Fantast, who turns from her lover Trim. Rendered jealous by this action, Trim challenges the count, who also is drawn into a duel with Sir Humphrey Noddy, by reason of the latter's plucking him by the nose. After waiting at the churchyard in vain for the coming of the Frenchman, Trim and Sir Humphrey go to the Fair with the intention of giving him a beating for his cowardice. Surprising

[1] Epistle Dedicatory to *Bury-Fair*.
[2] Genest, II, 400.
[3] *Ibid.*, II, 410.
[4] *Ibid.*, II, 604. In March, 1914, it was acted by the Harvard chapter of the Delta Upsilon Fraternity. Reviewed in *Harvard Crimson* of March 17, 1914.

him in busy conversation with the ladies, these men cudgel the pseudo-count soundly.

In the meantime, Lord Bellamy, who has taken lodgings at Bury, hopes to make Gertrude his wife. But the page Charles is not pleased with his master's suit, hints that she loves another, and presents him with a letter in Wildish's handwriting which she had dropped. Bellamy angrily orders him to return it immediately. When Bellamy and Wildish, who are friends, discover that each is in love with the same woman, they become involved in a duel, in the course of which Wildish drops his sword, but is given his life by Bellamy. The men then embrace and determine to allow Gertrude to decide their fate. Charles, who attends the interview unseen, faints when Gertrude refuses to answer Wildish favorably. Gertrude immediately runs to the page's assistance and discovers in Bellamy's attendant her sister Philadelphia, who had left home four months before in order to avoid marriage with a man she hated and who has since then fallen in love with Bellamy.

After his disgrace at the Fair, La Roch goes to Mrs. Fantast, whom he plans to marry on the morrow. While Lady Fantast is rejoicing in her daughter's good fortune, word is brought by the Frenchman's page that rumor of his being a barber has spread about the Fair. La Roch, after emphatically denying this accusation, hides in the closet when he hears approaching footsteps. Trim, Sir Humphrey, and Oldwit bring the same report concerning the "count," but Wildish, who corroborates the story, is faced down by La Roch. When finally Lady Fantast and her daughter are assured of the Frenchman's true profession, they make a hurried departure from Bury. The pseudo-count is arrested. Philadelphia, in woman's clothes, goes to her father, begs his pardon for running away, and receives his consent to marry Bellamy. Gertrude accepts Wildish. The play closes with Oldwit expressing joy at having found his daughter and at being rid of his wife.

Langbaine, echoing Shadwell's statement concerning the difficulty of finding a continual supply of new humour, would excuse the author of *Bury-Fair*, "if *Old Wit*, and Sir *Humphry Noddy*, have some resemblance with Justice *Spoil Wit*, and Sr. *John Noddy* in *The Triumphant Widow*." "Skilfull *Poets*," he continues, "resemble excellent *Cooks*, whose Art enables them to dress one

Dish of Meat several ways; and by the Assistance of proper Sawces, to give each a different Relish, and yet all grateful to the Palate. Thus the Character of *La Roche,* tho' first drawn by *Molliere,* in *Les Precieuses ridicules,* and afterwards copy'd by Sir *W. D'Avenant,* Mr. *Betterton,* and Mrs. *Behn;* yet in this Play has a more taking Air than in any other Play, and there is something in his Jargon, more diverting than in the Original it self."[5] That Shadwell's play is indebted to *Les Précieuses Ridicules* is quite obvious.[6] In Molière's comedy, the rejected suitors, Du Croisy and La Grange, in order to make ridiculous the affected young ladies, Cathos and Madelon, dress their valets, Mascarille and Jodelet, as a marquis and a viscount. The ladies are very easily taken in by Mascarille's discourse on poetry; they admire his clothing, smell his wig, and listen to his and Jodelet's talk about the wounds they have received upon the field of battle. When the game has proceeded far enough, the masters reappear, beat their valets, and strip them of their finery.

La Roch is in many ways as interesting a figure as his French prototypes. Unlike Mascarille, he is first introduced, not as a nobleman, but in his true profession of barber. When the idea of assuming the part of a count is suggested to him, he is chary of attempting it for fear he may lose money; but when he is told that all the town will run after him and that this will "help [his] Man to buy the Wenches Hair," he changes his tune and begins to act the rôle: "Begar, Monsieur, I have de Count of my Familee, I am a Gentilman of *Fraunce.* Indeed my Parents did condiscent to lette me makè de Peruke; for I delighted in it."[7]

The highly diverting scene[8] in which the pseudo-count meets the affected ladies at the Fair could not possibly be the work of a person who was habitually dull.

Mrs. Fantast: A most admirable Person of a Man! his Eyes briliant, and fièrre! my Heart is gone: He may say, as *Cæsar* did, *Veni, vidi, vici.*

[5] P. 445. Mrs. Behn's *The False Count; or, A New Way to play an Old Game* presents in Guiliom, the chimney-sweeper, a character based on Mascarille.

[6] The relationship of *Bury-Fair* to *Les Précieuses Ridicules* has been studied by Dr. Otto Seiler in his dissertation, *The Sources of Tho. Shadwell's Comedy, 'Bury Fair'* (Basel, 1904) and by Dr. Georg Heinemann in his *Shadwell-Studien* (Kiel, 1907), p. 69 ff.

[7] Shadwell, IV, 137-139.

[8] *Ibid.,* IV, 156 ff.

LADY FANTAST: My Eyes never beheld a Parallel.

MRS. FAN: Eh Gud! how the *French* Nobless outshines ours! methinks, they look like Tailors to 'em.

SIR HUMPHREY: Monsieur, your most humble Servant: welcome to *Bury*, as I may say.

OLDWIT: My Lord Count, you are heartily welcome to *Bury:* And I beg the Honour of your Company at Dinner, at my House.

COUNT: Messieurs, me kissè your Hands: me did tinke to invitè de Shief Majistrat, I don know vat you call him; Oh, is Alderman, to takè de Collation vid me; buttè me can no refusè de faveur.

MRS. FAN: I am transported with Joy!

L. FAN: Daughter, speak to him in *French;* he seems already Captivated with your Looks.

COUNT: You are appy in de Conversation of de very fine Ladeè; buttè to lette you know my Skill, my Cunning, me vil gage a hundred Pistole, dat dat fine Ladeè and her ver pretty Sister, are de *French* Ladeè.

OLDW: Ounds, this Count will make my damn'd affected Toad so proud, the Devil wou'd not live with her. *French,* and Sister, with a Pox!

L. FAN: We have often bewail'd the not having had the honour to be born *French.*

COUNT: Pardon me; is impossible.

MRS. FAN: *Mon foy, je parle vray:* we are meer English *assurement.*

COUNT: *Mon foy, je parle vray!* vat is dat Gibberish? Oh, lettè mè see; de Fadeer is de Lawyere, an she learne of him at de *Temple;* is de Law *French.*—I am amazè! *French* Lookè, *French* Ayre, *French* Mien, *French* Movement of de Bodee! Morbleau. Monsieur, I vill gage 4,500 Pistole, dat dese two Sister vere bred in *France*, yes. Teste bleu, I can no be deceive.

MRS. FAN: *Je vous en prie*, do not; we never had the blessing to be in *France;* you do us too much Honour. Alas, we are forc'd to be content with plain *English* Breeding: you will bring all my Blood into a Blush. I had indeed a *penchen* always to *French.*

COUNT: *Penchen!* vat is dat? Oh, is Law French.—You puttè de very great Confusion upon me: I tought it was impossible to find dat Mien, Ayre, Wit, and Breeding out of *France.*

OLDW: *French!* why, my Lord Count, this is my Wife; this is her Daughter.

COUNT: Daughtere! dis young Ladee havè de Daughtere! Begar, you makè my Head turn round, an mine Haire stand up: is impossible. Pardon me.

L. FAN: My dear sweet Lord Count, you pose me now with your grand Civilities: She is my Daughter; I was marry'd indeed exceeding young.

COUNT: Begar, Madam, den you be de pretty Modere, she de pretty Daughtere, in de whole Varle. Oh mine Art, mine Art! dose Eyes, dat

Ayre, ave killè me! I broughtè de Art out of *France*, and I ave lost it in dis place is gone, Madam; an Morbleau, you see now de *French* Count vidout a Heart. . . .

COUNT: Oh, Madam, you have de fine Haire, de very fine Haire! dose Tresses conquer de Lovere; *Cupid* makè his Net of dat Haire, to catchè de Art: de coleur delicat, better den my Peruke is great deal: Begar, if I had dat Haire, I vou'd makè two tree Peruke of dat.

WILDISH: Pox on you, you Rascal! You are no Barber, Sir; you are a Count.

COUNT: Havè de Patiance: dat is, me could makè de Peruke two tree; buttè I voud makè de Locket, de Bracelet, an de pretty Love-knack.

On two other occasions, La Roch nearly gives himself away. After he has kissed Sir Humphrey in order to become better acquainted, the mock count exclaims: "Ha! who Shavè your Facè? lettè me see: he leavè two, tree, four great Stumpè, dat prickè my Countenance. Oh fie! dese Barbiers *English* can do noting! If I wou'd take de Trade, Begar, I wou'd starvè dem all." Once more Wildish reminds him who he is; he replies, "I sometime takè delight to shavè de Nobless of *France* for my plaisir."[9] He is in greatest danger when he begins to talk business after allowing the ladies to smell of his peruke: "Is de ver fine Haire, Ladee: I have a great deal of de best in *England* or *France* in my Shop." Gertrude immediately asks him how he sells it. La Roch answers: "Shop! Shop! I no understand *English*, Shop! Vat you call de Place de Jentilman puttè his Peruke? Oh, his Cabinet, his Closet."[10]

In addition to *Les Précieuses Ridicules*, Dr. Georg Heinemann has indicated another possible source of *Bury-Fair* in *Les Femmes Savantes*. Oldwit and the two Fantasts are counterparts of Chrysale and his affected wife and daughter, Philaminte and Armande. The sensible woman Mrs. Gertrude, who can not abide the affectations of the others, plays a part in the action similar to that of Henriette in the French play.[11] In some of the scenes of Shadwell's comedy, Mr. Miles has found echoes of *Le Misanthrope*, *Le Bourgeois Gentilhomme*, and *La Comtesse d'Escarbagnas*.[12]

[9] *Ibid.*, IV, 162.

[10] *Ibid.*, IV, 180.

[11] Heinemann, *Shadwell-Studien*, pp. 71-72. He also sees a resemblance between Trim and Trissotin.

[12] Miles, *Influence of Molière on Restoration Comedy*, p. 226. Act I (p. 121 ff.) which Miles thinks "is freely adapted from *Le Misanthrope*, II, 4" is an old stage trick. Cf. *The Merchant of Venice*, I, 2.

Act V (p. 197 f.) may have been sug-

In his main plot, Shadwell incidentally satirizes two types of "wit"—that which displays itself in extravagant compliments, affectation of learning, artificial methods of expression, and exaltation of French breeding, and that which appears in horseplay, puns, and practical jokes.

Among the believers in the first kind of "wit" is Trim, described as "very wise, reserv'd, full of Forms, and empty of Substance; all Ceremony, and no Sense; more troublesomly ill-bred with his Formality, than a high-shoo'd Peasant with his Roughness." He considers Bury "the Habitation of the Graces and the Muses" and under the name of Eugenius exchanges verses with his Dorinda, Mrs. Fantast. The latter, who has learned French from an Irishman, sprinkles her conversation with phrases from that tongue. She acknowledges that she has ever had a tenderness for the Muses. "But Heroick Numbers upon Love and Honour are most ravissant, most suprenant; and a Tragedy is so Touchant! I die at a Tragedy; I'll swear, I do."[13] She designates Gertrude's sensible remarks against compliments as "Ill Breeding, *au dernier point!*" To her the Count is "*charmant*" and his air "*tuant.*"[14] Lady Fantast, her mother and Oldwit's third wife, "the most perpetual, impertinent, pratling, conceited, affected Jade, that ever plagu'd Mankind," bewails her "want of Poetry, *Latin*, and the *French* tongue." She reprimands Gertrude for her plain statement, "I . . . am now come to wait on you," by saying, "You shou'd have said; I assure you, Madam, the Honour is all on my Side; and I cannot be ambitious of a greater, than the sweet Society of so excellent a Person."[15] The "Wit and Breeding" of

gested by *Le Misanthrope*, V, 2. In the French play, Alceste and Oronte ask the capricious Célimène to decide between them. She leaves the matter for Éliante to judge. In *Bury-Fair*, Bellamy and Wildish ask Gertrude to make a similar decision. After some bantering, she is prevented from making an avowal by the fainting of the page.

In *Le Bourgeois Gentilhomme*, III, 4, Dorante persuades the unwilling M. Jourdain to put on his hat. Note stage direction in *Bury-Fair* (p. 124): "Wildish makes Signs to put his Hat on, and takes his own up. Trim strives . . . who shall put on his Hat last."

In *La Comtesse d'Escarbagnas*, scene 7, Julie and the Countess beg each other to be seated. Compare with passage between Wildish and Trim (p. 124).

[13] Shadwell, IV, 141. Mrs. Fantast's use of Frenchified expressions may owe something to Melantha in Dryden's *Marriage a la Mode*. Note Act II, scene 1; and Act III, scene 1. Both Melantha and Mrs. Fantast were acted by Mrs. Boutell.

[14] Shadwell, IV, 155.

[15] *Ibid.*, IV, 142.

the mistress is aped by the maid Luce, who announces that Madam Fantast has "attir'd herself in her morning Habiliments."

The second kind of "wit," that which shows itself in puns and practical jokes, is illustrated in the persons of Mr. Oldwit and Sir Humphrey Noddy—characters that had appeared earlier as Justice Spoilwit and Sir John Noddy in *The Triumphant Widow*.[16] Oldwit, described as a "paltry old-fashion'd Wit, and Punner of the last Age; that pretends to have been one of *Ben Johnson's* Sons, and to have seen Plays at the *Blackfryers*," is a dramatic exemplification of the "old fellows who value themselves on their acquaintance with the *Black Friars*," to whom Dryden refers in his *Defence of the Epilogue*. "The memory of these gentlemen," he writes, "is their only plea for being wits. They can tell a story of Ben Johnson, and, perhaps have had fancy enough to give a supper in the *Apollo*, that they might be called his sons; and, because they were drawn in to be laughed at in those times, they think themselves now sufficiently entitled to laugh at ours. Learning I never saw in any of them; and wit no more than they could remember."[17] In speaking of his younger days, Oldwit remarks: "My Friends soon perceiv'd I could not be a Divine; so they sent me to the Inns of Court; and there, i' faith, I pepper'd the Court with Libels and Lampoons: my Wit was so bitter, I 'scap'd the Pillory very narrowly . . . But then, for good Language and strong Lines, none out-did me."[18] When his wife tells him that his wit is "obliterated, antiquated, and bury'd in the Grave of Oblivion," he asks if he shall live to be deposed by her. "I cannot go to *London* yet, but the Wits get me amongst them, and the Players will get me to Rehearsal to teach them, even the best of them: And you to say I have no Wit," he adds.[19]

[16] For relationship of this play to *The Triumphant Widow*, see the dissertations by Seiler and Heinemann; also H. T. E. Perry, *The First Duchess of Newcastle and Her Husband as Figures in Literary History*, p. 156 ff. Many of the practical jokes played by Noddy are the same in both plays. Shadwell follows the earlier comedy in having this character pull a chair from a person as he is about to sit down, strike away a cane upon which someone is leaning, tell of thrusting a man into the water and of causing another to turn suddenly and bump his nose, make a pun on "rabbit," etc. In both plays Spoilwit (Oldwit) says he was sent to the inns of court when it was seen that he could not be a divine. The epitaph on Murial's horse and the translation of the poem on the fish are found in each comedy.

[17] *Essays of John Dryden* (ed. Ker), I, 175.

[18] Shadwell, IV, 131.

[19] *Ibid.*, IV, 145.

The "blunt, noisy, laughing, roaring, drinking Fellow," Sir Humphrey Noddy, is considered by Oldwit to be the "archest Wit and Wag." A great player of practical jokes, he causes his friend to hold his sides with laughter as he relates how he had pushed a man into the water. He indulges in such childish pranks as striking Oldwit's cane from under him and pinning Oldwit and Wildish together. He is guilty of a pun upon "rabbit" and "raw bit," and describes the day as "scabby," "because the Sun's broken out." This last sally is too much for Oldwit, who begs: "For the love of Heaven, dear Friend, not so fast: I cannot suffer it."[20] Through Wildish's remark, "his Mirth is the melancholiest thing in the World,"[21] Shadwell inserts his own comment upon Sir Humphrey.

Embodiments of a more sensible attitude are Wildish and Gertrude. Wildish resents being designated by Trim as "such a Top Wit, that all *England* rings out [his] Fame." He "had as lief be call'd a Pick-pocket, as a Wit." "A Wit is always a merry, idle, waggish Fellow, of no Understanding: Parts indeed he has, but he had better be without 'em," is his comment.[22] When Oldwit addresses him as "the chief Genius, the high Wit of the Age," he begs not to have that laid to his charge: "You had as good accuse me of Felony."[23] His aversion to the sort of "wit" represented by Lady Fantast and "her affected, conceited, disdainful Daughter" finds an outlet in his scheme to make them ridiculous through La Roch; his disgust with Oldwit and Sir Humphrey is given expression in his remarks to Bellamy on "Country Conversation."[24] Gertrude, likewise, is displeased with the affectations of her step-mother and replies when she is reprimanded for not showing breeding: "Breeding! I know no Breeding necessary, but Discretion to distinguish Company and Occasions; and common Sense, to entertain Persons according to their Rank; besides making a Curt'sie not aukwardly, and walking with ones Toes out." Her common-sense is further emphasized in her reply to Lady Fantast's statement that she has bred her daughter a linguist: "A Lady may look after the Affairs of a Family, the Demeanour of her Servants, take care of her Nursery, take all her Accounts every Week, obey her Husband, and discharge all the Offices of

[20] *Ibid.*, IV, 128, 154, 131, 164, 166.
[21] *Ibid.*, IV, 128.
[22] *Ibid.*, IV, 122.
[23] *Ibid.*, IV, 129.
[24] *Ibid.*, IV, 161.

a good Wife, with her Native Tongue; and this is all I desire to arrive at: and this is to be of some use in a Generation; while your fantastick Lady, with all those Trappings and Ornaments you speak of, is good for no more than a dancing Mare, to be led about and shown."[25]

In addition to the portrayal of the two kinds of "wit," Shadwell introduced a subplot recording the experiences of Oldwit's daughter Philadelphia, who has run away from home and who, in the guise of a page, has taken service with Bellamy. This episode resembles, in a general way, the central situation in *Twelfth Night*. Like Viola, who falls in love with Orsino, Philadelphia is enamoured of Bellamy. Like Viola, also, she is troubled because of her master's love for another woman. Like Viola, finally, she wins the hand of the man she loves.

Bellamy is an unusual character for a play of this time. After renouncing the loose practices of his early life, he has retired to the country where to his friend Wildish he appears in the rôle of sententious moralizer. He says, "I will no more suffer my Appetites to Master me, than Fire and Water; they are good Ministers, while they can be kept under"; "I must always think a Man a Slave, till he has conquer'd himself: For my part, I had almost as lief be in Subjection to another's Appetite, as to my own."[26] Thoroughly satisfied with life on his estate, where he can read the *Georgics* and contemplate the works of Nature, he disposes of city pleasures in this manner: "Your fine Women are a Company of proud, vain Fops and Jilts, abominably Daub'd and Painted; and I had rather kiss a Blackamoor, with a natural Complexion than any such: . . . Then, for your Wine, 'tis attended with such Surfeits, Qualms, Head-akes, late Hours, Quarrels and Uproars, that every Scene of Drunkenness is a very *Bedlam*."[27] The creation of this character, who argues for a higher standard of morality than that displayed by the average hero of Restoration drama, is another indication that Shadwell in the last years of his life was seriously interested in the reform of vices, as well as in the reform of follies.

Shadwell, who was always willing to introduce novelty into his setting, places his scene at Bury St. Edmunds during the time of

[25] *Ibid.*, IV, 142-143.
[26] *Ibid.*, IV, 135.
[27] *Ibid.*, IV, 172-173.

the fair. This town was well known to the dramatist, who, as a boy, had spent a year at the Edward VI Free Grammar School there.[28] Of the three annual fairs, the most important, that for which a charter had been granted by Henry III as early as 1272, was held for three days before and three days after the feast of St. Matthew, September 21. Gillingwater, the historian of Bury, writes that it was usual at the fair "to have different rows of booths assigned to the several manufacturers of Norwich, Ipswich, Colchester, London, etc., and even some foreigners, particularly the Dutch. The fair was then kept . . . on that spacious plain, Angelhill, betwixt the gate of the Abbey and the town, and occupied all the avenues leading to the Abbot's palace. Here were also minstrels, jugglers, mountebanks, etc., who were commonly allowed to perform their feats of dexterity during the fair, where used to assemble a great concourse of ladies and gentlemen from various parts of England." Among the more notable of the women whose attendance has been recorded was Mary Tudor, the sister of Henry VIII.[29]

The fair proper furnishes the actual setting for only two of the scenes.[30] Unlike the fair in *Bartholomew Fair*, it is incidental rather than necessary, to the action. Shadwell uses it as a background for the first appearance of La Roch in the rôle of count. The milliners, perfumers, and ginger-bread women, who cry their wares, and the Jack Puddings, who advertise the side-shows, although giving the scene an air of reality, are mere accessories to the setting and not individuals moulding the incidents.

According to Mr. Saintsbury, this comedy is "by far the best and liveliest of all Shadwell's plays."[31] I would modify this statement to read: "The episode in which the two Fantasts are rendered ridiculous by the barber-count is the best handled of any comic incident in Shadwell." In La Roch, the English writer produces a figure not inferior to his French original. With the exception of Trim, Wildish, and Gertrude, the other characters are less interesting than those which appear in the central situation. The

[28] See p. 9 ff.

[29] Edward Gillingwater, *An Historical and Descriptive Account of St. Edmund's Bury, In the County of Suffolk.* (Second edition. St. Edmund's Bury, 1811), pp. 270-275.

[30] Shadwell, IV, 147 ff., 192 ff.

[31] In the Mermaid Edition of Shadwell, p. 349.

tiresomeness of the puns and the horseplay of Oldwit and Sir Humphrey, the conventional handling of the stage-worn situation of the woman disguised as a page, and the tedious moralizings of Bellamy, in my opinion, militate against the unqualified acceptance of Mr. Saintsbury's praise. Considered in its entirety, *A True Widow* with its Jonsonian plot and variety of characters is in some ways the equal of *Bury-Fair*. *The Squire of Alsatia*, containing boisterous scenes of London life, is without doubt as lively a comedy as the play under discussion. One is justified, I think, in saying no more than that *Bury-Fair* is to be classed among Shadwell's best plays and is to be distinguished as containing the most amusing episode in any of his works.

CHAPTER XVII

THE AMOROUS BIGOT

THE AMOROUS BIGOT, *with the Second Part of Tegue O'Divelly*, although received at first in a manner not displeasing to the author,[1] failed to find continued favor with the theatrical public. Genest records no performance during the eighteenth century.

The plot of this play is rather complicated. Luscindo, a young gentleman of Madrid, is loved by the courtesan Levia, who, upon seeing his passion cool, determines to arouse his jealousy by transferring her affections to Doristeo. But Luscindo retaliates by pretending devotion to a certain Estifania, really the mistress of his attendant Hernando. The now jealous Levia tells of this affair to Doristeo, who becomes angry, thinking Estifania to be his sister. The two men are about to fight when Hernando reveals that the woman in question is a fish-seller's daughter and no relative of Doristeo's. In the meanwhile, Luscindo and Doristeo have become interested in Elvira and Rosania, the daughter and niece of Belliza, a widow who, after being deserted by her lover, has become very devout and would have all in her household emulate her. In this purpose, she is encouraged by the Irish priest, Tegue O'Divelly.

Colonel Bernardo, the father of Luscindo, upon his return from Flanders, visits the widow and proposes marriage, but when he sees Elvira, he is immediately smitten with love for her and writes a letter to Belliza, telling of the changed state of his affections. The mother appears pleased, urges her daughter to listen to his suit, and determines to win Luscindo for herself. When he hears of his son's devotion to Elvira, Bernardo decides to send him to the Low Countries, but desires him to receive the blessing of his future step-mother before departure. At this interview, Luscindo slips a note into Elvira's hand, revealing his love and asking her to prevail upon his father not to order him away from Spain.

[1] See pp. 82-83.

After her lover has left, Elvira tells her mother that he wishes to meet her (i.e., Belliza) in the balcony between eleven and twelve that night. Elvira then sends a note, written under her direction by Rosania, to Luscindo, with the information that she will await him at the wicket if he will have Hernando keep the appointment with Belliza. In the meantime, Doristeo has been exchanging notes with Rosania, thinking her name Elvira.

Levia, still bent on revenge, dresses herself in male attire and hires bravoes to attack Luscindo after his midnight interview with Elvira. Doristeo comes to the rescue and assists him in worsting the bravoes; but the two men soon commence fighting when each thinks the other is his rival. In the duel, Luscindo is victorious and spares Doristeo's life. Levia then tries another stratagem: she has her aunt Gremia inform Elvira and Belliza that Luscindo is contracted to a certain Henrietta de Sylvia. As a result, Elvira writes her lover that all is over between them. He, in turn, upbraids her for writing to Doristeo. Matters are soon straightened out, however, by Luscindo's explanation that Gremia is a bawd and by Elvira's avowal that her note of the previous evening was in the handwriting of Rosania in order to avert her mother's suspicions. The two lovers are then married.

As a last resort, Levia, still in man's clothing, goes to Bernardo, who is preparing for his wedding, and informs the old soldier that Elvira, who had been "his" mistress, has now forsaken "him" for Luscindo. The furious Bernardo hastens to his son and intended bride with the purpose of sacrificing them to his rage, but is restrained. In the meantime, Rosania has slipped out of the house and become quietly married to Doristeo. Belliza, after learning how Luscindo has deceived her, is ready to give herself up to a cloistered life; but, when Bernardo expresses a readiness to return to her, she abandons this purpose and agrees to become his wife.

In the prologue, the author expresses the opinion that some of the audience will think they have been tricked and "*for a new, shall find a damn'd old Play.*" After referring to *The Libertine* as the "Spanish Plot" on which he "*once writ before,*" he mentions the priest, an allusion of course to Tegue in *The Lancashire Witches.* Upon the foundation of this character in the earlier play, Shadwell built *The Amorous Bigot.*

But like Drake's *Ship, 'tis so repair'd, tis new;*
Newer than his Contemporaries show,
Who all to Novels or Romances owe,
And from whose Native Springs nought e'er did flow.

It is new in that it is not a slavish copy of any single comedy; it does, however, contain some incidents and characters that had already appeared in Shadwell's earlier plays.

But before examining Shadwell's borrowings from his own work, I must mention the echoes from Molière which Mr. Miles has found in this comedy.[2] He correctly sees in the rivalry of Bernardo and Luscindo a reminiscence of the mutual attitude of Harpagon and Cléante in *L'Avare.* Each play represents a father and son in love with the same woman. He furthermore finds in the passage in which Harpagon introduces his son to his future step-mother[3] a hint for the episode showing Bernardo in the act of presenting his son to Elvira.[4] Hernando's pretending that he is Luscindo and his making love to Belliza with speech composed of "Love-sick Language"[5] may have had its origin in the actions in *Les Précieuses Ridicules* of Mascarille, who recites impromptu verse to Cathos and Magdelon.[6] The resemblance, which is one in general idea rather than in specific circumstance, is not obvious enough to convince me that Shadwell had the French play in mind when he was writing this passage.

Except that each play presents the well-worn situation of a woman in love with a man who shows no interest in her, there is no relationship between Act I, scene IV, of *Les Femmes Savantes* and the designated passage in *The Amorous Bigot.*[7] In the former play, Clitandre begs Bélise to use her influence in urging his suit to her niece Henriette. Bélise, however, thinks he is making love to her in metaphor and refuses to understand the true purport of his conversation. In the latter comedy, when Bernardo would present his son to Elvira, Belliza interposes and bids him welcome. She becomes "enamour'd to the last Degree," and even believes,

[2] Miles, *Influence of Molière on Restoration Comedy*, p. 224.

[3] *L'Avare,* Act III, scenes VI, VII (ed. Lecour, Paris, 1876). In some editions of Molière, the scene in question is numbered XI.

[4] Shadwell, IV, 271.

[5] *Ibid.,* IV, 281.

[6] Scene IX.

[7] Shadwell, IV, 271 ff.

although she has no reason for doing so, that "he looks amorously upon [her]."

Mr. Miles finds another resemblance in the relationship of Elvira to Belliza and the *motif* of *L'École des Maris*. In Shadwell, Belliza keeps her daughter locked up; in Molière, Sganarelle treats his ward in a similar manner; in each play, the prisoner succeeds in duping the jailor. In the French play, also, Sganarelle carries a verbal message from Isabelle in which she explains to Valère the real state of her feelings. The message is so phrased that the guardian thinks it signifies one thing, while the lover knows it means something else. Sganarelle also delivers to his neighbor a box and letter, which Isabelle falsely tells him were thrust in her window by Valère's servant.[8] Similarly, Elvira informs Bernardo that his son has endeavored to corrupt her maid with a "Heart of Ruby set in Gold." She desires the older man to return this gift to Luscindo with the request that he find the owner, if it was not sent by himself, and with the advice that he leave no more letters under the loose board in the balcony. Although Bernardo thinks these words are a repulse to his son, the latter knows they are a proof of Elvira's love.[9]

In some of the remaining incidents, Shadwell was repeating devices which he had used in his earlier plays. The courtezan Levia is a reminder of Mrs. Termagant in *The Squire of Alsatia*. Both women, at first merely jealous, become desirous of vengeance and attempt to kill their former lovers: in *The Squire of Alsatia*, by snapping "*a Pistol at* Belfond, *which only flashes in the Pan*";[10] in *The Amorous Bigot*, by snatching Doristeo's sword, and running at Luscindo.[11] Both jealous women also dress as men and try to prevent the marriages their former lovers are contemplating. In the earlier play, Mrs. Termagant, in male attire, has two Alsatian Affidavit Men swear that they were witnesses to a contract of marriage between "him" and Isabella;[12] in the later comedy, Levia goes to Bernardo, tells him "he" is a cavalier in distress and that "his" mistress has sacrificed "him" to Luscindo.[13] The scene in which Levia orders the bravoes to kill Luscindo[14] is in line with

[8] *L'École des Maris*, Act II, scenes II-VII.

[9] Shadwell, IV, 263, 268.

[10] *Ibid.*, IV, 105.

[11] *Ibid.*, IV, 266.

[12] *Ibid.*, IV, 105.

[13] *Ibid.*, IV, 295-296.

[14] *Ibid.*, IV, 277.

the episode in *The Libertine* in which Maria, also in male costume, urges the bravoes to "dispatch" her betrayer, Don John.[15] The final words of Levia[16] are very similar to the concluding speeches of Goldingham in *The Miser*.[17]

The young women, Elvira and Rosania, like Miranda and Clarinda in *The Virtuoso* and Teresia and Isabella in *The Squire of Alsatia*, after being closely confined to the homes of their parents or guardians, are able to escape and marry the men of their choice. The amorous older woman whom we have met in Lady Loveyouth, Lady Gimcrack, and Lady Shacklehead also appears in this play. Unlike her predecessors in Shadwell's comedies, Belliza is a widow and therefore eligible to marry.

Gremia, the bawd, reminds one at times of Mrs. Termagant and Lady Busy. As Mrs. Termagant tells Isabella how she has been cast aside by Belfond in favor of an attorney's daughter,[18] so Gremia informs Belliza in the presence of Elvira that her niece to whom she gives the name of Henrietta de Sylvia has been abandoned by Luscindo in favor of another woman.[19] These revelations cause both Isabella and Elvira to become angry with their lovers. Gremia, in the passage just mentioned, uses a method of conversation similar to that employed by Lady Busy in *A True Widow* when she is attempting to argue Isabella into becoming the mistress of Bellamour.[20] She tries to be persuasive by continually larding her sentences with such interjections as "good," "very well."

The bluff soldier, Bernardo, is at times reminiscent of Sir Positive, although his boasts are extremely mild when compared with those of the universal pretender. He, however, "did last Campaign, without Pole, or any thing in [his] Hand, leap a Moat of 20 Foot wide, over a Fauxbray."[21] His attendant Hernando speaks of his prowess: "My Master is a Man of the greatest Activity of any Man in the Army." When Rosania asks if he can creep through a hoop, Hernando replies, "He shall do it with any Man in *Europe*," lines reminiscent of Sir Positive.[22] Hernando, in ridiculously backing his master's statements,[23] acts somewhat like

[15] *Ibid.*, II, 123.
[16] *Ibid.*, IV, 299.
[17] *Ibid.*, III, 100.
[18] *Ibid.*, IV, 81 ff.
[19] *Ibid.*, IV, 286 ff.
[20] *Ibid.*, III, 133 ff.
[21] *Ibid.*, IV, 261 ff.
[22] *Ibid.*, I, 43.
[23] *Ibid.*, IV, 261.

Jacomo who corroborates the words of Don John when the latter is wooing Clara.[24] Hernando is also the mouthpiece for the usual Shadwellian jest at the expense of the Heroic Play.[25] When, in disguise, he wooes Belliza and is at a loss what to say, he settles the matter thus: "I'll make Love in Rhime, out of Heroick Plays; 'tis even as natural here as upon the Stage." He then addresses her in a ridiculous poem, beginning

> *I am so dazzled with your radiant Eye,*
> *That like the silly, and unheedful Flye,*
> *(As sweetly the Heroick Poet sings;)*
> *At that bright Flame I've sing'd m' advent'rous Wings.*

Despite Shadwell's assertion in the prologue that he built this play upon the foundation of a "*foolish Priest,*" Tegue impresses the reader of *The Amorous Bigot* as being of slight importance to the action. His function in the plot is to encourage Belliza in her pious observances. But, in addition, he serves as the author's means for heaping further ridicule upon the Church of Rome. As in *The Lancashire Witches,* he has ambitions of being an "*Eerish* Cardinal"; he urges Rosania to "equivocate and maake use of mental Reservation"; and he also has the bottle of holy-water which he sprinkles upon Belliza while she is in a fainting fit and upon Bernardo when he would sacrifice his son to his fury. Tegue tells Gremia, the bawd, that she speaks like "a good pious Voman indeed," when she observes "dy *Lents,* dy Wigils and Embers." In those who love the Church, he will pass by "some Peccadillo's, as Shwearing, Wenching, and Lying, and de like." To Elvira he reads a list of the disreputable persons of whom he has made "braave Catholicks, gallant Catholicks." He is angry with Belliza for thinking of "Flesh upon a Fish-Day," when she leaves him in order to make herself ready for her suitor. He appears as a profligate in that scene where he attempts to ravish Rosania during confession. When, finally, against all his admonitions, Belliza decides to marry Bernardo, he "vill pronounce de Words of de maarriage without intention, and den it is no maarriage."[26]

[24] *Ibid.,* II, 142.

[25] *Ibid.,* IV, 281-282.

[26] *Ibid.,* IV, 229, 257, 288, 298, 241, 246, 245, 257 ff., 300. In *Wit for Money: or, Poet Stutter,* p. 15, Smith says to Stutter, "the List which the Lady

In short, *The Amorous Bigot* is a composite of dramatic devices which Shadwell by experience had found successful. It is a comedy of intrigue marked by action, rather than by characterization. Most of the figures are mere sketches depending for their vitality upon the skill of the actors. Although it may have pleased momentarily because of the opportunity afforded Tony Leigh to appear once more as Tegue, this play adds little to Shadwell's reputation as a dramatist.

Addleplot reads of their party, is the same thing almost with that which the *Irish* Priest reads in the *Amorous Bigott*, and though the words are somewhat different, the humour is the same." Both Lady Addleplot in D'Urfey's *Love for Money: or the Boarding School* (1691) and Tegue were acted by Anthony Leigh.

CHAPTER XVIII

THE SCOWRERS

WITH *The Scowrers* Shadwell returns to London for his scene, and writes a play in some ways reminiscent of *The Squire of Alsatia.*[1] Its life was longer than that of its predecessor, *The Amorous Bigot;* for it had at least one performance in the eighteenth century when it was revived with a fairly good cast at Drury Lane on August 22, 1717.[2]

The plot deals with the scouring exploits of Sir William Rant. This young roisterer is an object of aversion to his aunt, Lady Maggot, who has come to London with her daughters, Clara and Eugenia. While walking through Hyde Park in search of adventure, the lady meets one of Sir William's companions, Wildfire. This gallant, later to become a lover of Clara, accompanies her to her lodgings in order to protect her from the importunities of Tope. Sir William, himself a suitor to Eugenia, arranges a serenade and dinner at the home of Lady Maggot in order to welcome her daughters to the city. The mother, displeased by the noise, commands her husband, Sir Humphrey, to send the men from the house and threatens to pack the girls off to the country.

Clara and Eugenia, who are then locked up, determine to escape their mother's tyranny. Sir Humphrey's nephew, Whachum, repenting of his agreement to pay Lady Maggot five thousand pounds to be contracted to Clara, discovers that he loves Eugenia. In order to gain her interest, he describes his skill in scouring; but, when he acts on her suggestion that he show his metal by beating the governess Priscilla, he has to retreat, much the worse for the conflict. Later, Sir William, after beating Whachum, Bluster, and Dingboy, who had scoured at the Bear and Harrow before his arrival, appears in front of his lady's window with the intention of serenading her. During the uproar occasioned by the ensuing encounter with the watch, Mr. Rant, who has just come to the city, calls to his son. Sir William goes to his father, listens to a

[1] See pp. 85-86.

[2] Genest, II, 603.

well-deserved rebuke, and gives the assurance of his determination to repent and of his desire to marry Eugenia.

In order to be rid of Lady Maggot, Wildfire sends her a note in which he asks for a meeting. While the mother is at the rendezvous with Tope, who has taken the place of Wildfire, the girls throw themselves upon Mr. Rant for protection. When Lady Maggot discovers how she has been duped, her rage knows no bounds. She dare not pursue her vengeance, however, because Wildfire threatens to produce a ring she had given him at an earlier interview. Sir William and Wildfire finally renounce their old ways and look forward with joy to their marriages with Eugenia and Clara; on the other hand, Whachum, who has been beaten and arrested for his pranks, decides to continue his career of scouring and drinking.

Of the characters, the most original are Sir Humphrey Maggot, the Jacobite alderman, whose primary interest is in news-letters, particularly those which tell of the military successes of the King of France; Whachum, his loutish nephew, who pretends to be a law student, but who really spends his nights in emulating the scouring exploits of Sir William Rant; and Tope, a weather-beaten old sinner, who has drunk off two generations and who sees no reason for reforming at fifty-five. The others in general follow traditional lines. Lady Maggot is the amorous older woman found in many plays by Shadwell and his contemporaries. Like, Belliza, who loves Luscindo,[3] she is interested in Wildfire, the suitor of her daughter Clara. In depicting the results of Lady Maggot's behavior towards her daughters, Shadwell had a purpose similar to that in *The Squire of Alsatia*, for he writes in his epilogue:

But know all, by these Presents; there's no way
But Gentleness, to make ripe Girls obey:
Us'd ill, if they have Beauty, Wit, or Sense,
They will rebel in their own just Defence.[4]

Gildon thinks the character of Eugenia, the livelier of the two sisters, is copied from Harriet in Etherege's *The Man of Mode*.[5]

[3] *The Amorous Bigot.*
[4] Shadwell, IV, 391.
[5] P. 125. Gildon also thinks Sir William Rant is a faint copy of Dorimant and Sir Frederic Frolick.

Both women are high-spirited, fond of the city, and ready to fall in love with the men whom of all persons in the world their mothers would have them avoid. In my opinion, Eugenia and Clara, who, driven to rebel by harsh treatment, escape from the hands of their governess, play parts more like those of Teresia and Isabella in *The Squire of Alsatia*, and Clarinda and Miranda in *The Virtuoso*. Clara, like Mrs. Gripe in *The Woman-Captain*[6] and Isabella in *The Lancashire Witches*,[7] declares, "We are true *English* Women, . . . and are resolv'd to assert our Liberty and Property."[8] In the manner of Lucia, who talks against the country in the presence of her suitor, Clodpate,[9] Clara and Eugenia unite in deprecating to Priscilla the life of the "poor innocent Country Things, who never stir beyond the Parish, but to some Fair."[10] Although for different reasons, they follow the examples of Lucia and Carolina in *Epsom-Wells* and Theodosia in *A True Widow* by refusing to wed immediately the men with whom they obviously are in love. Lucia and Carolina, after observing the result of marriage in the lives of the persons at the Wells, receive Bevil and Raines as servants during good behavior.[11] Theodosia capriciously demands that Carlos serve as probationer for "a Month's Time" before entering into the order of benedicts.[12] Clara and Eugenia, however, determined that their intended husbands shall reform, insist that Sir William and Wildfire act as probationers for at least one year. In the meantime, they must renounce "the Pomps and all the Vanities of this wicked Town" and "Wine, Women, and base Company."[13]

As in *The Squire of Alsatia* Shadwell had the purpose of routing the "Knot of most pernicious Knaves" who infested Whitefriars, so in the play under consideration he would by ridicule expose scouring—a practice consisting of roistering through the streets, of beating the watch, of breaking windows, and in general of making the mid hours of the night hideous. Scouring was a very real menace to the London of the late seventeenth century. Luttrell records two disturbances in which young bloods were victorious in their conflicts with the watch. He relates how on the

[6] Shadwell, III, 360.
[7] *Ibid.*, III, 231.
[8] *Ibid.*, IV, 324.
[9] *Ibid.*, II, 208-209.
[10] *Ibid.*, IV, 324.
[11] *Ibid.*, II, 287.
[12] *Ibid.*, III, 210.
[13] *Ibid.*, IV, 389.

thirteenth of January, 1681-2, "at night, some young gentlemen of the Temple went to the Kings Head tavern in Chancery lane, committing strange outrages there, breaking of windowes, etc., which the watch hearing off, came up to disperse them; but they sending for severall of the watermen with halberts that attend their comptroller at the revells, were engaged in a desperate riott, in which one of the watchmen was run into the body with an halbert, and lies very ill; but the watchmen secured one or two of the watermen."[14] Also on May 31, 1691, he notes that the "lord Newburgh, sir John Conway, and some others, rambling in the night, fell upon the watch and beat them severely; and since, another scuffle has been with the watch, by two Mr. Stricklands and some others, where a watchman was killed; the latter were taken and committed to Newgate."[15]

Shadwell had represented scouring on the stage in *The Miser*[16] and *The Woman-Captain*,[17] and had referred to it in *The Squire of Alsatia*.[18] In *The Scowrers*, he not only ridicules the practice; but, through Mr. Rant, moralizes on the vice of drinking which leads to such extravagancies. His satire appears in the first act when the glazier, coming to Sir William Rant on the morning after a night of rioting, humbly petitions the scourer to allow him to take the position of his old glazier, who had died within the hour. "The Man indeed was an honest Man, but alack, alack! he had little to do for a long time, 'till your Business and your Friends, Sir, brought him into request: He has had a fine Time under you; for your Worship, I understand, has to Sash-Windows an utter Aversion, Sir, when you are in Beer." If Sir William will let him have the place, he will "see that all the Parish, when [Sir William pleases] to break their Windows, shall have as good Goods as any Man can furnish them with."[19] Further satire on scouring occurs in the delineation of the character of Whachum, who follows Sir William about in dumb admiration. After pricking up enough courage to address "the Prince of Drunkards and of Scowrers," he says, "I have seen you scowre so rarely, Sir, I

[14] Narcissus Luttrell, *Brief Historical Relation of State Affairs* (Oxford, 1857), I, 158.

[15] *Ibid.*, II, 238. Steele, in *The Tatler* No. 40 (July 12, 1709), has old Renault remember the time when "all your top wits were scowrers, rakes, roarers, and demolishers of windows."

[16] Shadwell, III, 84 ff.

[17] *Ibid.*, III, 379 ff.

[18] *Ibid.*, IV, 19, 25.

[19] *Ibid.*, IV, 316-317.

have had a mighty Ambition for the Honour of your Acquaintance; for my part, Sir, I am a very mad Fellow as any wears a Head, and I conceive, Sir, you love a mad Fellow." He then refers to his recent exploits: "Why, we have been bound over to the Sessions three times this Week. I suppose you may have heard of our roaring about *Holborn, Fetter-Lane, Salisbury Court.*"[20]

Sir William, determining to make examples of "such nauseous Rascals" as Whachum, accepts the latter's invitation to sup at the Bear and Harrow. Here in a riotous scene, Whachum, after kicking the drawers because of their slowness, threatening to toss the proprietor in a blanket, and plucking down the bar, resolves that the tradesmen, who are drinking in an adjoining room, should be at home with their wives. He and his henchmen act upon this decision and frighten away the harmless drinkers. While they are expressing pleasure in their success, Sir William and his comrades arrive. The arch-scourer observes that someone has usurped his privilege of cleansing the tavern. When Whachum enthusiastically informs him that he would have seen "such Scowring" had he arrived earlier, Sir William demands whether they think he "will suffer such awkward sneaking Coxcombs to wench, drink, and scower, to usurp the Sins of Gentlemen." Then, after tweaking the intruders by the nose, he kicks and cudgels them. Whachum, who feels certain that Sir William and his comrades are in jest, calls them "the finest Gentlemen in *Europe*." Such a misunderstanding of his motive arouses anger in the "noble Scavenger," who straightway cudgels the "damn'd dull imitating Dogs" out of the tavern. As they come to the door, the constable and watch, who have been aroused by the tradesmen, appear and force them back into the house. A "free for all" fight then takes place, with the result that Sir William emerges victorious over his imitators, the watch, and the tradesmen.[21]

Shadwell, in this play, does not assume the rôle of outraged reformer that he for a moment held in the person of Sir Edward Belfond when this worthy gentleman exclaimed against the evils of Alsatia.[22] Instead of hitting hard at the practice which gave the title to this comedy, he makes scouring a source of comic action.

[20] *Ibid.*, IV, 339.
[21] *Ibid.*, IV, 368 ff.
[22] *Ibid.*, IV, 109.

He appears as a moralist, however, when he represents his hero in the act of listening to a paternal lecture in blank verse on the evils of drink and sexual immorality.[23] The reproofs of the father touch the son, who gives assurance of his sincere repentance. The joy of Mr. Rant and the contrition of Sir William find their natural outlets in tears. The father's satisfaction is increased, moreover, when he learns of his son's love for Eugenia.

This conversation, although more consciously didactic, is very like the heart to heart talk in *The Squire of Alsatia* between Sir Edward and Belfond Junior. The older man persuades his adopted son that "there's nothing but Anxiety in Vice: . . . And every drunken Fit is a Short Madness, that cuts off a good part of Life."[24] At the close of each passage, the younger man confesses that he is passionately in love. In both plays, the wild youths, conquered by Cupid, tell their intended wives of the determination to relinquish their former habits. Belfond Junior bids farewell to the vice of the age and makes the assertion that there is no joy but in a tender wife.[25] Sir William closes *The Scowrers* with these lines:

> But where Wit, Beauty, Virtue keep the Field,
> As Prisoners at Discretion, all must yield;
> Those Forces joyn'd subdue all Vanities:
> The most compendious way of being Wise,
> Is to be Convert to a Lady's Eyes.[26]

In this comedy there are a few speeches which Shadwell, the Whig laureate, considered proper to insert against those turncoats from the rival party who were clamoring for office. Tope, after telling his friends that they lose the pleasure of the Park when they leave it for an adventure, says: "You shou'd be here in a Morning, and observe crouching Spaniels hastning to some great Man's Levee, whom they wish hang'd; and lean, assiduous Knaves of Business running from Office to Office, to get all they can under the Government they hate." Wildfire exclaims, "How many Villains, that wish the Government destroyed, yet crowd for Places in it"; and Sir William adds, "Such Rogues can do the Govern-

[23] *Ibid.*, IV, 377 ff.
[24] *Ibid.*, IV, 52.
[25] *Ibid.*, IV, 110.
[26] *Ibid.*, IV, 391.

ment no harm, if they be kept out." The desire of persons to curry favor at court, which Shadwell so excellently described in the epilogue to *Bury-Fair*, is again referred to when the spirited Eugenia tells her weaker-willed sister, if she does nothing to gain her freedom, that she is "like those unreasonable craven Fellows, that would do nothing towards the Deliverance of *England*, and yet would have all the Benefit of the Change; nay, would keep those that did, out of the Government."[27]

In *The Scowrers*, then, it seems as if Shadwell were attempting to repeat in a minor key the theme of the episode concerning Belfond Junior in *The Squire of Alsatia.* As in the earlier comedy, he represents a young scapegrace, won by love and parental pressure to repentance of his past misdeeds and a desire to live a better life. Scouring, a subject which he had previously treated, he here ridicules. The author does not, however, take the firm stand against the roistering "bloods" that he did against the cheats of Whitefriars. The scene between father and son, which concludes with a duet of weeping, is not usual in the drama of this time and should be classed among the forerunners of that *genre* which was to be so popular in the eighteenth century—sentimental comedy.

[27] *Ibid.*, IV, 329-330, 355-356.

CHAPTER XIX

THE VOLUNTEERS

THE *VOLUNTEERS; or The Stock Jobbers*, acted for the first time in the latter part of 1692,[1] was shorter lived than *The Scowrers*. It was revived on July 27, 1711, by the Summer Company at Drury Lane with a cast consisting of Pack, Bullock, Cross, Norris, Booth, Mills, Mrs. Bradshaw, Mrs. Porter, Mrs. Saunders, Mrs. Powell, and Miss Willis.[2] After the performance of October 22, 1711,[3] it appears to have been no longer in the repertory of Drury Lane.

The plot of this comedy is of the slightest structure. Major-General Blunt, an old Royalist soldier, has two daughters, the affected Teresia and the sensible Eugenia. The former is wooed by Sir Nicholas Dainty, a fop well suited to her tastes; the latter is loved by young Colonel Hackwell, the son of an old Anabaptist officer. Colonel Hackwell Senior is browbeaten by his second wife, who pursues an intrigue with a cowardly sharper Nickum. Her scornful daughter Winifred is sought by Sir Timothy Kastril; Colonel Hackwell's daughter Clara is admired by the brave volunteer Welford, who, like the younger Hackwell, has distinguished himself in the late war in Ireland. Through the influence of their step-mother, who desires to obtain all her husband's property, the younger Hackwell and his sister have been ordered from their father's house. Angered by the injustice of their treatment, the maid Lettice attempts to convince the colonel of his wife's infidelity. Nickum, when found by the colonel with his wife, pretends to be arousing her from a fainting fit. She turns this discovery to her advantage by feigning that her condition was caused by her step-son's solicitations. The Colonel then threatens to disinherit his son and to turn his property over to his wife and her daughter. When, however, he is later persuaded of her true character, he makes her guilt plain to all his friends. Son and daugh-

[1] See p. 91.

[2] Genest, II, 482.

[3] *Ibid.*, II, 489.

ter are received back into the good graces of their father. Winifred spurns Sir Timothy for Hop, a dancing master; Clara marries Welford; Eugenia weds young Hackwell; Teresia wins Sir Nicholas.

Certain situations and characters in this play are reminiscent of Shadwell's earlier work. The contrast between the affected and the sensible woman, which the author had shown in the characters of Mrs. Fantast and Gertrude in *Bury-Fair*, he repeats twice in *The Volunteers*. Teresia, "a foolish, confident, conceited and affected young Lady," thinks Sir Fopling the "best Character of a fine accomplish'd Gentleman" she had ever seen in a play, and vows she "can never be put out of Love with a good Mien and Air, and graceful Deportment, good Breeding, and such Things." Her sister Eugenia, who "love[s] nothing like the freshness, ease, and silence of the Country," cannot endure the pleasures of the London-bred Teresia, but is bored by "the piteous Dullness of new Plays, the Idleness of *Basset* and *Comet*, the most provoking Impertinence of how do you's, and visiting Days, with Tea-Tables."[4] By viewing with impatience the affectations of Teresia and by regarding Eugenia with tenderness, Major-General Blunt performs a function like that of Oldwit in *Bury-Fair*. A similar contrast is presented in Winifred, the step-daughter, and Clara, the daughter, of Colonel Hackwell. Winifred, "an ill-bred, scornful, affected Thing," shows fondness for the dancing-master Hop and considers that her step-sister lacks breeding because she has never learned to dance. Clara, "a Beautiful, Ingenious young lady," represents the more sensible attitude when she replies: "Breeding is in the Head, not in the Foot."[5] Mrs. Hackwell, "a most devilish imperious Wife, and the worst of Step-Mothers," is, like Lady Gimcrack, for a time able to deceive her husband. When, however, her true relationship with Nickum is discovered, she, like Mrs. Fantast, who runs away never to see the "Face of Man again,"[6] determines to "hide [her] Head in some dark Hole, and never see the Light again."[7] Her paramour Nickum is a cowardly sharper in the tradition of Hackum and his crew.

[4] Shadwell, IV, 403-405.
[5] *Ibid.*, IV, 413.
[6] *Ibid.*, IV, 211.
[7] *Ibid.*, IV, 486.

In the characters of Major-General Blunt, "an old Cavalier Officer, somewhat rough in Speech, but very brave and honest, and of good Understanding," and Colonel Hackwell Senior, "an old Anabaptist Colonel of *Cromwell*'s, very stout and Godly, but somewhat Immoral," Shadwell tapped a new vein. Soldiers of the Civil Wars had, it is true, been treated in earlier plays.[8] In Cowley's *Cutter of Coleman Street* (1661), the hero, who pretends to have been a colonel in the king's army, is represented as a "merry, sharking Fellow about the Town." Mrs. Behn in *The Roundheads; or The Good Old Cause* (1682), a play adapted from Tatham's *The Rump; or, The Mirror of the Late Times* (1660), gives an unfavorable portrayal of the opponents of the king as they appeared at the eve of the Restoration. Shadwell, however, pictures the former enemies as fast friends viewing their youthful adventures through the gilded haze of retrospect. The blood of Major-General Blunt is fired by the noise of war. He does not approve of present military methods, which are very different from those in vogue during his youth. "Now your *French* Trick is to lie secured in Passes, and not fight," and "Not Shot-Bags, but Money-Bags . . . do Grand *Lewis* his Business," are his comments.[9] At his birthday dinner he allows his cavalier friends to "be drunk, swagger, and fight over all [their] Battles, from *Edge-hill* to *Brentford*." He remembers with apparent relish how psalm-singing Roundheads "in high-crown'd Hats, collar'd Bands, great loose Coats, long Tucks under 'em, and Calves-Leather Boots" thrashed the "swearing, drinking, fine Fellows in lac'd Coats" of his party. He is diplomatic in quelling the dispute which arises between two of his drunken brothers-in-arms. One accuses the other of saying "he was nearer being hang'd for Plots for the King than I was." The second Cavalier replies: "Yes, and more, and better Plots, I'll justifie it; the Major-General knows it." Old Blunt understands how to deal with the matter: "Know!—adod, all the Plots, that I knew, ended in being damnable Drunk; and I believe you drank and spew'd in the King's

[8] In a note to *Peveril of the Peak* Scott writes: "The attempt to contrast the manners of the jovial Cavaliers, and enthusiastic, yet firm and courageous, Puritans, was partly taken from a hint of Shadwell, who sketched several scenes of humour with great force, although they hung heavy on his pencil when he attempted to finish them for the stage."

[9] Shadwell, IV, 410.

Service as much as most . . . Fools, put up your Swords . . . Go, go and drink, Friends, till you can't speak, and then you'll be good company."[10]

Shadwell represents the Cromwellian colonel, Hackwell, as interested primarily in turning a penny through stock-jobbing. When Welford comes to interview him on behalf of his son, Hackwell thinks his visitor to be "of the Vocation of Stock-jobbing" and immediately questions him as to whether the matter is about the linen manufacture, the glass, the copper, the tin, the divers, or the paper. The colonel's remarks when the subject is again treated do not present it in the best light. After his wife says that a "Patent . . . for one's walking under Water" "wou'd have been of great Use to carry Messages under the Ice this last Frost, before it wou'd bear," Hackwell replies: "it's no Matter whether it turns to Use or not; the main End, verily, is to turn the Penny in the way of Stock-Jobbing, that's all." Again, when the jobber questions whether the patent "of bringing some *Chinese* Rope-Dancers over" be lawful, Hackwell reassures him: "Look thee, Brother, if it be to a good End, and that we ourselves have no Share in the Vanity or wicked Diversion thereof, by beholding of it, but only use it whereby we may turn the Penny, and employ it for Edification, always considered that it is like to take, and the said Shares will sell well; and then we shall not care, whether the aforesaid Dancers come over or no."[11]

"The Stock-Jobbing Rogues" whom Nickum designates as "worse than . . . Sharpers with Bars and false Boxes" have projects hardly less ridiculous than those which had been derided by Jonson in *The Devil is an Ass*,[12] Brome in *The Antipodes*,[13] and Wilson in *The Projectors*.[14] Shadwell, however, in the brief scene just described, was the first dramatist to see the possibility of satire on stock-jobbing. Interest in this activity, says Houghton, writing in 1694, arose since the war with France, "for trade being obstructed at sea, few that had money were willing it should lie idle, and a great many that wanted employments studied how to dispose of their money, that they might be able to command it

[10] *Ibid.*, IV, 437-438, 481-482.

[11] *Ibid.*, IV, 416, 434-436.

[12] Act II, scene 1; Act IV, scene 1; Act V, scene 3.

[13] Act IV, scene 9.

[14] *Dramatic Works of John Wilson* (Maidment-Logan ed.), pp. 237 ff., 252 ff.

whensoever they had occasion, which they found they could more easily do in *joint-stock*, than in laying out the same in lands, houses, or commodities."[15]

As a contrast to the veterans of the Civil War, Shadwell introduces Sir Nicholas Dainty, "a most fantastick, conceited Beau, of drolling, affected Speech; a very Coxcomb, but stout; a most luxurious effeminate Volunteer." Like Shamtown in *The Fortune Hunters*,[16] he writes letters to himself which he pretends are sent by ladies. When he learns that the younger Hackwell's regiment in which he has enlisted as volunteer will be off for Flanders as soon as the wind is favorable, he is somewhat disturbed for fear that his points and laces will not be ready by that time.[17] The major-general, who is amused by these unwarlike preparations, is addressed by Sir Nicholas: "Pshaw, good Guardian, you are for your old-fashion'd slovenly War; War's another thing now; we must live well in a Camp, that's our business." He goes on to relate how he intends to carry "as good a Confectioner as any in *England*," and how he has provided garden seeds in order that he may be supplied with "fresh Sallets" every day. He later[18] affords the company much mirth by displaying the fringe and embroidery for his velvet bed and by reading the list of articles he is to carry with him upon the campaign: "Eight Waggons; one for my two Butlers, my Service of Plate and Table-Linnen; one for my two Cooks and Kitchin; one for my Confectioner; one for my Laundresses and Dairy-Maids, with all their Utensils . . . One for my Wardrobe, great and small, Valet de Chambers, and Upholsterers . . . The rest of the Waggons are for all Sorts of Wines and Drinks. I carry Fifty Horse, and Twenty-five Carters,

[15] John Houghton, *Husbandry and Trade Improv'd . . . Revised by Richard Bradley* (London, 1727), I, 261. In the *Gentleman's Journal* for January, 1691/2, is a story of "The Vain-Glorious Citt: Or The Stock-Jobber," in which "the modern Trade, or rather Game, called *Stoc-Jobbing*" is described. Thomas Gordon, in *The Humourist: Being Essays upon Several Subjects* (London, 1725), has an essay "Of Stock-Jobbers" (Vol. II, pp. 19-22). In the course of it, he says, "This Nation cannot, nor never did thrive but by Industry and Trading, *both of which, are much at a stand for the present,* by the ingenuous and publick-spirited Management of Stock-jobbers, and of those who abet them for the Sake of going Snacks."

[16] James Carlile, *The Fortune Hunters: or, Two Fools well met* (London, 1689), p. 18.

[17] Shadwell, IV, 428 ff. In his epilogue to Brady's *The Rape,* Shadwell ridicules the beaux who throng the theatre while their more warlike brethren are away fighting.

[18] *Ibid.,* IV, 441 ff.

Mowers, Reapers, Grooms, and two Gardiners." One thing only disturbs Sir Nicholas: "Tis Ice; there will be no drinking without Ice." The younger Hackwell suggests that there are ice-houses in France; whereupon the reassured beau asserts: "Then, I am resolv'd, one of the first Actions I shew my Valour in shall be in storming of an Ice-House."

The other beau, Sir Timothy Kastril, whose surname may have been suggested by that of the "angry boy" in *The Alchemist,* is at first far from quarrelsome. He replies to Blunt, when the latter asks why he does not go to war: "I? no, I thank you; if I do, I'll give 'em leave to ram me into a Cannon, and shoot me out at a Stone-Wall: No, thank Heaven, I am well enough here with the Ladies." His estate is good enough to pay the "Magnanimous Fellows . . . that love Roaring, Rattling, Gun-powder, and Cannon." As a child he suffered from chin-cough and the rickets, and is now troubled with colds and the toothache. He remains a confirmed coward until cudgelled by Nickum. Then he changes his tune: "A Knight, a Beau, a Wit Lugg'd by the Ears! Cudgel'd, Cuff'd, Boxt, Kick'd . . . Dam me, a Man had better be kill'd or hang'd: Well, Revenge shall be had, that's certain.—But how will Honour be had again, when I have lost it?—Besides, when this is known, I shall be buffeted every Day." After considering the matter, he resolves to fight: "For 'tis better to be kill'd, than to live such a beaten Life as I am like to live without it." At the approach of Nickum, he astonishes the sharper by asserting that he will make him fuller of holes than "e're pink't Sattin was," and by disarming him with slight difficulty. Offering him his sword, he orders the bully to fight again; but Nickum refuses to take arms against a person who has given him his life. Sir Timothy then cudgels his former assailant and refuses to return his sword.[19]

Puffed up by this success, the suddenly valiant beau threatens to run the brave Welford through the body. In this combat, however, he is worsted, a calamity which does not lessen his warlike desires. He boasts: "I'll fight with every Body that has ever frown'd upon me in his Life." After his tilt with the masqueraders from whom he has been rescued by the servants, he

[19] *Ibid.,* IV, 429-430, 456, 461-463.

replies to Sir Nicholas's warning that a beau should be "soft of Speech, very gentle and civil of Deportment, much joy'd with the Contemplation of himself, and well pleas'd with others" in these words: "Pish, Pox of a Beau! I'll have nothing to do with 'em; nor the Women neither; they have used me like a Dog: I would go to the War,—but that he that was my Tutor, that's a Non-swearer, has perplex'd my Conscience so, that I do not know which side to take.—But a Pox on me, if I don't fight at home;—I am out of Humour with the World." His final fit of pugnaciousness occurs when he "breaks" the head of Hop, the dancing master, whom Winifred prefers to himself. Seeing that everyone is contemplating marriage and that he is without a love, he determines to "Beau it no longer."[20]

Gildon has noticed the resemblance between the growing bravery of Sir Timothy and that of La Writ in *The Little French Lawyer* of Fletcher.[21] In the latter play, Cleremont, who needs a second for his duel, in vain asks several gentlemen to assist him. The peaceable lawyer La Writ, however, is, after considerable arguing, persuaded to accept the office. In the duel, he disarms not only his opponent Beaupre, but also Cleremont's adversary Verdone. Then giving both swords to Cleremont, he begs the latter to say nothing more about the affair. Try as he will, La Writ cannot keep this success from his mind. He antagonizes Dinant, who is standing near the west port of the city, and is prevented from fighting only by the coming of Cleremont. After neglecting his law business, he dispatches a challenge to the judge Vertaigne. The latter sends his nephew Sampson to take his place. The seconds, who prevail upon the duellists to remove their outer garments, run away with their clothes and swords. In this condition of undress, Sampson and La Writ come upon Champernel and his company. The lawyer, who ruffles this elderly gentleman, is struck down and beaten by him. The minute he sees blood, La Writ's bravery vanishes and it takes little urging to obtain from him the promise to "fall close to [his] trade again."[22] The likeness in general conception between Sir Timothy and La Writ is evident.

[20] *Ibid.*, IV, 463-464, 479, 482, 487.
[21] P. 125.
[22] Beaumont and Fletcher, *Works*, (ed. A. R. Waller), III, 393-397, 398-399, 426-428, 435 ff.

Sir Timothy, however, remains brave until the very end, "tho'," as Gildon notes, "we have not the Experiment whether the sight of his Blood would not have had the same Effect on him."

As laureate, Shadwell thought it fitting to insert a few patriotic remarks in compliment to Queen Mary. After the soldier, Hackwell Junior, has made love to Eugenia, she asks: "Wou'd you have me make my self so miserable, as to set my Heart upon one who may be lost in every Rencounter or Attack?" Hackwell replies: "Does not our Royal Mistress do the same, and bears it with a Princely Magnanimity? She and our Country have the greatest Stake in *Europe*, who will be sure to hazard himself with the bravest." Eugenia answers, "She is to be reverenc'd and admir'd, but hard it is to Imitate so Glorious an Example; and methinks a private Lady may be happier." Hackwell then avers: "We cannot in Gratitude pretend to be happier, than those from whom we have our Happiness; in them our Country's Cause, and yours, and all's at Stake."[23]

The Volunteers is a marked improvement upon Shadwell's two preceding comedies. The action, which at no moment lags, is concerned more with the portrayal of character than with the unfolding of an intricate plot. In the bluff old Cavalier officer, Major-General Blunt, the beau-warrior Sir Nicholas Dainty, and the suddenly valorous Sir Timothy Kastril, the author presents noteworthy dramatic figures. Through Colonel Hackwell Senior he inserts a satirical thrust at stock-jobbing, an activity here treated, I believe, for the first time in English drama. In this play, moreover, Shadwell throws aside the rôle of preacher, which he had assumed in the persons of Bellamy and Mr. Rant, and writes a comedy for the sole purpose of affording amusement.

[23] Shadwell, IV, 448.

CHAPTER XX

CONCLUSION

DURING the years following the Restoration of Charles II, no English playwright more consistently praised the work of Ben Jonson than Thomas Shadwell. Because of his admiration for Jonson and because of his desire to write comedies in accordance with the principles embodied in the practice of that dramatist, Shadwell merits the title of "grandson of Ben." Like his idol, he frequently states in preface or prologue his purpose of censuring some of the vices and follies of the age. In the manner of Jonson, he builds several of his characters upon the idea of the humour—a main trait or eccentricity which rules the possessor in all his actions.

In one of his dedicatory epistles, Shadwell describes a good comical humour as "such an Affectation, as misguides Men in Knowledge, Art, or Science, or that causes defection in Manners and Morality, or perverts their Minds in the main Actions of their Lives." His plays of humour emphasize character rather than plot —not the character of the normal representative man, but that of the eccentric man—the man who throws aside all pretences to normality in his desire to excel in that for which he is neither temperamentally nor physically fitted. The persons most prominent in this type of comedy are the pretenders to knowledge, science, or the arts, Sir Positive At-all, Sir Nicholas Gimcrack, and Ninny; the pretenders to wit, Drybob, Sir Formal Trifle, and Sir Samuel Hearty; the pretender to bravery, Briske; the old man who would play the lover, Snarl; the "light of love" who prates of virtue, Lady Vaine. To represent what he intends as a more normal attitude towards life, Shadwell usually introduces a pair of lovers who act the parts of the Jonsonian demonstrator and by contrast or characterizing speeches present the eccentricities of the humour-characters to the audience.

Plays constructed upon the principle of absolute consistency in character-portrayal are apt to become tiresome unless the author uses selection in the material he presents. Shadwell at times neglects to do this. Sir Positive At-all is omniscient on too many occasions; and Sir Nicholas Gimcrack is made the target for too many blows at the scientific movement. This piling up of characterizing details to the neglect of the plot may account in part for the fact that the public did not take kindly to Shadwell's comedies of humour. *The Sullen Lovers* pleased because the audience believed one of the figures to be a satire upon the boastful Sir Robert Howard. *The Humourists*, however, did not find favor and was saved only by the interpolation of "excellent Dancings." After a lapse of five years, Shadwell tempted fate with *The Virtuoso*, the success of which emboldened him to try once more with *A True Widow*. When the latter proved a failure, he accepted the rebuff and wrote no more comedies of humour strictly speaking, although he frequently introduced humour-figures in his later works. The plays in which Shadwell is not shackled to a theory —*Epsom-Wells*, *The Squire of Alsatia*, and *Bury-Fair*—are his best. In these, the action goes forward at a lively rate, the author not feeling the necessity of interrupting its progress in order to allow a character to "hold up his humour."

To the end, Shadwell continued to profess a moral purpose. Not only does he render his fools ridiculous, but he castigates the vices of the age. Through Bellamy and Mr. Rant, he argues for a higher standard of morality. In the person of Sir Edward Belfond, he assumes the rôle of a zealous reformer and determines that the dens of iniquity which infest Whitefriars shall be removed. Through the example of Belfond Junior he shows in a way satisfactory to his age that young men should be drawn to do right by love rather than by force. And, in *The Scowrers*, he administers the rebuke direct to the young rakes by causing Clara and Eugenia to refuse to marry them until they have proved by a year's renunciation of "Wine, Women, and base Company" that they have conquered themselves.

The influence of Molière upon Shadwell has been overemphasized. Like the other dramatists of his time, he of course could not escape being conscious of the writer of comedies across the channel. *Les Fâcheux* furnished the hint for *The Sullen Lovers*, a play which, in my opinion, does not imply a knowledge of *Le Misanthrope*. The situation of the girl who outwits her guardian, an episode treated in *L'École des Maris*, was presented frequently by Shadwell as well as by his contemporaries, Rhodes, Wycherley, and Otway. The general idea of *Les Précieuses Ridicules* is utilized in *Bury-Fair;* but Shadwell transplants his material perfectly to a background of English provincial life. In every one of his comedies except *The Miser*, which in the main plot is a close adaptation of *L'Avare*, Shadwell has used the situations derived from the French dramatist very freely.

Shadwell is in the line of the great tradition of English drama. His plays contain situations reminiscent not only of Jonson, but also of Shakespeare, Beaumont and Fletcher, Heywood, and Brome. In Sir Edward Hartfort, he represents a survival in Restoration times of the generous hospitality which marked the days of Queen Elizabeth. He is not, however, satisfied to have persons live entirely in the past. Less sympathetically presented than Sir Edward are Snarl, who decries the actions of the younger generation and can see good only in the days before the Civil Wars, and Mr. Oldwit, who, despite having been a friend of Cleveland and Randolph, shows by his approval of Sir Humphrey Noddy that he thinks puns and practical jokes the best form of wit.

Of the five dramatists whose works are included in the canon of Restoration comedy, but two, Etherege and Wycherley, wrote during the lifetime of Shadwell. The ceaseless brilliancy of the dialogue in *The Man of Mode* and the masterly innuendos of *The Country Wife* it was never Shadwell's lot to attain. If one must grant that his comedies lack the literary finish of the works of his two greater contemporaries, one should not therefore assume that his dialogue is inadequate. His "Men of Wit and Sense," who have been the subject of many sneering comments, are by no means dull. In their remarks on contemporary conditions and in their scenes of verbal fencing with the women characters, their lines have a frequent sparkle.

If Shadwell's plays do not possess the literary polish that is found in the comedies of Etherege and Wycherley, they do present a much larger gallery of characters. In addition to the lovers who are usually placed at the center of the action, such types appear as the cheat, the country gull, the cowardly hector, the hypocritical Puritan, the miser, the strumpet, the spendthrift, the beau, the foolish poet, the orator, the man of business, the sportsman, the veteran of the Civil Wars, the French surgeon, the Irish priest, the Church of England clergyman, the Jacobite alderman, the stock-jobber, the man or woman who affects French breeding, the pseudo-count, and the witch-finder. The older woman in pursuit of one of the younger men is a recurrent type. Worthy of special notice are Mrs. Gripe in *The Woman-Captain*, Isabella in *The Lancashire Witches*, and Clara in *The Scowrers*, all of whom on the strength of being "free English women" are ready to rebel at the man-made customs that hem them in.

Shadwell differs from Etherege and Wycherley also in his desire for novelty in setting. Almost alone among the dramatists of the Restoration, he was willing occasionally to lay the scenes of his English comedies outside the metropolis. He sets the action of *Epsom-Wells* at a popular watering-place; he uses the town where he had gone to school as the locale of *Bury-Fair;* he pictures the countryside in *The Lancashire Witches.* Other dramatists had frequently referred to Alsatia and the persons who inhabited that region; Shadwell, however, was the first playwright to make dramatic capital of the district. The interior of a theatre had been shown three times in Restoration drama before *A True Widow;* in the latter comedy Shadwell displayed his originality by depicting the actions of the audience.

As a satirist of contemporary fads and ideas, Shadwell is eminent among the dramatists of his time. In *The Sullen Lovers*, he ridicules the heroic tragedy, a type of play at which he was never tired of scoffing. In *The Virtuoso*, he jeers at certain aspects of the scientific movement. In *A True Widow*, he attempts to "expose" farce. In *The Lancashire Witches*, he derides countryside superstitions. In *Bury-Fair*, he presents the ridiculous results of French affectations in provincial society. In *The Scowrers*, he satirizes the rowdyism of wealthy and titled profligates. And finally, in *The Volunteers*, he has something to say about the recent craze of stock-jobbing.

What conclusions are we justified in drawing? Does Shadwell merit a higher place in literature than that assigned him by Dryden, or is he worthy merely of a seat on the dunces' bench by the side of Bavius and Maevius? In my opinion, there is but one answer. Shadwell, instead of scorn, deserves serious consideration. A wit in the sense that Etherege and Congreve are wits, he decidedly is not. On the other hand, he had wider interests than his more "literary" fellow-dramatists, and he was therefore ready to depict important details of everyday life which they ignored. He had a knack for finding novelty in character and in setting, and for presenting both entertainingly. Among the comic dramatists who wrote plays for the London stage between 1660 and 1692, a place next in importance to that occupied by Etherege and Wycherley belongs unquestionably to the author of *Epsom-Wells*, *The Squire of Alsatia*, *Bury-Fair*, and *The Volunteers*.

INDEX

INDEX